UNDERSTANDING THE
OF OBLIGATIONS

UNDERSTANDING THE LAW OF OBLIGATIONS

ESSAYS ON CONTRACT, TORT AND RESTITUTION

ANDREW BURROWS,
BCL, MA (Oxon), LLM (Harvard)
Norton Rose Professor of Commercial Law,
Oxford University, Fellow of St. Hugh's College

·HART·
PUBLISHING
OXFORD

Hart Publishing
Oxford
UK

Distributed in the United States by
Northwestern University Press
625 Colfax, Evanston
Illinois 60208-4210 USA

Distributed in Australia and New Zealand by
Federation Press
PO Box 45, Annandale
NSW 203, Australia

Distributed in the Netherlands, Belgium and Luxembourg by
Intersentia, Churchillaan 108
B2900 Schoten, Antwerpen
Belgium

Hart Publishing is a specialist legal publisher based in Oxford, England.
To order further copies of this book or to request a list of other publications
please write to:

Hart Publishing, Salters Boatyard, Folly Bridge,
Abingdon Road, Oxford OX1 4LB
Telephone +44 (0)1865 245533 or Fax: +44 (0)1865 794882
e-mail: mail@hartpub.co.uk
www.hartpub.co.uk

British Library Cataloguing in Publication Data
Data Available

ISBN 1-84113-183-0 (paper)

Typeset in 12pt Bembo
by Hope Services (Abingdon) Ltd.
Printed in Great Britain on acid-free paper
by Biddles Ltd, www.biddles.co.uk

For Charlotte

Contents

Foreword

This collection of essays explores issues that are of central importance in understanding the law of obligations. Each has a wide-ranging focus and, taken together, it is hoped that they provide the reader with a clear and stimulating guide to the present shape and likely future development of the law of obligations.

I have long held the belief that, in understanding the law of obligations, one should distinguish contract, tort, and restitution, while recognising concurrent liability between them. Essays 1 and 2 directly examine that belief. Essay 1 explains modifications in my thinking since the article I wrote on the same theme in the 1983 *Law Quarterly Review*. Essay 2 is an edited version of my inaugural lecture at UCL delivered on 16 November 1994 (and published in (1995) 48 *CLP* 103).[1] The postscript to essay 2 deals with two questions that are briefly touched on in that essay but merit more detailed consideration.

Essays 3–5 look at various aspects of the newly-recognised law of restitution, including likely future developments. They are lightly-updated versions of articles published at (1995) 18 *UQLJ* 149,[2] (1988) 104 *LQR* 576,[3] and (1997) 50 *CLP* 95[4] respectively. Versions of essay 3 were presented to a conference on *Equity, Restitution and the Banking Lawyer* at Bond University on 23 July 1994; to a staff seminar at the University of Queensland on 3 August 1994; to members of the Australian Banking Law Association in Melbourne on 24 August 1994 and in Sydney on 5 September 1994; and to Freehills, Sydney, on 6 September 1994. A version of essay 4 was presented to the Cambridge meeting of the SPTL Restitution Group in September 1987. Essay 5 was delivered in the series "Law and Opinion at the end of the Twentieth Century" in UCL on 13 March 1997.

---

[1] Reprinted by permission of Oxford University Press.
[2] Reprinted by permission of University of Queensland Press.
[3] Reprinted by permission of Sweet & Maxwell Ltd.
[4] Reprinted by permission of Oxford University Press.

Essay 6 defends tort against those (most notably Patrick Atiyah, most recently in *The Damages Lottery* (Hart Publishing, 1997)) who would seek to abolish much of it.

Essay 7 examines the structure, and legislative reform, of contractual remedies. It is an edited version of a paper delivered on 21 October 1995 at a joint seminar of the Scottish Law Commission and the Faculty of Law, University of Edinburgh (and published in (1997) 1 *ELR* 155).[5]

Essay 8 draws on my work at the Law Commission to look at where reforms are needed in contract and tort.

Occasionally I have found it convenient to deal with a development since an essay was first written by a square-bracketed footnote.

I would like to thank Kate Elliott for her meticulous copy-editing; and Richard Hart for preparing the tables and index and for his encouragement, enthusiasm and efficiency throughout.

I dedicate this book to Charlotte (now aged nearly three).

ANDREW BURROWS
6 March 1998
UCL

---

[5] Reprinted by permission of T. & T. Clark Ltd.

Table of Cases

Table of Statutes and Supra-national Legislation

1

Dividing the Law of Obligations

I. INTRODUCTION

The question of how, if at all, the law of obligations should be divided continues to generate interest and controversy. In recent times the debate has been fuelled by commentators who have suggested ways of dividing the law of obligations that contrast with the conventional distinction between contract and tort and, now, restitution.[1] Patrick Atiyah, for example, has argued that one should restructure the law of obligations around "reliance-based" and "benefit-based" liabilities.[2] Lord Cooke has advocated that duties of reasonable care should be recognised as a "distinct chapter of the law" whether they originate in contract, tort or otherwise.[3] More recently, Jane Stapleton has suggested categorising the law in terms of the different measures of damages, so that contract would alone be concerned with what she terms the "entitled result" measure, whereas tort would alone be concerned with what she terms the "normal expectancies" measure.[4] Renewed interest in how the law of obligations should be divided may also be a product of the recent calls for, and recognition of, an English law of restitution which have required lawyers to think carefully about the relationship between

---

[1] Apart from the commentators mentioned here, see Steve Hedley, "Contract, Tort and Restitution: or, On Cutting the Legal System Down to Size" (1988) 8 *LS* 137 who vociferously disagrees with the distinction between contract, tort and restitution. But even he thinks it important to classify the material into manageable chunks and suggests that we should focus on eight types of "asset" protected in the law of obligations.

[2] P.S. Atiyah, *The Rise and Fall of the Freedom of Contract* (1979) 4, 768, 778–9. See also P.S. Atiyah, "Contracts, Promises and the Law of Obligations" (1978) 94 *LQR* 193, 220–3.

[3] "Tort and Contract" in P. Finn (ed.), *Essays on Contract* (1987), 222, 228–32. See also "The Condition of the Law of Tort" in P. Birks (ed.), *Frontiers of Liability* Vol 2 (1994), 49, 60–1.

[4] J. Stapleton, "A New 'Seascape' for Obligations: Reclassification on the Basis of Measure of Damages" in P. Birks (ed.), *The Classification of Obligations* (1997), 193–231. See also "The Normal Expectancies Measure in Tort Damages" (1997) 113 *LQR* 257.

restitutionary and other obligations.[5] One can further argue that the increasing importance of European thought has been of relevance. In civil law jurisdictions, taxonomy has traditionally been taken far more seriously than in common law systems.[6]

In 1983 I wrote an article defending the division between contract, tort and restitution, principally against the attack on it made by Atiyah.[7] In part that defence rested on the need to recognise a law of restitution. The House of Lords has since done so.[8] Another major aspect of my defence was to counter Atiyah's claim that the law's fulfilment of expectations for binding promises (or, as it is often termed, protection of the expectation interest[9]) was in decline. He had argued that to fulfil such expectations reflected Victorian values that had no place in the modern welfare state; and that, as a consequence, contract had been, or was being, swallowed up by tort and restitution. I would suggest that legal developments over the last fifteen years support the view that the law's recognition of the need to fulfil expectations engendered by binding promises is not only alive but is flourishing. As Daniel Friedmann has recently written (in an article which uses the term "performance interest" in preference to "expectation interest"), "the main thrust of modern law has been in the very opposite direction . . . there are no signs of a weakening of the performance interest. On the contrary, one of the major trends in modern contract law is the strengthening of the protection accorded to the performance interest. Traditional limitations upon the availability of specific performance and upon the recovery of performance damages have either been removed or severely curtailed."[10]

But while I would abide by the essentials of what I wrote in 1983, I accept that there are modifications that need to be made. The purpose of this essay is, therefore, to explain afresh why I believe that the division between contract, tort and restitution is a satisfactory one.

---

[5] See R. Goff and G. Jones, *The Law of Restitution* (4th edn., 1993); P. Birks, *An Introduction to the Law of Restitution* (revised paperback edn., 1989); *Lipkin Gorman* v. *Karpnale Ltd* [1991] 2 AC 548.

[6] See, e.g., R. Zimmermann, *The Law of Obligations: Roman Foundations of the Civilian Tradition* (paperback edn., 1996).

[7] A. Burrows, "Contract, Tort and Restitution—A Satisfactory Division or Not?" (1983) 99 *LQR* 217.

[8] *Lipkin Gorman* v. *Karpnale Ltd* [1991] 2 AC 548.

[9] The term was coined by L. Fuller and W.R. Perdue, "The Reliance Interest in Contract Damages" (1936) 46 *Yale LJ* 52.

[10] "The Performance Interest in Contract Damages" (1995) 111 *LQR* 628, 648.

Amongst those who believe in the tripartite division of (at least most of[11]) the law of obligations into contract, tort and restitution, there would, I think, be general agreement with the following broad description. Contract is concerned with binding promises; tort is concerned with wrongs (other than breach of a binding promise); and restitution is concerned with unjust enrichment. In the next three sections, I use that description to provide a broad-brush and elementary picture of what makes up the law of contract, the law of tort, and the law of restitution.

2. CONTRACT

The law of contract is concerned with binding promises. It looks at what constitutes a binding promise and how such a promise is made; at the remedies for breach of such a promise; and at who is entitled to those remedies.

It has been a traditionally accepted feature of English law that only bargain promises—that is, promises supported by consideration—are binding. Gratuitous promises, apart from promises made by deed and those enforceable through proprietary or promissory estoppel, are not binding. But even if a bargain promise has been made and

---

[11] There are undoubtedly obligations that fall outside this tripartite division, most obviously the duty not to commit an "equitable wrong" (such as breach of fiduciary duty and breach of confidence): see pp. 14–15 below. It is also arguable that some wrongs arising under a statute cannot be classified as torts (e.g. unfair dismissal). The obligations to pay taxes and judgment debts also do not fall within contract, tort (and equitable wrongs), or restitution; see P. Birks, n. 5 above, 48. Some commentators argue that in some situations outside contract, tort and restitution, there is a duty to pay compensation for reliance loss on the basis of the plaintiff's "unjust sacrifice": see, e.g., S. Stoljar, "Unjust Enrichment and Unjust Sacrifice" (1987) 50 *MLR* 603; G.A. Muir, "Unjust Sacrifice and the Officious Intervener" in P. Finn (ed.), *Essays on Restitution* (Law Book Co., 1990), 297–351; J. Beatson, "Benefit Reliance and the Structure of Unjust Enrichment" in *Use and Abuse of Unjust Enrichment* (Clarendon Press, 1991), 21–44. For criticism of that approach, see A. Burrows, *The Law of Restitution* (Butterworths, 1993), 4–6. See also N. McBride, "A Fifth Common Law Obligation" (1994) 14 *LS* 35, who (i) treats as a fourth obligation, distinct from the primary obligations in contract, tort and restitution, the secondary obligation to pay damages for a breach of contract, tort (or other wrong); and (ii) argues that there is a fifth obligation exemplified by (a) the duty to pay a reasonable sum for requested non-contractual services performed on the understanding that those services would be paid for; (b) the duty to indemnify another against liability incurred by that other in acting as requested; (c) the duty to prevent detrimental reliance on a promise; and (d) the duty to restore losses to a trust fund resulting from a breach of trust. But I believe that it is more convenient to categorise together primary and secondary duties arising in contract and tort; and that (a)–(d) can probably be seen as falling within contract, tort (and equitable wrongs) or restitution.

accepted it may still not be binding for various reasons. For example, it may not be sufficiently certain; or it may be a social or domestic promise where it is presumed that the promisor does not intend to create legal relations; or it may have been induced by the promisee's misrepresentation or duress or undue influence; or the promisor may have made a mistake; or there may have been such a change of events subsequent to the making of the promise that the notion of "frustration" is brought into play; or the plaintiff may have broken his own promise in such a serious way as to make the defendant's promise, performance of which was conditional upon performance of the plaintiff's own promise, no longer binding. A number of these factors which render a promise that would otherwise be binding, non-binding, can be coherently linked by saying that a promise is not binding if it is unfair to the promisor to hold him or her to it. Using this notion of fairness, the expansion of invalidating factors that has taken place during the twentieth century, such as the widening of the doctrines of mistake and duress, and the passing of statutes such as the Unfair Contract Terms Act 1977, is readily explicable as reflecting the different view of fairness that holds sway today than in the past. That is, the laissez-faire/freedom of contract view of fairness is today tempered by a paternalistic/protection of the weak view of fairness.[12]

The remedies for breach of a binding promise are (almost always) concerned to fulfil the expectations engendered by that promise. This is most clearly shown by the remedy of specific performance where the defendant is ordered to carry out the promise made to the plaintiff. Although the courts have become more willing to grant specific performance,[13] the general position remains that it is a secondary remedy available only where damages are inadequate. However, the normal method of assessing damages for the breach of a binding promise is also concerned to fulfil the plaintiff's expectations.[14] This was made clear by Parke B in *Robinson* v. *Harman*.[15] He

---

[12] Burrows, n. 7 above, 260–1; A. Burrows, "The Will Theory of Contract Revived—Fried's 'Contract as Promise'" (1985) 38 *CLP* 141, 150.

[13] See, e.g., *Beswick* v. *Beswick* [1968] AC 58; *Sky Petroleum Ltd* v. *VIP Petroleum Ltd* [1974] 1 WLR 576; *Tito* v. *Waddell (No 2)* [1977] Ch. 106, 321–3; *Price* v. *Strange* [1978] Ch. 337; *Powell* v. *Brent London BC* [1988] ICR 176; Cf. *Co-operative Insurance Society Ltd* v. *Argyll Stores (Holdings) Ltd* [1997] 2 WLR 898.

[14] Less commonly, damages for breach of contract may be concerned to put the plaintiff into as good a position as if no contract had been made ("reliance damages") or to strip away gains made by the breach ("restitutionary damages"). On the latter, see *Surrey County Council* v. *Bredero Homes Ltd* [1993] 1 WLR 1361; *Att.-Gen.* v. *Blake*, [1998] 1 All ER 833; 140–5 below.

[15] (1848) 1 Exch. 850, 855.

said, "The rule of common law is that, where a party sustains a loss by reason of a breach of contract, he is, so far as money can do it to be placed in the same situation, with respect to damages, as if the contract had been performed."

Traditionally, under the doctrine of "privity of contract", only a party to the contract (that is, the promisee) can enforce it. A third-party beneficiary has no such entitlement. Although there are exceptions to the privity doctrine, it still basically holds sway. Whether that will still be so at the millennium is open to debate, particularly given the Law Commission's recent recommendations for legislative reform of the doctrine.[16]

It is important to add that the notion of "promise" that is being used, when one refers to the law of contract being concerned with binding promises, is a wide one. One can define a promise, in a wide sense, as "a statement or action by which the speaker or actor appears to accept an obligation to another (or others)[17] to do or not to do something."[18] So a promise may be made by an oral statement, by writing, or by conduct. Conduct constituting a promise will be context-specific but it may include, for example, a hand-shake, or a nod-of-the-head, or the delivery of requested goods (where, by delivery, one may be taken to have accepted an obligation to provide a certain quality or quantity of goods), or conduct encouraging another to perform services (where, by the encouragement, one may be taken to have accepted an obligation to pay for the services).

3. TORT

The law of tort is concerned with (common law) wrongs, other than breach of a binding promise. It identifies the various types of wrong and the remedies available for the victim of those wrongs. The internal structure of the law of tort leaves much to be desired, in that the different torts mix up descriptions of conduct with descriptions of the defendant's state of mind. Hence conduct–labelled torts, such as trespass to the person, libel and nuisance, exist alongside the tort of negligence (which refers to the defendant's state of mind, negligence

---

[16] *Privity of Contract: Contracts for the Benefit of Third Parties*, Law Com. No 242 (1996). See 166–8 below.

[17] A promise does not embrace, and must be distinguished from, a vow, which is an uncommunicated commitment to oneself not to another person: see C. Fried, *Contract as Promise* (Harvard UP, 1981), 41–2.

[18] See Burrows, n. 7 above, 244, 258.

belonging in a series which includes intention and strict liability).
There is also a distinction between torts which are actionable *per se*,
such as trespass and libel, and torts which are actionable only on proof
of damage, including nuisance and negligence. In relation to torts
actionable only on proof of damage, liability in tort can be broken
down into four main elements: (i) a duty; (ii) breach of duty; (iii)
non-remote damage; and (iv) defences. For torts actionable *per se*
there are three such elements, ((i), (ii) and (iv)).

Damages is the usual remedy for a tort, and the usual measure of
damages is compensatory. Hence the classic statement of Lord
Blackburn in *Livingstone* v. *Rawyard Coal Co*[19]: "Where any injuries
are to be compensated by damages, in settling the sum of money to
be given for reparation of damages, you should as nearly as possible
get at that sum, which will put the party who has been injured, or
who has suffered, in the same position as he would have been in if he
had not sustained the wrong, for which he is now getting his compensation or reparation." Less commonly, damages for a tort may be
concerned to punish the tortfeasor ("punitive damages") or to strip
away gains made by the tort ("restitutionary damages").[20] A further
important remedy for a tort is the injunction, which is essentially
concerned to prevent a tort being committed or continued, although
it can also be concerned to undo the effects of a tort that has already
been committed.

4. RESTITUTION

The law of restitution is concerned with unjust enrichment. It identifies what constitutes an unjust enrichment at the plaintiff's expense and
the remedies reversing such an enrichment. It deals, for example, with
when can one recover money paid, or the value of work done, by mistake, or under duress, or under a contract that is void, voidable, or
unenforceable, or that has been discharged for breach or frustration.
Most of the law of restitution comprises what used to be called quasi-
contract: the remedies are therefore principally the common law
remedies of the recovery of money in an action for money had and
received to the plaintiff's use, the recovery of money in an action
for money paid to the defendant's use, and a quantum meruit for the

[19] (1880) 5 App. Cas. 25, 39.
[20] See *Aggravated, Exemplary and Restitutionary Damages*, Law Com. No 242 (1997). See
169–71 below.

reasonable value of work done. But the law of restitution also includes areas of equity such as a fiduciary's liability to account for unauthorised profits, rescission of an executed contract (for example, for misrepresentation or undue influence), constructive or resulting trusts imposed to reverse unjust enrichment, equitable tracing and subrogation.

Several other essays in this collection explore and map out the newly-recognised law of restitution. Consequently I wish to confine my comments on restitution in this essay (which will hereinafter concentrate on the contract/tort division) to three main points.

First, it is now widely accepted, thanks to the work of Peter Birks, that the law of restitution is itself divisible into two areas.[21] One area, which overlaps with contract and tort, is concerned with when restitution may be given for a breach of contract or tort (or other wrong). But the primary area, often referred to as the independent law of restitution (or *autonomous* unjust enrichment) is where there is no overlap with contract and tort. The implications of that internal division (which not everyone accepts)[22] remain controversial.[23]

The second point is that the independent law of restitution is a division not only of the law of obligations but also of the law of property. That is, it is concerned not only with personal remedies but also with proprietary remedies (or, as one might otherwise express it, with the creation of proprietary rights). So it is that the reversal of autonomous unjust enrichment can sometimes be effected by the creation of proprietary rights through trusts (whether constructive or resulting), equitable liens, or subrogation to another's securities. In contrast, it would seem that remedies for torts or for breach of a binding promise (other than specifically enforceable promises, most obviously to transfer land) do not create proprietary rights (although restitutionary remedies for breach of fiduciary duty and other equitable wrongs may do so).[24]

---

[21] Birks, n. 5 above, 39–44, 132–3; P. Birks, *Restitution—The Future* (Blackstone, 1992), 1–2. Birks' terminology was used by the Court of Appeal in *Halifax Building Society* v. *Thomas* [1996] 2 WLR 63.

[22] For a major attack see P. Cane, "Exceptional Measures of Damages: A Search for Principles" in Birks (ed.), *Wrongs and Remedies in the Twenty-First Century* (1996), 312–23. See also J. Beatson, "The Nature of Waiver of Tort" in *The Use and Abuse of Unjust Enrichment*, n. 11 above, 206–43.

[23] For example, must a limitation period expressed as applying to an action for a wrong bar restitution for a wrong albeit that it need not bar an action in autonomous unjust enrichment? On this, see Law Commission Consultation Paper No 151 (1998), *Limitation of Actions*, paras. 5.16–5.19, 13.80.

[24] See, e.g., *Boardman* v. *Phipps* [1967] 2 AC 46, *Attorney-General for Hong Kong* v. *Reid* [1994] 1 AC 324.

Thirdly, Peter Birks has recently criticised putting restitution alongside contract and tort because this is to put a response-based category (restitution) alongside event-based categories (contract and tort). He writes, "the division [between contract, tort and restitution] is manifestly unsatisfactory, in a way that carries over into all our thought about the subject. 'Restitution' cannot align with 'Contract' and 'Tort', since restitution is a legal response to events (like compensation and punishment) and they are events to which the law responds."[25] In his view, the correct categorisation should be contract, wrongs, unjust enrichment (and other events). I would not seek to deny the logical force of Birks' argument, although it is an argument that would be greatly enhanced by practical proof that, in a series—contract, wrongs and unjust enrichment—the *only possible* analysis of restitution for wrongs is that the wrong (and not the wrong plus the enrichment) is the cause of action. However, I am not convinced that any confusion or practical difficulty is being caused by putting restitution alongside contract and tort. Even the labels "contract" and "tort" require further explanation in simpler language which draws out the principled division between obligations based on binding promises and obligations based on wrongs (other than breach of promise). Even if there is confusion about the divide between autonomous unjust enrichment (where unjust enrichment is the cause of action) and unjust enrichment by wrongdoing (where, following Birks, the wrong alone is the cause of action), this would not necessarily be eradicated by replacing the label "law of restitution" by "law of unjust enrichment". Indeed my fear is that it would cause greater confusion if one rejected, as a misnomer, the now familiar label "law of restitution".

5. THE DIVISION BETWEEN CONTRACT AND TORT

The division between contract and tort continues to be controversial. One can isolate two particular difficulties. One is the question whether the tort of negligence—particularly through the "assumption of responsibility" principle recognised initially in *Hedley Byrne & Co. Ltd* v. *Heller & Partners Ltd*[26] but given new life in more recent cases—is (at least sometimes) concerned to impose liability for the breach of a binding promise so that it is inaccurate to say that con-

[25] Birks in *The Classification of Obligations*, n. 4 above, 20.
[26] [1964] AC 465.

tract alone is concerned with such liability. That question is considered, *inter alia*, in the next essay, where I argue that a version of the "assumption of responsibility" principle does indeed blur the distinction between contract and tort and is only acceptable as a pragmatic "second-best" approach to direct reform of some unacceptable contractual rules.

The more fundamental difficulty (dealt with in the remainder of this essay) is whether one can justify dividing off breach of a binding promise from all other wrongs, rather than treating it as just another tort. Here we are asking, "Is there really something so distinctive about breach of a binding promise that merits it being treated in a distinct category of law from other wrongs?".

In seeking (implicitly) to answer this question, my 1983 *LQR* article focused on the different remedial principles of, or remedial interests protected by, contract and tort. I pointed out that contract was largely concerned to *fulfil expectations engendered* by a binding promise (that is, to protect the plaintiff's expectation interest by putting the plaintiff into as good a position as if the contract had been performed) and that tort was largely concerned *to compensate* for wrongful *harm* (that is, to protect the plaintiff's *status quo* interest by putting the plaintiff into as good a position as if no wrong had occurred).[27]

While I continue to believe that useful insights are to be gained by looking at the different remedial principles of, or remedial interests protected by, contract and tort I now think it important to stress two points. The first is that talk of tort "compensating for wrongful harm" is problematic. The second is that it should be made clear that differences in remedial principles or interests are of second-level importance in justifying the distinction between contract and tort.[28] In contrast, *it is of first-level importance that liability for breach of a binding promise (the concern of contract) rests on what, by convention,[29] is treated as a voluntarily*

---

[27] I also pointed out that restitution was concerned *to reverse* an unjust *enrichment* (that is, to protect the plaintiff's restitution interest by requiring the defendant to disgorge the value of a benefit gained at the plaintiff's expense).

[28] Stapleton treats the different remedial interests as being of first-level importance: see "The Normal Expectancies Measure in Tort Damages", n. 4 above; "A New Seascape for Obligations: Reclassification on the Basis of Measure of Damages", n. 4 above. For the preferable view that those differences are of second-level importance, see, e.g., Daniel Friedmann, "Rights and Remedies" (1997) 113 *LQR* 424; Ernest Weinrib, "The Judicial Classification of Obligations" in *The Classification of Obligations*, n. 4 above, 46–51. It seems to me, with respect, that a particular weakness of Stapleton's analysis is that she does not ask whether, and why, the difference in remedial interests is justified: see 13 below.

[29] It is important to recognise that one is concerned with what, by convention, is treated as a voluntarily undertaken obligation. That is, one is concerned with what "a reasonable

undertaken obligation whereas liability for all other wrongs (the concern of tort) has no such voluntary basis and is simply imposed.

What follows is an attempt to explain fully those two difficult, crucial (and linked) points.

The expression "compensation for wrongful harm" is problematic because, without further elaboration, it swallows up—and is not distinct from—the principle of fulfilling expectations engendered by a binding promise. That is, compensating the harm caused by breach of promise can be regarded as equivalent to fulfilling, so far as money can do it, the expectations engendered by the promise. As Atiyah has observed, "There is a sense in which even breach of contract is designed to provide 'compensation for wrongful harm', and until we have defined our terms more carefully, we cannot use them to justify [the division between contract and tort]".[30] Although I denounced the merger of contract and tort brought about by the single idea of putting the plaintiff into as good a position as if no wrong had occurred,[31] it was needlessly confusing to use a term that invited such a merger.

A less ambiguous term is "compensation for wrongful interference". Use of this phrase makes it clearer that the divide between contract and tort has traditionally marked a difference between a failure to benefit the plaintiff (the concern of contract) and harmful interference with the plaintiff (the concern of tort). The notion of interference neatly encapsulates the idea that in most areas of tort the defendant was a stranger to the plaintiff and that the plaintiff's entitlement was for the defendant to remain a stranger rather than wrongly coming into contact with the plaintiff. One is seeking to put the plaintiff into as good a position as if the defendant had done noth-

---

man" in a given society regards as a promise. It is irrelevant that the promisor does not regard himself as bound or that he has no intention of keeping his promise. Similarly it is irrelevant that the promisee does not think that the promisor will keep his promise. The promisor is bound because he has chosen to do that which by convention (i.e. by the standards of society) constitutes the method of morally binding oneself to another to do something. The law of contract gives legal force to the moral obligation to keep one's promise. Once one recognises the root objectivity of promising, it follows that there is no incompatibility between regarding contract as based on promise and the wide-ranging implication of terms into contracts. Although a promisor's subjective intentions will normally coincide with the objective intention, one is not looking at what the promisor has himself accepted an obligation to do but at what a reasonable man regards the promisor as having accepted an obligation to do. That it is important to regard promising as a convention is recognised by, e.g., Charles Fried, *Contract as Promise* (1981), ch. 2: but, at 61–3, he disputes that the objective standard of interpretation is based on the promise principle.

[30] *Essays on Contract* (Clarendon Press, 1986), 53.
[31] (1983) 99 *LQR* 217, 232.

ing (that is, had been passive) rather than committing the wrong in question.

The contrast to fulfilling expectations engendered by a binding promise is then immediately clear. The plaintiff's objection in contract is that the defendant has failed to benefit him: the defendant has failed to do what was promised. Plainly it would not avoid the wrong for the defendant to do nothing. To put the plaintiff into as good a position as if he and the defendant had remained strangers—that is, into as good a position as if no promise had been made—is not what is wanted. It is performance of the promise (not non-interference) that the plaintiff wants.

But once one substitutes a principle of "compensation for wrongful interference" for the ambiguously phrased principle of "compensation for wrongful harm", it also becomes clear that that single principle does not underpin significant areas of tort. While most of tort does indeed rest on a principle of compensation for wrongful interference, there are ever increasingly areas where that is not so and where tort is concerned with a failure to benefit. Examples are negligence cases, where the failure to benefit comprises a failure to prevent physical harm being caused by third parties under one's control[32]; and nuisance or negligence cases, where the physical harm has emanated from property within one's control.[33]

The question then becomes one of whether liability for failure to benefit in contract differs fundamentally from the instances of liability for failure to benefit in tort.

One argument is that it does fundamentally differ because the failure to benefit in contract comprises a failure to fulfil expectations engendered in the plaintiff by the defendant, whereas there is no tort liability for a failure to fulfil expectations engendered in the plaintiff by the defendant.[34] But one may counter-argue that that distinction is not illuminating because, with the exception of promises and representations, there are few fact situations where the question of tort fulfilling specifically engendered expectations could arise. Moreover, some may regard that distinction as inaccurate because a *possible* interpretation of some tort of negligence cases is that they fulfil

---

[32] E.g. *Dorset Yacht Co. Ltd v. Home Office* [1970] AC 1004; *Carmarthenshire CC v. Lewis* [1955] AC 549.

[33] E.g. *Goldman v. Hargrave* [1967] 1 AC 645; *Leakey v. National Trust for Places of Historic Interest and Natural Beauty* [1980] QB 485. Cf. *Stovin v. Wise* [1996] AC 923.

[34] See Burrows, n. 7 above, 221, 244–53.

expectations engendered in the plaintiff by the defendant (and independently of a promise made by the defendant).[35]

Perhaps a more satisfying or convincing argument, therefore, is that the liability for failure to benefit in contract differs fundamentally from the liability for failure to benefit in tort because liability for failure to benefit in contract can be—and is most commonly—a strict liability. The promisor is liable for failing to do what he or she promised to do irrespective of whether he or she used reasonable care to fulfil the promise. In contrast, while a defendant may be strictly liable in tort for wrongful interference,[36] he or she is rarely, if ever, strictly liable in tort for a failure to benefit.

This argument comes very close to Jane Stapleton's thesis that the measure of damages in contract differs from that in tort in that the former is an "entitled result" measure whereas the latter is a "normal expectancies" measure.[37] She writes, "Throughout the law of torts the only measure of compensatory damages available is the normal expectancies measure which I have therefore dubbed the 'tort measure'. What this illuminates clearly is the fundamental principle that, though a stranger may be under even a strict obligation not tortiously to damage the plaintiff's position and prospects, a plaintiff suing for breach of a common law tort obligation is never entitled to demand that a stranger positively achieve an improvement in his normal expectancies. Thus, while a stranger may be under a tort obligation, indeed a strict tort obligation, to avoid an outcome such as to avoid damage to my reputation, I am not entitled to demand he achieve an outcome such as improving my reputation. Similarly, if I am handed a free television in a commercial promotion I can sue for the injuries it causes me if it blows up but not at all if it simply does not work, even if the promoter had purported to 'guarantee' it. In tort there are also obligations of affirmative action but there are no common law tort obligations of affirmative action to secure a result (i.e. no strict obligations with regard to the achievement of a result): where there

[35] See, e.g., *Midland Bank Trust Co. Ltd* v. *Hett, Stubbs and Kemp* [1979] Ch. 384; *Junior Books Ltd* v. *Veitchi Co. Ltd* [1983] 1 AC 520; and *White* v. *Jones* [1995] 2 AC 207. However, my own view is that there is no satisfactory non-promissory interpretation of such decisions: see essay 2, and the postscript to it, below, especially at 30–1.

[36] E.g. in the tort of defamation, under the rule in *Rylands* v. *Fletcher* (1868) LR 3 HL 330, or for breach of statutory duty.

[37] "The Normal Expectancies Measure in Tort Damages", n. 4 above. But I do not agree with Stapleton's further argument (in "A New 'Seascape' for Obligations: Reclassification on the Basis of Measure of Damages", n. 4 above) that one should restructure the law of obligations according to these different measures. Rather I regard the difference in measures as an argument for continuing to distinguish breach of promise from other wrongs.

are duties of affirmative action here they relate only to the use of reasonable care not to the achievement of a result".[38]

But if one goes on to ask (which Jane Stapleton does not) whether that distinction between liability for failure to benefit in contract and liability for failure to benefit in tort is justified, it is submitted that one has to go back to the distinction between voluntary obligations and purely imposed obligations; and this shows why, as we emphasised earlier,[39] the distinction between voluntary and purely imposed obligations is of first-level, rather than second-level, importance in justifying the distinction between contract and tort. It makes perfectly good sense to say that the range of liability for failure to benefit in respect of purely imposed obligations should be narrow and should not extend to imposing strict liability because this would otherwise represent too great an infringement of individual liberty. There is no such objection to imposing wide-ranging strict liability for a failure to benefit where the basis of the liability is a voluntarily assumed obligation precisely because the defendant has chosen, or by convention is taken to have chosen, to restrict his or her freedom in that way.

The root distinction between voluntary and purely imposed obligations provides a satisfactory explanation for other subsidiary differences in remedies given for breach of contract as opposed to for torts. For example, it is clear that punitive (or, as they have traditionally been known, exemplary) damages cannot be awarded for breach of contract.[40] Similarly, restitutionary damages can rarely be awarded for breach of contract.[41] In contrast punitive and restitutionary damages can much more readily be awarded for torts.[42] We can now see that an explanation for this is that, being based on a voluntary undertaking, the courts ought to tailor the remedy in contract to what was voluntarily undertaken and should therefore be reluctant to invoke non-compensatory remedies, such as punitive and restitutionary damages. In contrast, where the liability is purely imposed, as in tort, there need be no such reluctance.

---

[38] "The Normal Expectancies Measure in Tort Damages", n. 4 above, 266–7. See similarly A. Burrows, *Remedies for Torts and Breach of Contract* (2nd edn., 1994), 6–7.

[39] See 9 above.

[40] *Addis* v. *Gramophone Co. Ltd* [1909] AC 488; *Perera* v. *Vandiyar* [1953] 1 WLR 672.

[41] *Surrey CC* v. *Bredero Homes Ltd* [1993] 1 WLR 1361. Cf. *Attorney-General* v. *Blake*, [1998] 1 All ER 833. See 140–3 below.

[42] See *Aggravated, Exemplary and Restitutionary Damages*, n. 20 above, Parts III and IV. See 169–71 below.

The conclusion, therefore, is that the distinction between voluntary obligations and purely imposed obligations—and hence between liability for breach of a binding promise and liability for all other wrongs—is of fundamental importance in understanding the law of obligations. Given that the division between contract and tort has traditionally been seen as differentiating breach of a binding promise from all other wrongs it should be regarded, alongside restitution, as a satisfactory division of the law of obligations.[43]

6. EQUITABLE WRONGS

Finally, a word needs to be said on equitable wrongs, such as breach of fiduciary duty (including breach of trust), breach of confidence and dishonest procuring or assisting a breach of fiduciary duty.[44] These equitable wrongs are analogous to torts but differ because of their historical roots in the Court of Chancery rather than the common law courts. Although restitution can readily be awarded, the main remedy for these wrongs is "equitable compensation" which seeks to put the plaintiff into as good a position as if no wrong had occurred. Although in the long-term, one can hope that such equitable wrongs will be absorbed as torts (as has happened for example, with breach of copyright and patent infringement) or, at least, that the differences between the remedy of equitable compensation and compensatory damages will be eliminated,[45] at the present time one cannot simply call these equitable wrongs "torts". They should be seen as alongside, rather than as within, the law of tort. To this extent,

[43] Peter Birks, "The Concept of a Civil Wrong" in D. Owen (ed.), *Philosophical Foundations of Tort Law* (Clarendon Press, 1985), 31–51, esp. 34 and 51, regards contract as distinct from tort only to the extent that it enforces (for example, by specific performance) a primary obligation: the obligation to pay damages for a breach of contract is a secondary obligation and to that extent breach of contract is no different from torts (and can be added to the list of torts). My view, in contrast, is that both primary and secondary obligations in contract belong together as stemming from a voluntary obligation. All other obligations (whether stemming from wrongs or unjust enrichment) are purely imposed.

[44] The last of these was recognised and labelled in this way (in contrast to the traditional "knowing assistance in a fraudulent and dishonest scheme") by the Privy Council in *Royal Brunei Airlines Sdn. Bhd.* v. *Tan* [1995] 2 AC 378. I agree with Birks that undue influence and non-disclosure are not wrongs: see A. Burrows, *The Law of Restitution* (Butterworths, 1993) 377–9; P. Birks, "Unjust Factors and Wrongs: Pecuniary Rescission for Undue Influence" [1997] *RLR* 72.

[45] Important cases moving in the direction of removing distinctions between these two remedies are *Target Holdings Ltd* v. *Redferns* [1996] 1 AC 421; *Swindle* v. *Harrison* [1997] 4 All ER 705.

it is an oversimplification to talk merely of contract, tort and restitution. Strictly speaking one should instead be talking of a tripartite division between contract, tort and equitable wrongs, and restitution. This serves to show that, as illustrated by the debate on the relationship between consideration and promissory estoppel,[46] and as shown in relation to several aspects of the law of restitution,[47] a major challenge still facing the English law of obligations is to integrate properly common law and equity. More than a century after the Judicature Acts 1873–5 that historical divide continues to hamper the law's rational development.

[46] See n. 7 above, 239–44.
[47] See 105–8 below.

2

Solving the Problem of Concurrent Liability

I. INTRODUCTION

Everyone, to some extent, uses categories to make facts or ideas comprehensible and manageable. For lawyers, categorisation is particularly important because it is through categorisation—or as one might otherwise label it "principled reasoning"—that we attempt to adhere to that essential requirement of the rule of law that like cases should be treated alike. No doubt Professor John Dawson was correct to warn us against excessive formalism which he derided as "that well-known ailment of lawyers, a hardening of the categories".[1] But to reject the discipline of clarity and rationality imposed by categorisation is to slide from the rule of law into a potentially disastrous regime of decision-making by pure intuition.

Given the central importance of legal categorisation, it is not surprising that a fertile source of interest and controversy for lawyers is the situation where existing categories of the law overlap. The topic of this essay is one such area of overlap, namely that between the three main causes of action in civil law: contract, tort, and restitution. The phrase "concurrent liability" precisely refers to where there are overlapping causes of action; i.e. on the same facts the plaintiff, on the face of it, can frame his or her claim in more than one way. The problem posed by concurrent liability is whether the plaintiff has a free choice as to which cause of action to pursue. More particularly, to what extent, if at all, is a claim in tort or restitution ruled out because there is a contract between the parties.

So, for example, if my solicitor or architect gives me incorrect advice, have I a free choice whether to sue for the tort of negligence or for breach of his or her contractual obligation to advise me using reasonable care? Or if I have paid for goods that have not been deliv-

---

[1] J. Dawson, "Restitution or Damages" (1959) 20 *Ohio St. LJ* 175, 187.

ered, have I a free choice whether to sue in restitution for the recovery of the payment or to sue for damages for breach of contract?

In giving the leading speech of the House of Lords in *Henderson* v. *Merrett Syndicates Ltd*,[2] which dealt with the liability of Lloyd's underwriting agents to Names at Lloyds, Lord Goff said this: "My own belief is that, in the present context, the common law is not antipathetic to concurrent liability, and that there is no sound basis for a rule which automatically restricts the claimant to either a tortious or contractual remedy." Eight years earlier, in *Tai Hing Cotton Mill Ltd* v. *Liu Chong Hing Bank*,[3] which concerned customers' duties to their banks in respect of forged cheques, Lord Scarman, giving the opinion of the Privy Council, had put forward the diametrically opposite view saying, "Their Lordships do not believe that there is anything to the advantage of the law's development in searching for a liability in tort where the parties are in a contractual relationship." Expressing the same sentiment as Lord Scarman, but using rather more colourful language, Tipping J in a product liability case in the New Zealand High Court said, "if the parties have chosen a contractual bed they should ordinarily be expected to lie in it alone, without the seductive company of tort."[4]

One of my aims in this essay is to explain why, in my view, the House of Lords in *Henderson* was justified in rejecting Lord Scarman's infamous and influential dictum and in accepting concurrent liability between tort and contract. More generally my aim is to bring restitution into the frame of concurrent liability[5] and to develop a thesis for solving the concurrent liability problem whichever overlapping causes of action are in issue.

2. ADVANTAGES

Why might a plaintiff want to choose one, as opposed to another, of the three causes of action, assuming that he can establish the basic ingredients of more than one of the three?

Leaving aside matters of procedure and private international law, the most significant advantages are threefold.

---

[2] [1994] 3 WLR 761, 788.
[3] [1986] AC 80, 107.
[4] *Simms Jones Ltd* v. *Protochem Trading New Zealand Ltd* [1993] 3 NZLR 369, 381.
[5] For the basic features of a cause of action in restitution, see 6–8 above and essay 3 below.

(1) The plaintiff may be entitled to a higher quantum of recovery because the principal aim of the remedies for each cause of action differs. So for breach of contract, the remedies are principally concerned to protect the plaintiff's expectation interest by putting the plaintiff into as good a position as if the contract had been performed. For tort, the remedies are principally concerned to protect the plaintiff's status quo or reliance interest by putting him or her into as good a position as if no tort had occurred. And in restitution the remedies are concerned to protect the plaintiff's restitution interest by reversing the defendant's unjust enrichment at the plaintiff's expense. As the quantum of the expectation, status quo and restitution interests may differ it follows that one cause of action rather than another may be advantageous for the plaintiff. It should be added that there may be further quantum advantages flowing from subsidiary remedial aims of the different causes of action. For example, exemplary damages concerned to punish the defendant can be awarded for certain torts but not for breach of contract.

(2) The plaintiff may be entitled to a higher quantum of recovery because the principles limiting damages are not applied in the same way to claims for breach of contract as they are for tort. For example, the rules on remoteness and on whether one can recover for mental distress or loss of reputation are traditionally more favourable to plaintiffs in tort than in contract; whereas the law on contributory negligence is less favourable to plaintiffs in tort than in contract.

(3) The plaintiff may be entitled to a longer limitation period for commencing one cause of action rather than another. This may be because the statutory time period is longer. Or it may be because the different causes of action accrue at different dates so that the statutory time period starts running at different dates. Or it may be because of the application of the Latent Damage Act 1986, with its discoverability test, which applies to the tort of negligence but not to breach of contract.[6]

In so far as one is talking about tort and contract, the second and third of those three advantages seem to me highly controversial. Unless one wishes to defend awards of nominal damages, why should a contractual cause of action, but not a tortious negligence claim, accrue without any loss being suffered? Can it be right that a cause of action in contract, but not in the tort of negligence, may be lost before the plaintiff could have known that he or she had that action?

[6] *Iron Trade Mutual Ins. Co. Ltd* v. *J.K. Buckenham Ltd* [1990] 1 All ER 808; *Islander Trucking Ltd & Hogg Robinson* v. *Gardner Mountain (Marine) Ltd* [1990] 1 All ER 826.

And why should the fact that one is suing for a breach of contract rather than a tort mean that the more restrictive remoteness rules of *Hadley* v. *Baxendale*[7] rather than *Wagon Mound*[8] apply? On that last issue, who can forget the desperate pleas of Lord Denning MR in *Parsons (Livestock) Ltd* v. *Uttley Ingham & Co. Ltd*[9] in which the question at issue was whether the supplier of a defective pig hopper should be held liable in contract for the loss of 254 pigs that had died from a rare intestinal disease after eating nuts that had gone mouldy in the hopper? After referring to the different remoteness tests in contract and tort, Lord Denning said, "I find it difficult to apply those principles universally to all cases of contract or to all cases of tort: and to draw a distinction between what a man 'contemplates' and what he 'foresees'. I soon begin to get out of my depth. I cannot swim in this sea of semantic exercises—to say nothing of the different degrees of probability—especially when the cause of action can be laid either in contract or in tort. I am swept under by the conflicting currents. I go back with relief to the distinction drawn in legal theory by Professors Hart and Honoré . . ." which he then explained to be a distinction between whether the type of damage suffered was physical damage or pure economic loss rather than whether the cause of action was contract or tort.

In contrast to the second and third advantages, the first advantage—that the principal aims of the remedies differ—is, in my view, entirely justified and is one way of explaining the validity and vitality of the contract, tort, restitution taxonomy. Of course, as far as contract and tort are concerned, one can unite the principal aims by saying that in both one is primarily concerned with compensation by aiming to put the plaintiff into as good a position as if no breach of contract or tort had occurred. But that formulation has the disadvantage of tending to obscure the crucial fact that most obligations in contract are for nonfeasance—i.e. a failure to benefit—whereas most obligations in tort are for misfeasance—i.e. harmful interference. As Mr Tony Weir has written in his incomparable comparative law analysis of the problems of concurrent liability in the *International Encyclopedia of Comparative Law*: "Human good, for which the law exists, depends on the maintenance and development of human goods—[such as] life, health, property, and wealth. . . . To ensure their maintenance we have the law of tort, and to promote their

[7] (1854) 9 Exch. 341.
[8] [1961] AC 388.
[9] [1978] 1 All ER 525, 534.

development we have the law of contract. Contract is productive, tort law protective. In other words, tortfeasors are typically liable for making things worse, contractors for not making them better."[10]

This distinction between a failure to benefit and harmful interference is of fundamental importance, for while imposing liability for the latter is straightforwardly justifiable on the basic libertarian principle that one can do what one likes provided it does not harm anyone else, to impose a liability for failure to benefit is in general regarded as an unwarranted interference with an individual's freedom of action. True there are, ever increasingly, exceptional situations in which tort liability is imposed for a failure to benefit. Classic illustrations are negligence cases, where the failure to benefit comprises a failure to prevent physical harm being caused by third parties under one's control.[11] But the essential difference between such tort examples of a failure to benefit and the failure to benefit imposed in contract—and reflected in contract's standard protection of the plaintiff's expectation interest—is that the liability in contract flows naturally from the parties' own voluntarily assumed obligations. By imposing a liability for a failure to benefit, the law of contract is essentially merely upholding the parties' own commitments.[12]

3. CENTRAL THESIS

I now want to turn to my central thesis. Given that it may be advantageous to a plaintiff to frame a claim on one cause of action rather than another, how should the law solve the concurrent liability problem? My suggested solution, based on respecting party autonomy, is as follows: the plaintiff should have a free choice to sue in tort or restitution, irrespective of a contract between the parties, subject to three restricting principles which I label the independence principle, the exclusion principle, and the anti-circularity principle.

According to the independence principle, if a claim for tort or restitution is not independent of a claim for breach of contract, the rules governing contractual claims, as a matter of logic, should apply.

---

[10] *International Encyclopedia of Comparative Law*, Vol XI, ch. 12, *Complex Liabilities*, para. 6. See 10–11 above.

[11] Eg *Dorset Yacht Co. Ltd* v. *Home Office* [1970] AC 1004; *Carmarthenshire CC* v. *Lewis* [1955] AC 549. See 11 above.

[12] See essay 1 above; A. Burrows, *Remedies for Torts and Breach of Contract* (2nd edn., Butterworths, 1994), 6, 20.

That is, if in essence the claim is one to enforce a contract, it would be illogical not to apply contractual rules.

By the exclusion principle, if the parties in their contract have validly excluded liability in tort or restitution, that must be respected. It clearly cannot be right to override the parties' intentions by ignoring valid exclusion clauses. Where there is an express exclusion clause, the acceptance and application of this principle are straightforward and well understood. Much more problematic, and central to the concurrent liability dilemma, is whether the parties to a contract have *impliedly excluded* liability in tort or restitution. On a very wide view of implied exclusion, the mere existence of the contract could be read as an implied exclusion of non-contractual liability, thereby automatically denying concurrent liability. In my opinion, that would go too far and would have the effect of undermining, rather than respecting, the autonomy of the parties. The preferable view is that it must be clear, over and above the mere existence of the contract, that the parties intended to exclude non-contractual liability. The most obvious illustration of this is that the parties can normally be taken to have intended that no more onerous standard of performance liability should be imposed by tort than is laid down by the express or implied terms of the contract.

According to the anti-circularity principle, a plaintiff seeking restitution of a benefit conferred under a contract or apparent contract must first establish that that contract is invalid, whether because it is void, voidable, or unenforceable, or because it has been discharged for breach or frustration. This is required in order to break the circularity of holding a party contractually liable to confer a benefit which the law of restitution requires the other party to return.

I would like to add two points at this stage. First, while I am confining my attention in this essay to overlaps between contract, tort and restitution, the thesis I am putting forward is equally applicable to other examples of concurrent liability, in particular to overlaps between the equitable wrongs of breach of fiduciary duty or breach of confidence and contract.[13] Secondly, the free choice thesis does not touch on the question whether a plaintiff can *combine* remedies for more than one cause of action. Combining remedies raises

---

[13] For this kind of overlap see, e.g., *Aquaculture Corpn.* v. *New Zealand Green Mussel Co. Ltd* [1990] 3 NZLR 299.

different questions, and requires different answers, than does the problem of concurrent liability.[14]

For the rest of this essay I want to test, and illustrate, my suggested thesis by considering in detail the two most problematic areas of concurrent liability. First, should a plaintiff be able to escape from a bad bargain by suing the defendant in restitution for a failure of consideration rather than suing the defendant for breach of contract? Secondly, should a plaintiff be able to sue the defendant for the tort of negligence rather than suing the defendant for breach of contract?

4. SHOULD A PLAINTIFF BE ABLE TO ESCAPE FROM A BAD BARGAIN BY SUING THE DEFENDANT IN RESTITUTION FOR A FAILURE OF CONSIDERATION RATHER THAN SUING THE DEFENDANT FOR BREACH OF CONTRACT?

Say, for example, P contracts to buy a bicycle from D for £900 and pays £100 in advance but that D fails to deliver the bicycle albeit that its market price is only £700. Or say P contracts to build a tunnel for D, and half way through D repudiates the contract even though the contractual rate for the work is below the market rate. In either case is P entitled to discharge the contract and claim restitution of the advance payment or the value of the work done even though, because the bargain was a bad one for P, this would give him or her a higher sum than contractual damages?

This question has never been definitively decided by the English courts. In some other jurisdictions, however, restitution has been allowed to trump contract by allowing the plaintiff to escape from a bad bargain. In the Connecticut case of *Bush* v. *Canfield*[15] the plaintiff contracted to buy flour from the defendant seller for $14,000. Although the market price dropped to $11,000 the seller failed to deliver the flour. The plaintiff buyer terminated the contract and sought restitution of the $5,000 part payment that had been made. This was granted even though the plaintiff buyer would have lost $3,000 on the transaction (and his expectation damages would therefore have been $2,000). And in the Californian case of *Boomer* v. *Muir*[16] the plaintiffs recovered a quantum meruit of $257,000 for

[14] See the postscript to this essay.
[15] 2 Conn. 485 (1818); Hosmer J dissented.
[16] 24 P 2d 570 (1933).

work in building a dam even though they were entitled to only another $20,000 under the contract.

Applying my suggested thesis, restitution should indeed here trump contract by allowing the plaintiff a free choice to sue in restitution unaffected by what his remedies would have been had he sued for breach of contract. The anti-circularity principle is not infringed provided one insists that the plaintiff can only claim restitution where he or she has validly discharged the contract for the defendant's breach. And subject to there being an express exclusion clause or perhaps a liquidated damages clause one cannot normally say that the parties have excluded restitution. Normally their attention will have been focused on performance and not on what the consequences of a breach should be. This leaves as the key issue the independence principle. Is the claim in restitution independent of a claim for breach of contract? I would argue that it is. The thrust of the plaintiff's claim for failure of consideration is not that the defendant has committed a breach of contract but rather that the defendant has been unjustly enriched by receiving a benefit from the plaintiff that was rendered on the basis of a counter-performance by the defendant that has not been forthcoming. So it is that the same, or a very similar, restitutionary claim for failure of consideration can be brought irrespective of any breach, for example where there was never a valid contract between the parties or where there was a valid contract but it has been discharged by frustration rather than breach.

Of course the fact that the restitutionary claim is independent does not mean that one has to ignore the contract price in working out the value of *services* rendered to the defendant. A recurring theme throughout the law of restitution is that to measure the defendant's enrichment by the objective value of non-monetary benefits is often too harsh to defendants.[17] Normally—but not always—defendants can legitimately argue that they have only been enriched in line with the value they placed on the services in the contract or purported contract. It is for this reason, and not because contract should override restitution, that the actual decision in the dam case of *Boomer* v. *Muir* can be criticised. Could it really be said that the services in building the dam were worth to the defendant their objective market value rather than the price agreed in the contract?

In this respect, it is interesting to contrast the claim in restitution with a claim for reliance damages for breach of contract. It has been

---

[17] See essay 4 below; and A. Burrows, *The Law of Restitution* (Butterworths, 1993), 7–16, 268–70.

clearly established by cases such as *CCC Films (London) Ltd* v. *Impact Quadrant Films Ltd*,[18] where the plaintiffs did not receive films that they had paid for, that a plaintiff cannot escape from a known bad bargain by claiming reliance damages for breach of contract rather than the usual expectation damages. And this is precisely because, unlike the restitutionary claim for failure of consideration, reliance damages are dependent on, and not independent of, the breach of contract.

5. SHOULD A PLAINTIFF BE ABLE TO SUE THE DEFENDANT FOR THE TORT OF NEGLIGENCE RATHER THAN SUING THE DEFENDANT FOR BREACH OF CONTRACT?

This, the second testing ground for my thesis, is the area where there has been most controversy.[19] It is also the area most lawyers think of when hearing the phrase "concurrent liability".

In the leading case of *Henderson* v. *Merrett Syndicates Ltd*,[20] it was decided that concurrent liability between the tort of negligence and contract should be accepted whatever the relevant form of damage but, for the purposes of exposition and for more substantial reasons that will become clear in due course, I am going to rely on the distinction familiar to all tort students between negligently caused physical damage, whether personal injury or damage to property, and negligently caused pure economic loss.

---

[18] [1985] QB 16.

[19] There is a large body of literature on this topic. See, e.g., C. French, "The Contract/Tort Dilemma" (1982) 5 *Otago LR* 236; J. Holyoak, "Tort and Contract After Junior Books" (1983) 99 *LQR* 591; F.M.B. Reynolds, "Tort Actions in Contractual Situations" (1985) 11 *NZULR* 215; A.J.E. Jaffey, "Contract in Tort's Clothing" (1985) 5 *Legal Studies* 77; B.S. Markesinis, "An Expanding Tort Law—The Price of a Rigid Contract Law" (1987) 103 *LQR* 354; W. Lorenz and B.S. Markesinis, "Solicitors' Liability Towards Third Parties" (1993) 56 *MLR* 558; K. Barker, "Are we up to Expectations? Solicitors, Beneficiaries and the Tort/Contract Divide", (1994) 14 *OJLS* 137; Sir Robin Cooke, "Tort and Contract" in P. Finn (ed.), *Essays on Contract* (The Law Book Co., 1987); P. Cane, "Contract, Tort and Economic Loss", ch. 6 in M. Furmston, *The Law of Tort* (OUP, 1986); P. Cane, *Tort Law and Economic Interests* (2nd edn., Sweet & Maxwell, 1996), 129–49, 307–34; *Chitty on Contracts* (27th edn., 1994), paras. 1–042 to 1–029; R. Jackson and J. Powell, *Professional Negligence* (4th edn., Sweet & Maxwell, 1997), paras. 1–50 to 1–57.

[20] [1994] 3 WLR 761.

(1) *Negligently Caused Physical Damage*

This can be dealt with very briefly because concurrent liability has
here been long accepted and I do not think anyone seriously thought
that Lord Scarman's dictum in *Tai Hing*, that I referred to earlier, was
intended to affect cases of physical damage.

Of the numerous decisions that could be used to illustrate the
courts' traditional acceptance of the plaintiff's free choice, subject to
exclusion, in this sphere, I pick just one. In *Jackson* v. *Mayfair Window
Cleaning Co. Ltd*,[21] the defendants had contracted to clean the plaintiff's chandelier. While they were doing so, the chandelier fell from
the ceiling and smashed. The plaintiff sued for the negligently caused
property damage and the question was whether that claim could lie
in tort. Barry J said, "What I have to ask myself . . . is whether, in
essence, the plaintiff must rely on [the] contract in order to establish
her claim or whether she can properly treat the contract as a mere
matter of history, explaining the presence of the defendants' work-
man in her flat, and establish a breach of duty independent of any
obligations undertaken by the defendants to her under that contract.
In my judgment, the present claim falls within the latter category.
The plaintiff does not complain . . . that the defendants failed to clean
her chandelier at the time or in the manner stipulated by their contract. Her case is based on a broader duty, independent of any contractual obligation undertaken by the defendants. She says that if the
defendants, through their workmen, interfere with her property—
whether with or without her permission and whether in pursuance
of a contract or otherwise—they are under an obligation not to damage that property as a result of their negligence. . . . This is, I think,
the true foundation of the plaintiff's claim."[22]

Barry J was stressing, therefore, the independence of the
negligence claim from that for breach of contract. And this is surely
correct.[23] Where one is concerned with negligently caused physical
harm, the liability is almost invariably based on the defendant's

---

[21] [1952] 1 All ER 215. See also, e.g., *Donoghue* v. *Stevenson* [1932] AC 562, 610 (*per* Lord
MacMillan); *Matthews* v. *Kuwait Bechtal Corp.* [1959] 2 KB 57, 67 (*per* Sellers LJ).

[22] *Ibid.*, at 217–18.

[23] That the tortious negligence claim is independent is strengthened when one considers
the situation where P is a third party who has been injured or has suffered property damage
as a result of negligence by D in performing its contract with X: for it is clear that the tort
of negligence may in that situation impose a higher standard of care than that contractually
undertaken by D to X. See, e.g., *Junior Books Ltd* v. *Veitchi Co. Ltd* [1983] 1 AC 520, 533
E–F (*per* Lord Fraser).

harmful interference and not on a failure to benefit the plaintiff. Correspondingly there will rarely be any difficulty in accepting that the obligation to take reasonable care for one's neighbour is justifiably imposed independently of any binding promise made by the defendant. And even where exceptionally the tort liability is imposed for a failure to benefit, the very fact that the relevant harm is physical, and hence in general more serious, renders an independent non-promissory justification for liability less problematic than where the loss involved is purely economic.[24]

(2) Negligently Caused Pure Economic Loss

When one turns to negligently caused pure economic loss, the picture of a long well-established acceptance of concurrent liability dramatically changes. Coming in to *Henderson* there was support in the tangled case law for both the rejection of concurrent liability and its acceptance in this context.[25] From the mass of cases, the most influential were, on the one hand, *Tai Hing*, rejecting concurrent liability and, on the other hand, *Midland Bank Trust Co.* v. *Hett Stubbs and Kemp*,[26] in which Oliver J held that a solicitor who negligently failed to register as a land charge his client's option to purchase a farm, with the result that the farm was acquired by someone else, was concurrently liable in contract and tort.

---

[24] I.e. we may well consider it an acceptable interference with individual liberty to be required in certain situations to step in to save another's health or perhaps property when, analogously, requiring intervention to save another from pure economic loss would be thought unacceptably intrusive. If there are situations in which a liability for negligently caused physical damage cannot be justified independently of the defendant's binding promise, the case for allowing concurrent liability would to that extent rest on pragmatism not principle, as is explained below at 31–3.

[25] Decisions or dicta rejecting concurrent liability included *Groom* v. *Crocker* [1939] 1 KB 194; *Bagot v. Stevens Scanlon* [1966] 1 QB 197; *Tai Hing Cotton Mill Ltd* v. *Liu Chong Hing Bank* [1986] AC 80, 107 (*per* Lord Scarman); *Banque Financiere* v. *Westgate Insurance Co.* [1989] 2 All ER 952, 1011 (*per* Slade LJ); *Lee* v. *Thompson* [1989] 2 EGLR 150, 153 (*per* Lloyd LJ); *Bell* v. *Peter Browne & Co.* [1990] 3 WLR 510, 524 (*per* Mustill LJ); *Scally* v. *Southern H & S Services Board* [1991] 4 All ER 563. Decisions or dicta accepting concurrent liability included *Midland Bank Trust Co.* v. *Hett Stubbs and Kemp* [1979] Ch. 384; *Ross* v. *Caunters* [1980] Ch. 297; *Forsikringsaktieselskapet Vesta* v. *Butcher* [1988] 2 All ER 43, 47 (*per* O'Connor LJ); *South* v. *Eric Bush* [1990] 1 AC 831, 870 (*per* Lord Jauncey); *Caparo Industries Plc* v. *Dickman* [1990] 2 AC 605, 619 (*per* Lord Bridge); *Youell* v. *Bland Welch & Co. Ltd (No. 2)* [1990] 2 Lloyd's Rep. 431; *Punjab National Bank* v. *De Boinville* [1992] 3 All ER 104; *Lancashire & Cheshire Assoc. of Baptist Churches Inc.* v. *Howard & Seddon Partnership* [1993] 3 All ER 467, 477.

[26] [1979] Ch. 384.

Henderson has now settled the controversy by supporting *Midland Bank* and rejecting *Tai Hing*. There are three key strands in the leading speech of Lord Goff. First, that Oliver J in *Midland Bank* had correctly interpreted the House of Lords' decision in *Hedley Byrne & Co. Ltd v. Heller & Partners Ltd*[27] as supporting concurrent liability in this context; secondly, that this was also the approach persuasively adopted in other Commonwealth jurisdictions;[28] and, thirdly, that in terms of principle and policy respect for the will of the parties to the contract did not require more than recognising that a concurrent tort liability should not outflank an exclusion or limitation in the contract. Lord Goff also went on to apply an analogous approach to what one might call the "privity" question, beyond our immediate concern in this essay, of whether the indirect Lloyd's Names (i.e. those who had no contract with the defendant managing agents) had a tortious negligence claim despite the chain of agency and sub-agency contracts that had been set up.

Lord Goff expressed his central conclusion as follows: "given that the tortious duty is imposed by the general law, and the contractual duty is attributable to the will of the parties, I do not find it objectionable that the claimant may be able to take advantage of the remedy which is most advantageous to him, subject only to ascertaining whether the tortious duty is so inconsistent with the applicable contract that, in accordance with ordinary principle, the parties must be taken to have agreed that the tortious remedy is to be limited or excluded."[29]

The burning theoretical question is whether their Lordships in *Henderson* got it right, or whether on the contrary *Tai Hing* exemplified a preferable approach. In answering this my suggested thesis requires one to focus on the independence and exclusion principles, the anti-circularity principle having no role to play, being concerned entirely with overlaps between restitution and contract.

The exclusion principle featured prominently in Lord Goff's speech. As is apparent in the passage just cited, and there are other passages to similar effect, his Lordship's acceptance of concurrent liability was explicitly qualified by the idea that tort should not impose a liability inconsistent with the contract. Although what is

---

[27] [1964] AC 465.
[28] Most notably by the Supreme Court of Canada in the solicitors' negligence case of *Central Trust Co.* v. *Rafuse* (1986) 31 DLR (4th) 481. See also *BG Checo International Ltd* v. *British Columbia Hydro & Power Authority* (1993) 99 DLR (4th) 577.
[29] [1994] 3 WLR 761, 788.

meant by inconsistency is open to interpretation, I have already suggested that, leaving aside express exclusion clauses, what should principally be in mind is that the tort of negligence should not impose a more onerous performance liability than that contractually undertaken. On the facts that was not so; the purported tort liability of the managing agents to the direct names at Lloyds was no more onerous than their implied contractual obligation to use reasonable care and skill in the exercise of their functions as managing agents.

Much more perplexing is the application of the independence principle. In what sense was the tort obligation in *Henderson* independent of the contractual obligation to use reasonable care and skill? As a matter of logic, if the essential basis for the tort was the defendant's contractual promise, the contractual rules should have applied; it would be illogical to have two causes of action founded on the same basis.

Lord Goff described the governing tort principle as being "an assumption of responsibility coupled with reliance by the plaintiff", which he regarded as the wider principle established in English law thirty years ago by the House of Lords in *Hedley Byrne* v. *Heller*.[30] In that case it was held that, subject to their disclaimer, bankers would have been liable in tort for the gratuitous provision to the plaintiff of a negligently favourable reference for one of their customers.

The difficulty is to know what is meant by an "assumption of responsibility". Other Law Lords in cases subsequent to *Hedley Byrne*, such as Lord Griffiths in *Smith* v. *Eric Bush*[31] and Lord Roskill in *Caparo Industries Plc* v. *Dickman*,[32] have rejected it as unhelpful; and its ambiguity has been subjected to penetrating scrutiny and attack by Mr Kit Barker writing in the 1993 *Law Quarterly Review*.[33]

In analysing what is meant, it cannot be emphasised too strongly that in so far as one merely means that the defendant in a professional or business context has given advice or information for the benefit of the plaintiff that has been relied on by the plaintiff, as was directly in issue in *Hedley Byrne*, there is no difficulty in regarding the imposition of a duty of care in tort as independent of any contractual liability of the defendant.[34] This is essentially because the objection to

---

[30] [1964] AC 465.

[31] [1990] 1 AC 831, 864–5.

[32] [1990] 2 AC 605, 628.

[33] "Unreliable Assumptions in the Modern Law of Negligence" (1993) 109 *LQR* 461.

[34] Cf. where the plaintiff's complaint is not that he has detrimentally relied on the defendant's misrepresentation but that the defendant has failed to make the statement that reasonable care required and the plaintiff needs such a statement to be made in order to make

negligent misrepresentation is that the defendant has harmfully interfered with the plaintiff, not that the defendant has failed to benefit the
plaintiff. So it is that, as established by numerous cases, whether on
the common law tort or the analogous tort of deceit or the analogous
statutory tort created by section 2(1) of the Misrepresentation Act
1967, damages for tortious misrepresentation protect the plaintiff's
reliance and not his expectation interest.[35]

However, once one moves from statements to the performance of
beneficial services, a complaint of negligently caused pure economic
loss naturally embraces a complaint of failure to benefit. So, for
example in *Midland Bank* v. *Hett Stubbs and Kemp* the complaint was
not that the plaintiff was in a worse position than if no services had
been rendered by the solicitor but rather that the plaintiff was in a
worse position than if the solicitor had registered the option to purchase. In other words the claim was one for a failure to benefit—a
claim for the expectation interest—and not one for harmful interference, i.e. for protection of the reliance interest.[36]

So we return to the question, now leaving aside misstatements,
what is meant by an assumption of responsibility?

It would appear that what their Lordships had in mind was that a
defendant has promised, by words or conduct, to render services for
the benefit of the plaintiff: the independence from contract being
perceived to be that, provided relied on, that promise may be gratuitous and need not be supported by consideration. This fits precisely
with Lord Devlin's speech in *Hedley Byrne*. In passages cited and
relied on by Lord Goff, Lord Devlin said, "A promise given without
consideration to perform a service cannot be enforced as a contract
by the promisee: but if the service is in fact performed and done negligently, the promisee can recover in an action in tort."[37] And later

---

a gain. In that situation the aim of damages is to put the plaintiff into as good a position as
if a statement using reasonable care had been made rather than into as good a position as if
no statement had been made. An example, but one where the statement is made to a third
party rather than to the plaintiff, is *Spring* v. *Guardian Assurance Plc* [1994] 3 WLR 354, where
it was held that a duty of care is owed to one's former employee in writing a reference that
was an essential requirement for the plaintiff's employment by a new employer.

[35] See, e.g., *Gran Gelato Ltd* v. *Richcliff (Group) Ltd* [1992] 1 All ER 865, 876; *Royscot Trust
Ltd* v. *Rogerson* [1991] 2 QB 297, 304–5; *Cemp Properties (UK) Ltd* v. *Dentsply Research &
Development Corp* [1991] 2 EGLR 197, 201. See generally Burrows, n. 12 above, 172–6.

[36] To argue that *Midland Bank* was a case of harmful interference would seem to lead to
the untenable conclusion that there is no difference between the expectation and reliance
interests, i.e. that every failure to benefit (at least of an obligation to use reasonable care) represents the loss of the same benefit elsewhere.

[37] [1964] AC 465, 526.

he continued, "the categories of special relationships which may give rise to a duty to take care in word as well as in deed are not limited to contractual relationships or to relationships of fiduciary duty, but include also relationships which in the words of Lord Shaw in *Nocton* v. *Lord Ashburton*[38] are 'equivalent to contract', that is, where there is an assumption of responsibility in circumstances in which, but for the absence of consideration, there would be a contract."[39]

But if this promissory explanation is correct, it carries with it certain difficulties. For example, there seems no stopping point short of saying that every negligent breach of contract for services causing loss, including an expectation loss, is now actionable as a tort. The builder who negligently completes a job late or the car mechanic whose workmanship is negligently defective surely falls as squarely within the promissory assumption of responsibility principle as does the professional rendering services. And is there a sufficently clear distinction between the rendering of services and the performance of other beneficial acts? If not, is it the case that the seller of goods who negligently fails to deliver them to the purchaser, or negligently delivers them late, or negligently delivers goods that are not of merchantable quality can now be sued by the purchaser in the tort of negligence? Most importantly for the theme of this essay, it is all very well to treat gratuitous promises as independent of promises supported by consideration where there is no consideration—although even that runs counter to the views of academics as poles apart doctrinally as Professors Atiyah and Fried, who convincingly argue that the present doctrine of consideration should be abandoned—but it is another matter entirely to regard there as being any continuing independence for a tort action where the relevant promise *is* supported by consideration.

Is there any alternative explanation of "assumption of responsibility" that avoids falling foul of the independence principle in this way? I think not. Any idea that the law of tort simply imposes an obligation to use reasonable care where the defendant is performing services, analogously to its imposition of liability for statements, fails to provide any convincing justification for why the defendant is held liable not merely for harmful interference but also for a failure to benefit the plaintiff.

One might have thought that some help would be gleaned from a consideration of the law on fiduciaries, where, conventionally, oblig-

[38] [1914] AC 932, 972.
[39] [1964] AC 465, 528.

ations are imposed for a failure to benefit. Indeed the kernel of Lord Browne-Wilkinson's short speech in *Henderson* was that fiduciary liability should be regarded as an example of, and subsumed within, the wider tort liability being imposed.[40] Intriguingly, however, this line of enquiry merely leads one back to the same dilemma, this time in trying to clarify who is a fiduciary. So, for example, Professor Austin Scott's classic definition, "A fiduciary is a person who undertakes to act in the interests of another person"[41] is clearly similar to their Lordships' "assumption of responsibility". But what does that definition signify beyond a promise, by words or conduct, to benefit another?

I have also considered whether anything could turn on whether the defendant has started to perform the services or not: on the distinction, in other words, between executed and executory services. But if a solicitor has induced a plaintiff, by his words or conduct, to rely on his registering an option, it surely cannot matter in establishing a duty of care whether any steps have been taken to register that option or not. Analogously I have always found puzzling the suggestion that, while a stranger is not under a legal obligation to use reasonable care to rescue a drowning child, the stranger who starts to effect the rescue may come under a legal obligation to complete it, irrespective of whether the child's position has been worsened by the intervention (e.g. by pre-empting rescue attempts by more competent rescuers).[42]

One is driven to the conclusion, therefore, that applying the strict logic of the independence principle, the decision in *Henderson* may be found wanting. Nevertheless it seems that the decision is correct and that the Lords were right to accept concurrent liability. To understand how this can be, we must return to the earlier part of this essay where I suggested that it was hard to see why restrictions on damages, such as remoteness and, particularly importantly, limitation periods, should be less favourable to plaintiffs suing for breach of contract than for the tort of negligence. The strictly logical development would be to reform the law of contract so as to eliminate its unwarranted disadvantages thereby removing the incentive to sue in tort. But this would presumably require legislation and, even from my seat at the

---

[40] For criticism of this, see J.D. Heydon, "The Negligent Fiduciary" (1995) 111 *LQR* 1.

[41] "The Fiduciary Principle" (1949) 37 *Calif. LR* 539, 540. See also P. Finn, "The Fiduciary Principle" in T.G. Youdan (ed.), *Equity, Fiduciaries and Trusts* (Carswell, 1989), 1–56, esp. 54.

[42] See the postscript to this essay.

Law Commission, that seems an unlikely development. The pragmatic solution is to allow plaintiffs to evade those unwarranted disadvantages by framing what is in essence a contractual claim as a claim in tort. That, it seems to me, is the true justification for *Henderson* and is reflected in various passages in the speech of Lord Goff and in the judgment in the Court of Appeal of Sir Thomas Bingham MR. After referring to the injustice that can be produced by, *inter alia*, the English limitation rules in contract, the Master of the Rolls said, "The present law [on concurrent duties in contract and tort] has developed, untidily but pragmatically, to enable the courts to do justice despite these rules."[43] And in the words of Lord Goff, after referring, *inter alia*, to the different rules, as between contract and tort, for limitation and remoteness of damage, "It can of course be argued that the principle established in respect of concurrent liability in contract and tort should not be tailored to mitigate the adventitious effects of rules of law such as these, and that one way of solving such problems would no doubt be 'to rephrase such incidental rules as have to remain in terms of the nature of the harm suffered rather than the nature of the liability asserted'.[44] But this is perhaps crying for the moon. . . ."[45] And although written in respect of the analogous question whether the tort of negligence can outflank the doctrine of privity by enabling a third party to sue for an intended benefit,[46] the following passage from an essay by Donald Harris and Cento Veljanovski perfectly describes the position: "The rational way forward would be to [reform contract] . . .: this reform, however, would probably need legislation, which might be indefinitely delayed. A 'second-best' solution is to use the law of torts to plug the gaps left by contract law, but this should be done with full realisation of what we are doing."[47]

So it seems to me that the independence principle shows that the contrast between *Tai Hing* and *Henderson* is ultimately a contrast between the forces of logic and those of pragmatism.

---

[43] Transcript, 16.

[44] Lord Goff here referred to Weir, n. 10 above, para. 72.

[45] [1994] 3 WLR 761, 781.

[46] Although outside the central theme of this essay, I would argue that, in contrast to claims for negligently caused physical damage, claims in the tort of negligence by third parties to a contract for pure economic loss measured by the expectation interest are not independent of the contract. The claim in negligence is a pragmatic way round the privity doctrine. For support for the view that the claim in the tort of negligence is not independent of the contract, see e.g. *Junior Books* v. *Veitchi* [1983] AC 520, 551–2 (*per* Lord Brandon, dissenting). Cf. n. 24 above.

[47] "Liability for Economic Loss in Tort", ch. 3 in M. Furmston (ed.), *The Law of Tort* (Duckworth, 1986), 59.

Of course, the pragmatic solution is limited, in that it leaves untouched the law on the non-negligent breach of strict contractual obligations. Yet the victim of such a breach has an equally strong case for saying, for example, that the law of limitation operates too harshly in leaving him time-barred even though he could not reasonably know that he had a claim. Analogously, no-one has ever suggested, as far as I am aware, that one should confine reform of the doctrine of privity to where the contract to benefit the third party has been negligently broken. So unless one believes that a more principled categorisation of the law of obligations is between strict obligations and obligations of reasonable care rather than between contractual and tortious obligations—a view advanced, most famously, by Lord Cooke[48]—the pragmatic solution in *Henderson* should not be regarded as ending the need for reform of, for example, contractual limitation periods.

6. CONCLUSION

If one does not believe in the division between contract, tort and restitution, an acceptance of concurrent liability can be presented as showing the break-down of that categorisation. I have approached the topic as a long-committed believer in that division and have sought to develop a thesis that is applicable whatever overlapping causes of action are in issue. In applying the thesis that plaintiffs should be free to choose their cause of action subject to the principles of exclusion, anti-circularity and independence, my conclusions have been that always subject to exclusion: first, an innocent plaintiff, after discharge for breach, should be free to escape from a bad bargain by claiming restitution for failure of consideration; secondly, a party to a contract should be free, largely as a matter of principle, to sue in tort for negligently caused physical damage and negligent misstatements; and thirdly, in respect of the negligent rendering of services causing pure economic loss, concurrent liability is an acceptable pragmatic solution pending legislative reform of, for example, contractual limitation periods. Whether one agrees with those conclusions or not, I hope at the very least that my suggested thesis can

---

[48] "Tort and Contract" in P. Finn (ed.), *Essays on Contract* (Law Book Co., 1987), 222, 228–32; "The Condition of the Law of Tort" in P. Birks (ed.), *Frontiers of Liability* (Clarendon Press, 1994), ii, 49, 60–1.

provide a scheme of analysis by which the complex problem of concurrent liability can be rationally debated and solved.

This postscript deals with two questions that were briefly touched on
in the above essay but merit more detailed consideration. First, can a
liability for failure to benefit justifiably arise from starting to perform
services rather than from a promise (made by words or conduct) to
perform the services? Secondly, what should be the law on combining
remedies for one (or more) cause(s) of action?

1. *Starting to Perform Services*

In the above essay, I indicated that I found unconvincing the idea that
a liability for failure to benefit could justifiably arise from starting to
perform services rather than from a promise to perform the services;
and that I therefore found puzzling the suggestion that a stranger who
starts to effect a rescue of a drowning child (perhaps unknown to the
child) comes under a legal obligation to complete it, irrespective of
whether the child's position has been worsened by the intervention.[1]

I would like to take the opportunity to analyse this issue in greater
detail for two reasons. First, it has central importance to the relationship between contract and tort. If there is a valid reason for imposing
a liability for failure to benefit based on starting to perform the services, that is independent of any promise made by words or conduct,
it means that there is a principled (rather than a pragmatic) reason for
allowing a tort claim for pure economic loss (protecting the expectation interest) in many situations that overlap with contract. Secondly,
there have been relevant academic and judicial comments on this
issue since the above essay was written.

I suggested in the above essay that what their Lordships in
Henderson v. *Merrett Syndicates Ltd* appeared to have in mind was a
promissory interpretation of "assumption of responsibility", and that
this fits precisely with Lord Devlin's speech in *Hedley Byrne & Co. Ltd
v. Heller & Partners Ltd*.[2]

---

[1] See 31 above.
[2] [1964] AC 465. See 29–30 above.

But although not specifically cited by their Lordships, the following passage from the speech of Lord Morris of Borth-y-Gest in *Hedley
Byrne* suggests a different interpretation of "assumption of responsibility". He said, "Quite apart . . . from employment or contract
there may be circumstances in which a duty to exercise care will arise
if a service is voluntarily undertaken. A medical man may unexpect-
edly come across an unconscious man, who is a complete stranger to
him, and who is in urgent need of skilled attention: if the medical
man, following the fine traditions of his profession, proceeds to treat
the unconscious man he must exercise reasonable skill and care in
doing so".[3]

One can interpret this *obiter dictum* of Lord Morris as recognising a
principle that, independently of any promise, there can be liability for
a negligent failure to benefit where one has started to perform—has
undertaken[4]—services for that other. It would seem fictitious to
regard the hypothetical doctor as having promised the injured person
to administer treatment. Moreover, at least on the face of it, Lord
Morris was not confining the doctor's liability to where his interference made the patient worse off than if he had done nothing.

Yet the predominant legal view is that, in this sort of "rescue" situation, a defendant's liability in negligence is confined to not making
the plaintiff worse off and does not comprise a liability for failure to
benefit. This is shown in two cases; the first Canadian and the second
English.

In *Horsley* v. *McLaren, The Ogopogo*,[5] a guest (M) on the defendant's
boat had fallen overboard and another guest (H) had dived overboard
to try to help. M and H both died. Their dependants sued the defendant for the wrongful deaths on the basis that the defendant had
negligently manœuvred the boat in a rescue attempt. At first instance
Lacourcière J held that, while there was no general duty to rescue,
where one had undertaken a rescue, one would be liable in the tort
of negligence for negligently carrying it out or for negligently
abandoning it.[6] And as against H, in contrast to M, the defendant's

---

[3] [1964] AC 465, 494–5. Lord Morris referred for support to *Banbury* v. *Bank of Montreal*
[1918] AC 626, 689; *Shiells* v. *Blackburne* (1789) 1 H Bl. 158; and *Wilkinson* v. *Coverdale*
(1793) 1 Esp. 75.
[4] The word "undertake" has two different meanings which precisely correlate to the
"promissory" or "commencement of performance" interpretations of "assumption of
responsibility". That is, "to undertake to do X" is "to promise to do X". "To undertake X"
is "to start to perform X".
[5] [1971] 2 Lloyd's Rep. 410.
[6] [1969] 1 Lloyd's Rep. 374.

negligence caused the death. But on appeal by the defendant, the decision in favour of H's dependants was overturned by the Ontario Court of Appeal[7] (and this, in turn, was upheld by a majority of the Supreme Court of Canada[8]). Schroeder JA, giving the leading judgment of the Ontario Court of Appeal, said the following: "The learned judge held that whether there was a duty on the appellant to rescue Matthews or not, he had voluntarily assumed that duty; that is he had entered into a relationship which cast responsibility upon him, and hence was liable for failure to use reasonable care in dealing with Matthews. This reasoning, however, disregards the principle that even if a person embarks upon a rescue and does not carry it through, he is not under any liability to the person to whose aid he had come so long as discontinuance of his efforts did not leave the other in a worse condition than when he took charge".[9]

In the recent case of *Capital and Counties plc* v. *Hampshire CC*[10] a number of premises were destroyed by fire. In actions against separate fire brigades, the Court of Appeal analysed the common law duty of care owed by a fire brigade (and analogously other "rescue services"[11]) to those whose buildings are on fire. It was held that a fire brigade is under no common law duty to do anything. In Stuart-Smith LJ's words, "the fire brigade are not under a common law duty to answer the call for help, and are not under a duty to take care to do so. If, therefore, they fail to turn up, or fail to turn up in time, because they have carelessly misunderstood the message, got lost on the way or run into a tree, they are not liable".[12]

[7] [1970] 1 Lloyd's Rep. 257.

[8] [1971] 2 Lloyd's Rep. 410 (*per* Ritchie, Judson and Spence JJ, Laskin and Hall JJ dissenting). All the members of the Supreme Court adopted a different approach from Schroeder JA in regarding there as being a special duty to rescue Matthews arising out of his position as guest and passenger.

[9] [1970] 1 Lloyd's Rep 257, 263. Schroeder JA here relied on *East Suffolk Rivers Catchment Bd.* v. *Kent* [1941] AC 74.

[10] [1997] 3 WLR 331.

[11] The Court of Appeal's decision was applied by May J in *OLL Ltd* v. *Secretary of State for Transport* [1997] 3 All ER 897 in deciding that no duty of care was owed by a coastguard who, in respect of the Lyme Bay tragedy (when four out of eight children on an adventure holiday died when their canoes capsized), was alleged to have conducted a search and rescue operation negligently. May J said, at 905, "There is no obvious distinction between the fire brigade responding to a fire where lives are at risk and the coastguard responding to an emergency at sea. On this basis, the coastguard would be under no enforceable private law duty to respond to an emergency call, nor, if they do respond, would they be liable if their response was negligent, unless their negligence amounted to a positive act which directly caused greater injury than would have occurred if they had not intervened at all."

[12] [1997] 3 WLR 331, 344.

More importantly to the theme of this postscript, it was held that, even if a fire brigade does start to fight a fire, its duty of care is confined to not making the position worse. In this, the Court of Appeal followed *East Suffolk Rivers Catchment Board* v. *Kent*[13] in which the House of Lords held that a local authority was not liable where it had negligently carried out repair work to a sea wall so that flooding continued for 178 days instead of fourteen days. Viscount Simon LC (in a passage cited by Stuart-Smith LJ) said: "If . . . the appellants, by their unskilful proceedings had caused a further area of the respondents' land to be flooded, or had prolonged the period of flooding beyond what it would have been if they had never interfered, they would be liable. But . . . nothing of this sort happened. The respondents would have gained if the flooding had stopped sooner; their complaint against the appellants is that they did not act with sufficient skill to stop it more promptly; but the respondents cannot point to any injury inflicted upon them by the appellant Board, unless it be the Board's want of success in endeavouring to stop the flooding at an earlier date".[14]

Stuart-Smith LJ, in discussing the concept of "assumption of responsibility", also drew an analogy with a doctor who, although under no legal obligation to do so, goes to the assistance of someone who he sees injured in a road accident: "If he volunteers his assistance, his only duty as a matter of law is not to make the victim's condition worse".[15] And later he said, "It is not clear why a rescuer who is not under an obligation to attempt a rescue should assume a duty to be careful in effecting the rescue merely by undertaking the attempt. It would be strange if such a person were liable to the dependants of a drowning man who but for his carelessness he would have saved, but without the attempt would have drowned anyway. In Canada, it has been held that he is not: *The Ogopogo*. This is consistent with the *East Suffolk* case."[16]

In applying these principles to the facts, only one of the five fire brigades was held liable in the tort of negligence. This was the brigade that had negligently turned off the automatic sprinklers. On the face of it, this made the plaintiff's position worse and the brigade was unable to prove—the burden being held to be on it—that the

---

[13] [1941] AC 74. See also *Stovin* v. *Wise* [1996] AC 923, 949F (*per* Lord Hoffmann).
[14] [1941] AC 74, 84–5.
[15] [1997] 3 WLR 331, 349.
[16] [1997] 3 WLR 331, 351.

building would still have been burned down completely had it done nothing and the sprinklers had been left on.

These two cases therefore show that, contrary to Lord Morris' *obiter dictum* in *Hedley Byrne*, the courts have not accepted the notion that "assuming responsibility", in the sense of starting to perform a beneficial service for the plaintiff, puts a defendant under a duty to use reasonable care to benefit the plaintiff. Absent something more, for example, a promise or a statutory duty,[17] the defendant who starts the task is liable for harmful interference not for a failure to benefit.

This issue has recently been academically recognised as having central importance for understanding the distinction between contract and tort. Jane Stapleton has in effect argued that liability for a negligent failure to benefit is *commonly* imposed in the tort of negligence and should not therefore be seen as the province of promissory/contractual liability as opposed to tort.[18] The key to this analysis is her idea that, once the defendant has started to perform a beneficial service, the plaintiff's normal expectancies are shifted, so that the defendant is under an obligation to use reasonable care to benefit the plaintiff.

She gives the illustration of a doctor who finds a person on a deserted moor who has accidentally fainted face down. If left, the person is certain to die. The doctor attempts the rescue but bungles it, so that the victim is left paralysed. In so far as there is any liability on a doctor who carries out a rescue, Stapleton's view is that the liability cannot be confined to not making the victim worse off, but should extend to a failure to benefit the victim. She argues that a typical example of negligent surgery is the same: we are concerned with the position the plaintiff would have been in if the surgery had been carried out carefully, not the position the plaintiff would have been in if the defendant had not carried out the surgery at all. It then further follows that cases like *Junior Books Ltd* v. *Veitchi Co. Ltd*[19] and

---

[17] The statutory duty on the National Health Service (or equivalent health trusts) to provide care to patients appears to explain why, absent contract, a doctor and hospital authority owe a duty to an admitted patient to take reasonable care to effect a cure. On that "liability for failure to benefit", see *Cassidy* v. *Ministry of Health* [1951] 2 KB 343, 360; *Barnett* v. *Chelsea and Kensington Hospital Management Committee* [1969] 1 QB 428, and *Capital and Counties Plc* v. *Hampshire CC* [1997] 3 WLR 331, 349.

[18] Jane Stapleton, "The Normal Expectancies Measure in Tort Damages" (1997) 113 *LQR* 257. See also Jane Stapleton, "A New 'Seascape' for Obligations: Reclassification on the Basis of Measure of Damages" in P. Birks (ed.), *The Classification of Obligations* (Clarendon Press, 1997) 193–231.

[19] [1983] 1 AC 520 (owners held to have tort claim against sub-contractors for negligent laying of a floor).

White v. *Jones*[20] (and we can add, for example, *Midland Bank Trust Co.* v. *Hett Stubbs and Kemp*[21])—in which the defendants were held liable in the tort of negligence for the plaintiff's "expectation interest"— have been wrongly regarded as controversial in awarding a "contractual" measure of damages. Rather, in Stapleton's view, the plaintiffs in those cases received a standard tort "normal expectancies" measure of damages. So, taking *White* v. *Jones* as an example, she writes, "once a task is undertaken it is normally the case that it is done with care. Thus, the plaintiff did have a normal expectancy that the task would be done with care. . . . *White* v. *Jones* is therefore, a conventional case in terms of measure of damages, a case of damage to normal expectancies and there is no need to see it as a revolutionary case in which tort required a defendant to improve a plaintiff's normal expectancies".[22]

But Stapleton's thesis not only contradicts the predominant legal view, as shown by the two cases set out above; it also fails to explain convincingly why starting to perform a task should make a difference. It is particularly for the latter reason that her thesis has been persuasively rejected by Stephen Smith. He writes, "According to Dr Stapleton . . . although the doctor is not liable if he does nothing, he is liable if he helps carelessly. This seems odd. In some cases, carelessly attempting to help an injured person . . . can leave that person worse off than doing nothing. If by attempting to help someone, I either induce him or her not to seek alternative aid or make alternative offers of aid unlikely or impossible, I will have made that person worse off if my attempt is unsuccessful. The victim misses out on alternative opportunities for (more effective) help. . . . The point [in Stapleton's hypothetical example] of the hiker being on a deserted moor . . . is precisely to avoid foregone opportunity arguments. The hiker clearly will die if the doctor does nothing. So why is the doctor held liable for doing something which made the hiker better off, when the doctor would not have been liable for doing nothing, even though doing nothing would have left the hiker worse off than he in fact ended up?"[23] And he later writes, "*White* v. *Jones* should be understood . . . as exactly what it appears to be: a pragmatic attempt

---

[20] [1995] 2 AC 207 (intended beneficiaries under a will held to have tort claim against solicitors, who negligently delayed in drawing up a will, their client dying before they had done so).

[21] [1979] Ch. 384. See 26–9 above.

[22] [1995] 2 AC 207, 282.

[23] "Rights, Remedies and Normal Expectancies in Tort and Contract" (1997) 113 *LQR* 426, 427–8.

to get around either the privity rules or the rules on wills and estates".[24]

In conclusion, I derive comfort from the fact that my puzzlement over the significance of a defendant starting to perform a service is shared by others and is consistent with the predominant judicial view. I continue to believe that the awarding of pure economic loss protecting the expectation interest in the tort of negligence rests on breach of a promise (made by words or conduct) and hence constitutes a pragmatic and not a principled development.[25] Having said that, the contrary view does have some support (for example, from Lord Morris and Jane Stapleton) and cannot, I think, be dismissed out of hand. It can perhaps be argued that the reason starting to perform a beneficial service makes a difference is that, once one has started to perform, it is less of an infringement of liberty to be required to use reasonable care to benefit the plaintiff than it is if one were required to intervene in the first place. But that is a controversial suggestion and there is no doubt that, where the defendant has promised to perform a service for the plaintiff, that promise provides an altogether more convincing reason for the defendant being required to benefit the plaintiff. By making the promise the defendant has, as a matter of convention, already curtailed his or her freedom of action.

2. Combining Remedies

In the above essay, I said that combining remedies raises different questions, and requires different answers, than does the problem of concurrent liability.[26] I now have the opportunity to indicate, albeit

---

[24] *Ibid.*, 430.

[25] For a similar thesis, see the excellent article by Simon Whittaker, "The Application of the 'Broad Principle of Hedley Byrne' as between Parties to a Contract" (1997) 17 *LS* 169. In the unreported decision in *Holt* v. *Payne Skillington*, 18 Dec. 1995, referred to by Whittaker, the Court of Appeal appeared to accept that a tort duty of care founded on "assumption of responsibility" could impose a liability for *failure to benefit* that was more extensive than that in the contract between the parties. It is hard to understand the basis of such a liability. In contrast, the proposition that a tort duty of care can be more extensive than the contractual liability between the parties would have been uncontroversial had the Court of Appeal confined itself to tort liability for negligent advice given: see 28–9 above. The actual decision was so confined, the Court of Appeal holding that negligent advice given by estate agents, concerning the use to which property could be put, had not been relied on by the purchasers of the property.

[26] See 21–2 above.

briefly, how the question of combining remedies for one (or more) cause(s) of action should be dealt with.[27]

The law draws a distinction between remedies that can be combined (for example, termination of a contract for breach of contract plus damages for breach of that contract; or an injunction to prevent the continuation of a tort plus damages for the tort) and "alternative and inconsistent" remedies that cannot be combined. In relation to the latter, a plaintiff must "elect" between inconsistent remedies. In the case of remedies given by the courts that election can be made until judgment or even satisfaction of a judgment.[28]

My thesis is that "election" has traditionally been given too wide a scope, and that a plaintiff should always (or nearly always) be able to combine judicial remedies (that is, remedies given by the courts) albeit that the courts should be careful, in assessing quantum, to avoid double recovery. In other words, to label some remedies as "alternative and inconsistent", and to force a plaintiff to make an election, is to adopt an unnecessarily blunt method of avoiding double recovery.

Before illustrating this thesis, it is first necessary to identify situations where a plaintiff should not be able to combine remedies because any combination of the remedies would be inconsistent. The following are two classic examples, in both of which, it should be noted, one of the remedies was a "self-help" rather than a judicial remedy: rescinding *ab initio* a contract at the same time as claiming damages for breach of the contract[29]; and terminating a contract for breach of contract and seeking specific performance of it.[30] These are situations where the purposes of the two remedies are inconsistent with each other so that it is only right that a plaintiff should be required to elect which to pursue. The effect of the plaintiff's election in these situations is akin to a plaintiff being barred from a remedy for an infringement of his or her rights because the plaintiff has affirmed, waived or acquiesced in the infringement.[31] All rest on the

[27] I have derived much assistance from discussion of this question with Stephen Watterson, research assistant at the Law Commission.
[28] The classic authority is *United Australia Ltd* v. *Barclays Bank Ltd* [1941] AC 1.
[29] See G. Treitel, *The Law of Contract* (9th edn., Sweet & Maxwell, 1995), 342.
[30] *Johnson* v. *Agnew* [1980] AC 367, 392, *per* Lord Wilberforce. His Lordship said, "if the vendor treats the purchaser as having repudiated the contract and accepts the repudiation, he cannot thereafter seek specific performance. This follows from the fact that, the purchaser having repudiated the contract and his repudiation having been accepted, both parties are discharged from further performance."
[31] For the close link between election, affirmation, waiver and acquiescence, which indeed are often used in overlapping senses, see Treitel, n. 29 above, 354–6, 725–6; and Meagher, Gummow and Lehane, *Equity Doctrines and Remedies* (3rd edn., Law Book Co., 1992), paras. 3611–12, 3618.

justifiable policy that it is unfair to a defendant for a plaintiff "to blow hot and cold". Having made a choice, it would not be fair to allow a change of mind.

In contrast, when one turns to combining judicial remedies, the need for an election is far less obvious, and on close analysis seems to melt away. This can be illustrated by focusing on combining restitutionary and compensatory remedies for an equitable wrong or a tort.

This question has been most commonly discussed in relation to whether a plaintiff can be awarded both an account of profits and (compensatory) damages for an intellectual property tort. The law is clear: a plaintiff cannot be awarded both an account of profits and damages but must choose between them.[32] Similarly, in *United Australia Ltd* v. *Barclays Bank Ltd*[33] Viscount Simon LC considered that, before judgment or possibly satisfaction of judgment, the plaintiff must elect, as a remedy for the tort of conversion, between restitution (in that case, through the action for money had and received) and compensatory damages. Again, in *Mahesan* v. *Malaysia Government Officers' Co-op Housing Society Ltd*,[34] the agent of a housing society, in return for a bribe, caused the society to buy land at an overvalue. The society sued the agent for both the amount of the bribe ($122,000) and damages for the tort of deceit for the loss sustained by the society (assessed at $443,000). The Federal Court of Malaysia awarded both the amount of the bribe and the damages. On appeal, this was overturned by the Privy Council which held that the society was bound to elect between its claims under the two heads. Since the society would obviously have elected to take damages, judgment was entered for $443,000.

Perhaps the clearest analysis of this issue is contained in the Privy Council's judgment in *Tang Min Sit* v. *Capacious Investments Ltd*,[35] which concerned a breach of trust. Lord Nicholls relied on a distinction between alternative and cumulative remedies and said: "The law frequently affords an injured person more than one remedy for the

---

[32] *Neilson* v. *Betts* (1871) LR 5 HL 1: *DeVitre* v. *Betts* (1873) LR 6 HL 319; *Colbeam Palmer Ltd* v. *Stock Affiliates Pty. Ltd* (1968) 122 CLR 25; *Island Records Ltd* v. *Tring International plc* [1995] 3 All ER 444. S. 61(2) of the Patents Act 1977 reads: "the court shall not, in respect of the same infringement, both award the proprietor of a patent damages and order that he shall be given an account of the profits."

[33] [1941] AC 1, 18–19. See also *Ministry of Defence* v. *Ashman* (1993) 66 P & CR 195, 200–1.

[34] [1979] AC 374. See A. Tettenborn, "Bribery, Corruption and Restitution—The Strange Case of Mr Mahesan" (1979) 95 *LQR* 68.

[35] [1996] 4 All ER 193. See P. Birks, "Inconsistency Between Compensation and Restitution" (1996) 112 *LQR* 375.

wrong he has suffered. Sometimes the two remedies are alternative and inconsistent. The classic example, indeed, is (1) an account of the profits made by a defendant in a breach of his fiduciary obligations and (2) damages for the loss suffered by the plaintiff by reason of the same breach. The former is measured by the wrongdoer's gain, the latter by the injured party's loss. . . . . Faced with alternative and inconsistent remedies a plaintiff must choose, or elect, between them. He cannot have both."[36]

It is therefore clear law that a plaintiff cannot be awarded both compensation and restitution for a wrong and must elect between them. But why should this be so?

The answer appears to be that this ensures that a plaintiff cannot recover both *full* restitution and *full* compensation for a wrong. And to award both *full* restitution and *full* compensation would be unacceptable because (unless one or other award is nil) a combination fails to achieve either *just* a reversal of the defendant's unjust enrichment or *just* a compensation of the plaintiff's loss. An award of either changes the position of both the defendant and the plaintiff. So, for example, if D has received a bribe of £1,000 and has caused loss to P of £2,000, the effect of requiring D to pay P £3,000 would be that P is neither *just* compensated for its loss (but instead receives a windfall of £1,000), nor is D *just* stripped of its unjust enrichment (but rather has an extra £2,000 stripped away). As alternatively expressed, an award of £3,000 would be inconsistent with either of the remedial purposes being pursued and would constitute "double recovery".

But *provided the one takes account of the other* there is no inconsistency, or double recovery, in allowing both restitution and compensation to be awarded.[37] In the example given, the correct result should be that D is required to pay P £2,000. This could be justified as full compensation alone. But it could also be justified as full restitution (£1,000) plus partial compensation (£1,000).

The best that can be said of a requirement of election is that it conveniently saves the courts from having to become embroiled in the issue of the extent to which an award of restitution and an award of compensation would entail "double recovery". And justice will normally be done because a plaintiff will almost inevitably elect to claim

---

[36] *Ibid.*, at 197.

[37] For the same conclusion, in respect of combining compensation for breach of contract with restitution of money paid for failure of consideration, see G. Treitel, n. 29 above, 850. See also *Baltic Shipping Company* v. *Dillon* (*The Mikhail Lermontov*) (1993) 176 CLR 344; K. Barker, "Restitution of Passenger Fare" [1994] *LMCLQ* 291.

the remedy with the higher measure of recovery on the facts.[38] But
ultimately the law is requiring an election where it is not really necessary; the two remedies are not inevitably inconsistent. The principled approach would be to recognise this, to remove any mandatory
requirement of election, to allow a plaintiff to claim compensation
and restitution, and for the court to resolve the problem of double
recovery at the stage of assessing quantum.

---

[38] The chances of justice not being done have been reduced by the decision in *Island
Records Ltd* v *Tring International Plc* [1995] 3 All ER 444 according to which a plaintiff is entitled to defer election until after there has been an enquiry as to the amount of profits.

3

Understanding the Law of Restitution:
A Map Through the Thicket

1. INTRODUCTION

In the Michigan Court of Appeals in *Snider* v. *Dunn*,[1] Levin J in a dissenting judgment said that: "Those who venture into the restitution thicket not infrequently become lost. It is part of our task to see that they are heard from again." As someone who has for a number of years been wandering through the restitutionary forests of the common law world, I see my central task in this essay as being to provide some sort of map through what at times does indeed appear to be an impenetrable jungle. In so doing I shall focus on Australian, as well as English, cases

2. WHAT IS THE LAW OF RESTITUTION ABOUT?

Although some may disagree, there is general consensus that the law of restitution is the law concerned with reversing a defendant's unjust enrichment at the plaintiff's expense. It deals with such issues as when can one recover money paid, or the value of work done, by mistake, or under duress, or under a contract that is void or voidable or that has been discharged for breach or frustration; or when is one entitled to the disgorgement of gains made by a wrongdoer rather than compensation for one's loss.

To cite from two restitution enthusiasts, first Peter Birks and secondly Andrew Tettenborn:

> "Restitution is an area of the law no smaller and no less important than, say Contract, Tort, or Trusts. A series of intellectual and historical accidents has, however, scattered its raw material to the fringes of other subjects. Homes have been found for it under dishonest or

[1] 160 NW 2d 619, 628 (1968). I would like to thank Dr Joachim Dietrich, for drawing my attention to this case.

opaque labels: quasi-contract, subrogation, constructive trust, money had and received, and so on. Dispersed in this way, Restitution has escaped the revolution in legal learning which has happened over the past century. It has been the age of the textbook. Successive editions have settled the case-law of other subjects into well-tried and now familiar patterns. The case-law of Restitution remains disorganized: its textbooks have only just begun to be written. . . . It is the last major area to be mapped and in some sense the most exciting subject in the modern canon. There is everything to play for".[2]

And from the first page of Tettenborn's *Law of Restitution*[3]:

"Gains, like losses, prima facie lie where they fall. If I make you a gift of £100 or a car, that is your good luck: if I pay you £1,000 for goods supplied, or clean your windows because I have contracted to do so, you are merely receiving what is due to you. That is what economic life is about. But some cases are different. With some gains, you cannot simply pre-empt the issue by putting them down to good luck, or business, or the nature of things, or the important presumption running through English law that gifts are irrevocable. For example, when I gave you £100, I might have forgotten that I had already transferred £100 to your account last week, and thus was making the same gift twice: I might equally have only done so because I thought I was richer than I was. I may have cleaned your windows, not from any feeling of benevolence or because I intended to benefit you, but for some entirely different reason. You might have asked me to do so pending the outcome of negotiations for a long-term window-cleaning contract between us: or I might have mistaken your house for that of your neighbour, whose windows I had agreed to clean. Again, take the payment of £1,000. Although this was made for goods supplied, this is not the end of the story: I may have refused to accept the goods concerned; it may turn out that you only delivered part of them, or that what you did deliver were sub-standard; and so on. This is what the law of restitution is about. More formally, restitution is the response of the law to enrichment which it regards as unjustified."

Adopting a more technical approach, the bulk of the law of restitution comprises that area of the common law that used to be called quasi-contract and covers remedies such as the action for money had

---

[2] This illuminating passage appears on the fly-sheet of the hardback copy of P. Birks, *An Introduction to the Law of Restitution* (Clarendon Press, 1985). One can safely assume that it was written by Birks and not by an employee of the Oxford University Press.

[3] A. Tettenborn, *Law of Restitution* (Cavendish Publishing Limited, 1993), 1. [A different passage, making similar points, appears in A. Tettenborn, *Law of Restitution in England and Ireland* (2nd edn., Cavendish Publishing Ltd., 1996) 1.]

and received to the plaintiff's use, the action for money paid to the defendant's use, a quantum meruit and a quantum valebat. But it also includes areas of equity such as a fiduciary's liability to account for unauthorised profits, rescission of an executed contract (for misrepresentation, undue influence or duress), equitable tracing and subrogation. The principle against unjust enrichment therefore pulls together (and fights against) the historical divide between common law and equity.

Although it incorporates elements of the law of property as well as the law of obligations, restitution is most obviously located alongside contract and tort as a third division of the law of obligations.

3. THE RECOGNITION OF THE PRINCIPLE AGAINST UNJUST ENRICHMENT

English and Australian law traditionally did not recognise a law of restitution based on reversing unjust enrichment and dicta of great judges, like Lord Mansfield[4] and Lord Wright,[5] tended to fall on deaf ears. On the traditional approach, the areas of common law and equity mentioned above were treated as having no relationship to each other; and the implied contract theory (hence "quasi-contract") was primarily put forward to explain most of the relevant common law. If the plaintiff pays the defendant £1,000 under a mistake of fact, his legal remedy to recover the £1,000 was said to rest on the defendant's implied promise to pay it back. But that promise cannot rest on the defendant's actual intention and the theory provides no explanation for why the promise should be implied.

In 1966 Goff and Jones published *The Law of Restitution*[6] which attacked the traditional approach and sought to demonstrate that there is a coherent and principled English (and Australian) law of restitution based on reversing unjust enrichment. Their thesis slowly gained acceptance in academia and amongst some practitioners and judges. In Australia this culminated in the acceptance in 1986 by the High Court of the principle against unjust enrichment and the rejection of the implied contract theory in *Pavey & Matthews Pty. Ltd* v. *Paul.*[7] Six years later this was followed by *David Securities Pty. Ltd* v.

---

[4] *Moses* v. *Macferlan* (1760) 2 Burr. 1005.
[5] *Fibrosa Spolka Akcynja* v. *Fairbairn Lawson Combe Barbour Ltd* [1943] AC 32, 61.
[6] R. Goff and G. Jones, *The Law of Restitution* (Sweet & Maxwell, 1966). Now in its 4th edn. published in 1993.
[7] (1986) 162 CLR 221.

Commonwealth Bank of Australia,[8] in which the High Court took Australian law further along the true restitutionary road by accepting the defence of change of position and by abolishing the mistake of law bar. England lagged slightly behind but in 1991 in *Lipkin Gorman* v. *Karpnale Ltd*[9] the House of Lords accepted the unjust enrichment principle and recognised a change of position defence. And a year later in *Woolwich Equitable Building Society* v. *Inland Revenue Commissioners*,[10] their Lordships relied on unjust enrichment thinking to reach the radical decision that a citizen is entitled as of right to restitution of payments demanded by a public authority *ultra vires*.

In the next section I shall look at that quartet of cases in a little more detail not only to give those who are unfamiliar with the law of restitution a firmer grasp of the sort of issues in play but also to prove to sceptics the importance now being attached by the highest courts in England and Australia to the principle against unjust enrichment. Before doing so there are three further points I would like to make on the recognition of the law of restitution.

First, it should not be thought that Australia and England are the first jurisdictions to recognise unjust enrichment. On the contrary, in civil law systems, such as Germany and France, a law of unjust enrichment has been long established. And within the common law world, North America has led the way: in the United States, restitution based on unjust enrichment was accepted in 1932 with the publication of the *Restatement of Restitution*; and in Canada, the principle was accepted in *Deglman* v. *Guaranty Trust Co.*[11] in 1954.

Secondly, that the law of restitution has only been recently recognised in England and Australia does not mean that one has no concern with cases prior to 1986 or 1991. Rather it is believed that, whatever the overt language used, the courts have long been applying the principle against unjust enrichment. The modern approach must therefore be to explain how most past decisions can be rationalised using the language of unjust enrichment, while acknowledging that the open acceptance of the principle may enable unwarranted traditional restrictions to be more easily evaded.

Thirdly, it is important to concede that the recognition of the principle against unjust enrichment is not a development favoured by everyone. Some argue that that principle is misleading or unhelpful

---

[8] (1992) 175 CLR 353.

[9] [1991] 2 AC 548.

[10] [1993] AC 70. [See also now *Westdeutsche Landesbank Girozentrale* v. *Islington London BC* [1996] AC 669.]

[11] [1954] 3 DLR 785.

or, at least, that the ambit of the law in which it has any validity is very small indeed. In England most of that sort of scepticism has disappeared. Practitioners and judges are now increasingly aware of the importance of restitution. It is also creeping into an increasing number of undergraduate courses. Indeed the English Law Society has recently recommended that an understanding of the law of restitution should be a compulsory part of any law degree for intending solicitors.

I must confess, therefore, that it was something of a shock, in teaching in Australia in 1994, to find how relatively undeveloped is the Australian interest in, and knowledge of, the subject. Sitting in Oxford, reading the judgments of Mason CJ and Deane J, and knowing that *Pavey & Matthews Pty. Ltd* v. *Paul* gave Australia a five-year lead, I had expected the importance of the subject to be taken for granted.

It is interesting to speculate why this should be. It may be that the Federal system means that it takes longer for developments through the High Court to filter down to grass-roots level. It may also be that the role of restitution in Australia has been clouded by the burgeoning use made by the courts of the notion of "unconscionable conduct". It has also been suggested to me that the difference is a reflection of the academic communities in the two countries. In England we have had for thirty years or so very strong postgraduate courses at, e.g., Oxford and Cambridge, turning out into the profession high-powered lawyers attuned to restitutionary thinking. In contrast some of the most influential voices in the academic community in Australia have been, and are, restitution-sceptics.

4. A QUARTET OF LEADING ANGLO–AUSTRALIAN CASES

(i) *Pavey & Matthews Pty. Ltd* v. *Paul*[12]

The plaintiff builders had renovated a cottage for the defendant pursuant to an oral contract by which they were to be remunerated according to prevailing rates. When the work was done, the defendant paid the plaintiffs $36,000. The plaintiffs maintained that she should pay a further $27,000 as an overall payment of $63,000 was the

---

[12] (1986) 162 CLR 221.

prevailing rate for the job. The contract was unenforceable by builders under the Builders Licensing Act 1971 (NSW). It was therefore indisputable that a claim by the plaintiffs to enforce the express oral contract would have failed as falling directly foul of the Act. But the question at issue was whether a quantum meruit claim for the work done was sufficiently independent of a contractual claim to avoid the provisions of the Act. The High Court (Brennan J dissenting) held that it was and that the plaintiffs were therefore entitled to an extra $27,000.

There were two main strands in the reasoning. First, the Court rejected the traditional view that the quantum meruit was based on an implied oral contract, which would have fallen directly foul of the Act. Instead the quantum meruit was viewed as a non-contractual claim to restitution based on unjust enrichment, the essential feature of which was not Mrs Paul's promise but the carrying out for payment of the work by the builders and its acceptance by Mrs Paul. Secondly, it was held that the restitutionary claim did not indirectly undermine the policy of the Act for, while the Act was concerned to allow building owners to withdraw from their oral commitments, it was not designed to permit owners to pay nothing for requested building work that had been carried out. In contrast, the builders would have had no claim if, for example, Mrs Paul had withdrawn her promise to pay before the renovation work had started and yet the builders had gone on to carry out the work. Nor could the builders have reaped the benefit of a good bargain by recovering a quantum meruit higher than the objective market rate for the work, even if Mrs Paul's promise had been to pay them at that higher rate. In the words of Mason and Wilson JJ[13]:

> "Deane J . . . has concluded that an action on a quantum meruit, such as that brought by the appellants rests, not on implied contract, but on a claim to restitution or one based on unjust enrichment, arising from the respondent's acceptance of the benefits accruing to the respondent from the appellant's performance of the unenforceable oral contract . . . [T]he shortcomings of the implied contract theory have been rigorously exposed and the virtues of an approach based on restitution and unjust enrichment . . . widely appreciated. . . . We are therefore now justified in recognising, as Deane J has done, that the true foundation of the right to recover on a quantum meruit does not depend on the existence of an implied contract."

And according to Deane J:

[13] (1986) 162 CLR 221, 227.

"[U]njust enrichment in the law of this country . . . constitutes a unifying legal concept which explains why the law recognises, in a variety of distinct categories of case, an obligation on the part of a defendant to make a fair and just restitution for a benefit derived at the expense of a plaintiff and which assists in the determination, by the ordinary processes of legal reasoning, of the question whether the law should, in justice, recognise such an obligation in a new or developing category of case. . . ."[14]

And later, after reference to the Act, he continued:

"[T]he survival of the ordinary common law right of the builder to recover, in an action founded on restitution or unjust enrichment, reasonable remuneration for work done and accepted under a contract which is unenforceable by him does not frustrate the purpose of the section to provide protection for a building owner. The building owner remains entitled to enforce the contract. He cannot, however, be forced either to comply with its terms or to permit the builder to carry it to completion. All that he can be required to do is to pay reasonable compensation for work done of which he has received the benefit and for which in justice he is obligated to make such a payment by way of restitution. In relation to such work, he can rely on the contract, if it has not been rescinded, as to the amount of remuneration and the terms of payment. If the agreed remuneration exceeds what is reasonable in the circumstances, he can rely on the unenforceability of the contract with the result that he is liable to pay no more than what is fair and reasonable."[15]

The great significance then of *Pavey & Matthews Pty. Ltd v. Paul* is its recognition that there is an Australian law of restitution based on the principle against unjust enrichment which operates independently of claims to enforce a contract.

It was another five years before the equivalent English case, to which we shall now turn.

(ii) *Lipkin Gorman v. Karpnale Ltd*[16]

Cass, a partner in a firm of solicitors, had drawn on the partnership account at Lloyds Bank (he was an authorised signatory) to pay for his gambling at the Playboy Club. The partners had thereby suffered

[14] *Ibid.*, 256–7.
[15] *Ibid.*, 262–3.
[16] [1991] 2 AC 548.

a loss of some £220,000. The club had overall won £154,695 from the money stolen and used for gambling by Cass: that is, although the stolen money staked by Cass was a lot higher, the club had paid out winnings to Cass thereby reducing its net gain. The solicitors succeeded before the House of Lords in being awarded £150,960 in an action for money had and received against the club. The club was also held liable to pay the solicitors damages of £3,735 for conversion of a banker's draft that on one occasion had been used for gambling by Cass instead of cash.

The prime importance of the case is that all their Lordships explicitly based the decision on unjust enrichment. And they accepted for the first time a defence to restitution of "change of position" which can only be rationalised through unjust enrichment reasoning: that is, it was the club's net enrichment that was to be disgorged taking into account losses it had incurred (payment out of winnings) in the good faith belief that Cass was using his own money for the gambling.

According to Lord Templeman:

> "The club was enriched as and when Cass staked and lost to the club money stolen from the solicitors amounting in the aggregate to £300,000 or more. But the club paid Cass when he won and in the final reckoning the club only retained £154,695 which was admittedly derived from the solicitors' money. The solicitors can recover the sum of £154,695 which was retained by the club if they can show that in the circumstances the club was unjustly enriched at the expense of the solicitors."[17]

And he concluded:

> "When Cass lost and paid £154,695 to the club as a result of gaming contracts, he made to the club a completed gift of £154,695. The club received stolen money by way of gift from the thief; the club, being a volunteer, has been unjustly enriched at the expense of the solicitors from whom the money had been stolen and the club must reimburse the solicitors."[18]

In Lord Goff's words:

> "[T]he solicitors' claim in the present case is founded upon the unjust enrichment of the club, and can only succeed if, in accordance with the principles of the law of restitution, the club was indeed unjustly enriched at the expense of the solicitors. . . . Whether change of position is, or should be recognised as a defence to claims in restitution, is

---

[17] [1991] 2 AC 559.
[18] Ibid., 565.

a subject that has been much debated in the books. It is however a matter on which there is a remarkable unanimity of view, the consensus being to the effect that such a defence should be recognised in English law. I myself am under no doubt that this is right."[19]

Lipkin Gorman and *Pavey & Matthews* should have put to rest the long-running but arid debate as to whether there is an Anglo–Australian law of restitution based on unjust enrichment. Instead all attention can, and should, now be focused on the content of the subject. Moreover, the way has been cleared for the courts to ensure that like cases are truly being treated alike and to reject unwarranted historical restrictions on restitution. It is precisely that challenge of reform that we see at work in the final two cases of the quartet.

(iii) *David Securities Pty. Ltd* v. *Commonwealth Bank of Australia*[20]

The plaintiff companies had defaulted in repaying foreign currency loans to the defendant bank. The loan agreements had turned out badly for the plaintiffs and they claimed compensation for their loss based on an alleged breach of a duty by the bank to advise them of the risks associated with such loans. The bank counterclaimed for the sums still owing under the loan agreements. The plaintiffs' claim failed but the subject matter of the appeal to the High Court of Australia was the decision that the plaintiffs could not set off against the bank's counterclaim the payments they had made pursuant to an allegedly void clause (clause 8(b)) of the loan agreements. In accordance with that clause the plaintiffs were bound to pay, and had paid, the tax that the bank was liable for in respect of the interest on the loan. The plaintiffs argued that the obligation was void under section 261 of the Income Tax Assessment Act 1936 (Cth.) and that they were entitled to repayment of the money paid under it on the ground that it was paid by mistake. The lower courts decided that, while clause 8(b) was void, restitution should be denied because the plaintiffs had paid under a mistake of law not fact. The High Court agreed that the clause was void but it remitted the case to the trial judge to consider the evidence in the light of its ruling that, first, mistake of law is a valid ground for restitution; and, secondly, change of position is a valid defence to restitution.

---

[19] *Ibid.*, 578.
[20] (1992) 175 CLR 353.

The second aspect of the decision follows *Lipkin Gorman* in recognising that even though the defendant may have received an unjust enrichment the amount of that enrichment, and hence the quantum of restitution, may be reduced or eliminated by causally related losses incurred by the defendant in good faith subsequent to the receipt. But *David Securities* represents a significant advance from the position in England in its recognition that a claim for restitution can be grounded on a mistake of law as well as fact.

In England the restitution of mistaken payments is still restricted according to the type of mistake made. If the mistake is one of fact, it is only clearly recoverable if it is a "mistake as to liability", that is, if on the facts as the plaintiff believed them to be he would have been under a liability to the payee to make that payment. And, subject to some exceptions, there can be no restitution if the payment was made by mistake of law. The first of these restrictions was departed from by Robert Goff J in *Barclays Bank Ltd* v. *W.J. Simms Son & Cooke (Southern) Ltd*[21] in favour of a causation test: did the mistake cause the payment? But that decision has yet to be applied by an appellate court. And there has been no equivalent judicial rejection of the mistake of law bar.[22]

In *David Securities* the High Court adopted the causation test for both mistakes of law and fact. In Australia therefore the type of mistake no longer matters. It is its effect on the payer that counts. The fear that this may lead to too many claims and may destabilise security of receipt was felt to be adequately met by recognising, as Robert Goff J had done, a number of qualifications and defences: (i) most notably, change of position; (ii) that restitution cannot be applied if the payment was made in return for good consideration (i.e. in accordance with a valid contract or contractual term); (iii) waiver of the right to recover by paying suspecting that one might be mistaken but electing not to check the true position.

It may be that the decision in *David Securities* could have been reached without any reference to the principle against unjust enrichment. However recognition of that principle as underpinning the law on mistaken payments made rejection of the mistake of law bar that much more obvious; for once one sees that the relevant objection in mistake cases is that the defendant is unjustly enriched in the sense

---

[21] [1980] 1 QB 677.

[22] In *dicta* in *Woolwich Equitable Building Society* v. *Inland Revenue Commissioners* [1993] AC 70, 199, Lord Slynn thought that the mistake of law bar was "open to review by your Lordships' House". For a contrary view, see Lord Keith at 154.

that the plaintiff did not mean the defendant to have the money, there is no obvious justification for treating mistakes of law differently from mistakes of fact. As the majority (Mason CJ, Deane, Toohey, Caudron and McHugh JJ) said, "If the ground for ordering recovery is that the defendant has been unjustly enriched, there is no justification for drawing distinctions on the basis of how the enrichment was gained, except in so far as the manner of gaining the enrichment bears upon the justice of the case."[23]

Before moving on, one should note an important link between *David Securities* and *Lipkin Gorman*. In both, restitutionary liability was strict, subject to defences: that is, it did not turn on any fault or unconscionable behaviour by the defendant. The essential thrust of the claims was not condemnation of the defendant's behaviour but rather that the plaintiff did not mean the defendant to have the money. In *David Securities*, the vitiation of the plaintiff's intention was brought about by mistake; in *Lipkin Gorman* the plaintiff's intention was vitiated in the even more extreme sense that the firm of solicitors was ignorant of the fact that its money was being stolen and used for gambling by Cass. This pattern of restitutionary liability being strict, subject to defences, and resting on a factor vitiating the voluntariness of the plaintiff is to be found throughout much of the law of restitution. One impact of it is to cast severe doubt on the validity of the traditional insistence in several equity restitutionary cases,[24] usually discussed under the heading of "knowing receipt and dealing", that a defendant (even though a volunteer) receiving money transferred in breach of fiduciary duty is only liable to account for the money if he had *knowledge* of the breach.

(iv) *Woolwich Equitable Building Society* v. *Inland Revenue Commissioners*[25]

This, the final case of the quartet, is also the most radical. The plaintiff was charged tax which, from the outset, it objected to paying on the ground that the regulation authorising it was *ultra vires* the Inland Revenue. Having paid the tax demanded (some £57m) the plaintiff

---

[23] (1992) 175 CLR 353, 375.

[24] See, e.g., *Carl-Zeiss Stiftung* v. *Herbert Smith & Co. (No. 2)* [1969] 2 Ch. 276; *Belmont Finance Corpn* v. *Williams Furniture Ltd (No. 2)* [1980] 1 All ER 393; *Re Montagu's Settlement Trusts* [1987] Ch. 264. Cf. *Ministry of Health* v. *Simpson (sub nom Re Diplock)* [1951] AC 251. See also essay 5, 106–7 below.

[25] [1993] AC 70.

straight away issued judicial review proceedings to establish the invalidity of the charge and, shortly thereafter, issued a writ claiming restitution. The judicial review proceedings were successful before the House of Lords in establishing that the demand was *ultra vires*.[26] The Revenue thereupon repaid the principal sum of tax but it refused to pay interest on that sum (agreed by the parties to be £6.73m). Under section 35A of the Supreme Court Act 1981 the plaintiff would only be entitled to interest at the court's discretion if it could establish that it had been legally entitled to restitution of the principal sum. Although relating to a dispute over interest, the question at issue was, therefore, whether the plaintiff was entitled as of right to restitution of the principal sum. The majority of the House of Lords held that it was so entitled.

The difficulty for the plaintiff was that the facts fell just outside the standard grounds allowing restitution. First, a claim based on mistake could not succeed because the plaintiff had argued from the outset that the regulation was *ultra vires*. It was therefore not mistaken or at least had waived its right to rely on any mistake. In any event, any mistake was one of law, not fact. Secondly, a claim based on duress could not succeed because the only realistic threat that the Inland Revenue was making was to sue Woolwich for non-payment and a threat to sue is legitimate, not illegitimate, pressure. Nor could it be said that the pressure exerted fell within the notion of duress *colore officii* because the Inland Revenue was not impliedly threatening to withhold performance of a duty owed to Woolwich.

So applying the traditional grounds for restitution, Woolwich's claim should have failed and that was the approach taken by the minority, Lords Keith and Jauncey. But the majority (Lords Goff, Browne-Wilkinson and Slynn) considered that it was appropriate to push the law forward by recognising that the fact that a demand for payment has been made by a public authority *ultra vires* is itself a good ground for restitution. In Lord Goff's words, "I would therefore hold that money paid by a citizen to a public authority in the form of taxes or other levies paid pursuant to an ultra vires demand by the authority is prima facie recoverable by the citizen as of right."[27] This was in essence to recognise a special public law ground for restitution based on the policy or constitutional principle that there should be no taxation without Parliament.

---

[26] *R. v. IRC, ex parte Woolwich Equitable Building Society* [1990] 1 WLR 1400 (HL).
[27] [1993] AC 70, 177.

This clear example of judicial legislation, and the departure from the traditional more restrictive approach, could have been reached without reliance on a principle of unjust enrichment. The advantage of the principle is that it made it easy to see the direct links between payments by mistake and by duress and the extent of the incremental development needed in order to enable Woolwich to succeed.

5. RESTITUTIONARY REMEDIES

Before proceeding further, a word is needed on restitutionary remedies. For what can cause an unnecessary amount of confusion, especially for those unfamiliar with the subject, is that there is a host of different personal (i.e. substitutionary) remedies concerned to effect restitution. In an ideal world these would be rationalised. Unfortunately at the present time one cannot simply talk of claiming personal (or substitutionary) restitution. Rather differently described personal remedies are applicable to different situations of unjust enrichment. For example, the most common restitutionary remedy covering the recovery of money paid to the defendant is the action for money had and received to the plaintiff's use. This was the remedy in *Lipkin Gorman, David Securities* and *Woolwich*. For the value of services one claims a quantum meruit, as in *Pavey & Matthews Pty. Ltd v. Paul*, and for the value of goods a quantum valebat. Where one has discharged another's debt under legal compulsion, one may claim restitution in an action for money paid to the defendant's use or an indemnity. For restitution for breach of fiduciary duty or breach of confidence or an intellectual property tort one normally claims an account of profits, whereas for restitution for other torts one will normally simply be awarded restitutionary damages (i.e. damages measured according to the gain made by the tortfeasor).

While this panoply of often archaic sounding remedies is unfortunate, it should not be allowed to obscure the straightforward position that, while some of those remedies can be used in other contexts, a plaintiff choosing one of them is almost always seeking personal restitution of the defendant's unjust enrichment at the plaintiff's expense.

In addition to personal (substitutionary) remedies, some restitutionary remedies are proprietary (i.e. concerned with specific property). Proprietary restitution is a particularly difficult topic but probable examples of restitutionary proprietary remedies are the equitable lien, some constructive and resulting trusts, and

rescission of a contract or deed of gift under which title to property
has passed.

6. THE CONCEPTUAL STRUCTURE OR MAP OF RESTITUTION

I now want to turn more specifically to the map of restitution. That
is, to provide an overview of how the many apparently disparate elements making up the subject can be viewed as a coherent whole or,
to put it another way, to indicate the key elements in any restitutionary claim.

Recognition of the principle against unjust enrichment does not
mean that Anglo–Australian law has moved to a discretionary system
whereby the judges simply ask themselves, "is this enrichment
unjust?". On the contrary, the unjust enrichment principle operates
at a high level of generality and the approach of the courts is still very
much an incremental one, whereby what is meant by unjust enrichment is heavily dependent on past cases. This has been emphasised by
both Deane J and Lord Goff. In *Pavey & Matthews* the former said:

> "To identify the basis of such actions as restitution and not genuine
> agreement is not to assert a judicial discretion to do whatever idio-
> syncratic notions of what is fair and just might dictate. The circum-
> stances in which the common law imposes an enforceable obligation
> to pay compensation for a benefit accepted under an unenforceable
> agreement have been explored in the reported cases and in learned
> writings and are unlikely to be greatly affected by the perception that
> the basis of such an obligation, when the common law imposes it, is
> preferably seen as lying in restitution rather than in the implication of
> a genuine agreement where in fact the unenforceable agreement left
> no room for one."[28]

Similarly in *Lipkin Gorman* Lord Goff said:

> "I accept that the solicitors' claim in the present case is founded upon
> the unjust enrichment of the club. . . . But it does not, in my opin-
> ion, follow that the court has carte blanche to reject the solicitors'
> claim simply because it thinks it unfair or unjust in the circumstances
> to grant recovery. The recovery of money in restitution is not, as a
> general rule, a matter of discretion for the court. A claim to recover
> money at common law is made as a matter of right; and even though
> the underlying principle of recovery is the principle of unjust enrich-

---

[28] (1986) 162 CLR 221, 256.

ment, nevertheless, where recovery is denied, it is denied on the basis of legal principle."[29]

In seeking to link the underlying principle of unjust enrichment to the black letter law laid down in the cases, the most rational and helpful approach is to analyse any restitutionary claim in terms of four distinct questions:

(1) Has the defendant been *benefited* (i.e. enriched)?
(2) Was the enrichment *at the plaintiff's expense*?
(3) Was the enrichment *unjust*?
(4) Are there any *defences*?

If the first three questions are answered affirmatively, and the fourth negatively the plaintiff will be entitled to restitution.

These four stages constitute the fundamental ingredients of a restitutionary claim. The equivalent conceptual structure of a tort claim comprises the duty of care, breach of duty, non-remote damage, and defences.

(1) *Benefit*

The benefit received usually comprises money but it can comprise, e.g., services, goods or land.

Where the benefit comprises money, as is usually the case and was so in *Lipkin Gorman*, *David Securities* and *Woolwich*, there is no great difficulty. If P pays D £100 D is clearly benefited and benefited to the tune of £100.

Much more problematic are non-money benefits (i.e. benefits in kind), especially services as were in issue in *Pavey & Matthews Pty. Ltd v. Paul*. If P increases the objective market value of D's land by building something on it, D may well say that what P has built is of no value to D or, at least, is not worth to D the objective value. Or if P cleans D's car, D may legitimately say that he did not want it cleaned or did not want it cleaned at the price that P is demanding. This is the argument that Birks has labelled "subjective devaluation".[30]

Whether using that label or not, the courts do accept that defendants are entitled to subjectively devalue objective benefits. This means that where benefits in kind are in issue, plaintiffs must identify facts that overcome the subjective devaluation argument. What those

---

[29] [1991] 2 AC 548, 578.
[30] Birks, n. 2 above, 109–10.

facts are is a matter of theoretical dispute. Goff and Jones, followed by Birks, have suggested the two tests of whether the defendant has been *incontrovertibly benefited* or has *freely accepted* the benefit.[31] An incontrovertible benefit is one that no reasonable person could seriously deny was beneficial, for example, an improvement to property that has been sold at a higher price because of the improvement, the discharge of another's debt, or the rendering of necessary services. The language of incontrovertible benefit has now been used by some courts.[32] Free acceptance—that is, where a recipient knows that a benefit is being offered to him non-gratuitously, and where he, having the opportunity to accept, elects to accept—is more controversial and has spawned an extensive academic debate.[33] Suffice it to say here that a less controversial test, supplementing incontrovertible benefit, is where the defendant has *requested* the benefit in kind. So, in *Pavey & Matthews*, there was no difficulty in saying that Mrs Paul was benefited by the renovation work on her cottage because she had requested that work.

(2) At the Plaintiff's Expense

In the vast majority of cases within the law of restitution, including the quartet of cases examined above, the benefit to the defendant is at the plaintiff's expense in the sense that the benefit represents a loss to the plaintiff. For example, if the plaintiff mistakenly pays the defendant £100, the plaintiff's loss of £100 becomes the defendant's gain of £100.

Alternatively, however, the plaintiff may be able to establish that the defendant's gain is at his expense because the defendant has committed an established wrong against the plaintiff (be it a tort, breach of contract, breach of fiduciary duty, or breach of confidence). For example, it has long been settled that a plaintiff is entitled to an account of profits for a breach of fiduciary duty, or breach of confidence, or tortious infringement of his intellectual property rights, irrespective of whether the defendant's profits (that the plaintiff is seeking) do not match, and are greater than, the plaintiff's loss.

---

[31] Goff and Jones, above n. 6, 18–27; Birks, above n. 2, 114–24.

[32] E.g., *BP Exploration Co. (Libya) Ltd v. Hunt (No. 2)* [1979] 1 WLR 783; *Procter & Gamble Philippine Manufacturing Corpn. v. Peter Cremer GmbH* [1988] 3 All ER 843; *Peel (Regional Municipality) v. Canada* [1992] 98 DLR (4th) 140.

[33] See A. Burrows, *The Law of Restitution* (Butterworths, 1993), 11–16; and essay 4 below.

Indeed it is this potential of a higher award that constitutes the major advantage of restitution for a wrong over a normal award of compensation for a wrong. Similarly it has now been clearly established by the Court of Appeal in England that damages for a proprietary tort, such as trespass to land, can be measured in terms of reversing gains made by the tortfeasor rather than compensating the plaintiff for his loss.[34]

This dual meaning of "at the expense of" lies behind the great division of the law of restitution advocated by Professor Birks between what he calls "unjust enrichment by subtraction", which is an entirely independent cause of action, and "unjust enrichment by wrongdoing" which is dependent on proving a wrong.

Normally, once one has recognised that central division, the question of "at the expense of" is straightforward. However, one difficulty within unjust enrichment by subtraction occurs where money received by the defendant goes through a third party's hands rather than being paid directly by the plaintiff to the defendant. In that situation, is the defendant's gain at the expense of the plaintiff or the third party? This was one of the difficulties in the *Lipkin Gorman* case: was the Playboy Club's enrichment, in receiving the money, at the expense of the plaintiff firm of solicitors or at the expense of Cass? In particular how could it be said that the loss was the solicitors' when well-established authorities laid down that when Cass withdrew the money from the partnership account at Lloyds Bank he took good title to that money (i.e. the money belonged to him).

One way to answer this is to take a broad-brush factual approach and to say that the solicitors had suffered a loss which, as a matter of factual causation, had become the club's gain. However, the House of Lords preferred a more technical approach under which the club's gain was held to be a loss to the solicitors because, applying the common law rules of tracing, the solicitors could trace their loss through to the money received by the club. More specifically, there was a common law tracing chain from (i) the loss in value of the solicitors' chose in action, underpinning their account with Lloyds Bank, to (ii) the money drawn out by Cass, and, as that money was not mixed with other money by Cass, to (iii) the club's receipt of the money from Cass.

[34] *Ministry of Defence* v. *Ashman* (1993) 66 P & CR 195; *Ministry of Defence* v. *Thompson* [1993] 40 EG 148.

(3) *Was the Enrichment Unjust?*

This is the question which requires the most detailed analysis of past cases, for to avoid the charge that the subject encourages "palm-tree justice" and idiosyncratic judicial discretion, it is important that the complex value-laden decision on injustice is essentially distilled from the existing case law.

As regards unjust enrichment by subtraction, the cases show that the main grounds for restitution or, as we might say, the main "unjust factors", can be listed as follows: mistake (as in *David Securities*), fail-ure of consideration (as in *Pavey & Matthews*), duress, legal compul-sion, necessity, undue influence, unconscionable dealing, incapacity, ignorance (as in *Lipkin Gorman*), and *ultra vires* demands by public authorities (as in *Woolwich*).

It is those factors that, *at a general level*, establish that the defendant's enrichment at the plaintiff's expense is unjust. But to isolate those unjust factors does not end the investigation. On the contrary, only detailed examination of the case law will reveal, e.g. whether all kinds of mistake trigger restitution; what kinds of pressures constitute duress; and what the law means by failure of consideration and in what factual contexts it operates. It is primarily with the task of elu-cidating such details of *unjust* enrichment that books and courses on restitution are concerned.

Similarly with regard to unjust enrichment by wrongs, only detailed examination of the cases will show which wrongs trigger restitution. For example, in English law the position is that, while equitable wrongs and some torts, especially proprietary torts, trigger restitution, restitution for breach of contract (i.e. requiring the dis-gorgement of gains made by breaking a contract) will generally not be awarded.[35]

The heavy reliance on past cases is not meant to suggest that there is no scope for an expansion of the law of restitution. On the con-trary it is believed that the categories of unjust factor are not closed (the decision in *Woolwich* supports this) and that, as has been stressed above, within the existing categories the open recognition of the underlying principle against unjust enrichment in *Pavey & Matthews* and *Lipkin Gorman* will make it easier for the courts to discard unwar-ranted historical restrictions (as shown by *David Securities*).

[35] The leading case denying restitution for breach of contract is *Surrey County Council* v. *Bredero Homes Ltd* [1993] 3 All ER 705. [But see now the *obiter dicta* of the Court of Appeal in *Attorney General* v. *Blake*, [1998] 1 All ER 833] See 140–3 below.

It is sometimes suggested that the "unjust" question is better approached by looking for reasons why an enrichment at the plaintiff's expense is not unjust rather than reasons why it is unjust. That is, an approach of "unjust enrichment unless . . ." rather than "unjust enrichment if . . .". It may be doubted whether the two different approaches lead to different results, particularly if it is accepted that on the "unjust enrichment if . . ." view the law is not static. Of the two it is more in keeping with the traditions of the common law, and makes it easier to describe the present law on restitution, to put the onus on the plaintiff to bring his claim within the interpretative reach of past cases. It is therefore the "unjust enrichment if . . ." approach that is traditionally preferred and is adopted in the above list of unjust factors.

(4) *Defences*

Even if the plaintiff has established an enrichment, at the plaintiff's expense, that is unjust, the defendant may be able to avail himself of a defence. The general restitutionary defences include change of position, estoppel, limitation, incapacity, illegality, and *bona fide purchase*. Again the details of these defences can only be ascertained by detailed examination of the cases.

Of greatest significance, in practice and theoretically, is change of position which, as we have seen, was accepted for the first time in England in *Lipkin Gorman* and in Australia in *David Securities*. The defence has a privotal role to play in counterbalancing the sweep of *prima facie* restitutionary liability. Now that it has been recognised, the courts are likely to feel less constrained in pushing forward the range and content of the unjust factors knowing that defendants have the security of receipt guaranteed by the defence.

While it is clear that a mere spending of money does not constitute change of position—rather the defendant must have acted differently than he otherwise would have done—the precise ingredients of change of position were left open for case law development by the House of Lords and High Court respectively. In *Lipkin Gorman* itself the defence, as we have seen, was successful: the club had paid out winnings to Cass which were deducted in determining the value of the unjust enrichment claim. In *David Securities* the question whether the bank had changed its position, after receipt of the mistaken payment, was remitted to the trial judge.

The sort of issues on change of position that the courts are likely to be required to resolve in the future include:

    (i) can a defendant rely on the defence where, although he has spent the money buying property which he would otherwise not have bought, he retains that property?

    (ii) can a public authority rely on the defence?

    (iii) is the defence applicable where the defendant has not detrimentally relied on the money being his but has nevertheless lost it, e.g., it has been stolen?

    (iv) what is the relationship between the new defence of change of position and the long-established defence of estoppel?

7. MORE DIFFICULT TERRAIN

It may appear from all this—and indeed I would have partly failed in my task if I have conveyed any contrary impression—that the main features on the map of restitution are relatively clear and obvious. In this final section I want to push on into areas where that is not so: where no clear map can be drawn.

Probably the commonest claim for restitution is that money was paid by a mistake of fact. Following *David Securities* it may be thought that, leaving aside the precise content of defences such as change of position, the restitutionary position on mistaken payments is straightforward. In fact some complex questions remain unanswered which can be illustrated by reference to the facts of two English cases concerning payments made by banks under mistakes of fact: (1) *Chase Manhattan NA Ltd* v. *Israel–British Bank (London) Ltd*[36] and (2) *Barclays Bank Ltd* v. *W.J. Simms Son & Cooke (Southern) Ltd*.[37]

(1) *Chase Manhattan NA Ltd* v. *Israel–British Bank (London) Ltd*[38]

Facts: P mistakenly makes two payments of $2m to X bank for the account of D bank. Only one such payment should have been made and the second was the result of a clerical error by one of P bank's employees.

---

[36] [1981] Ch. 105.
[37] [1980] QB 677.
[38] [1981] Ch. 105.

On the face of it this is a simple case. P bank would *prima facie* (i.e. subject to defences) be entitled to succeed in an action for money had and received against D bank. Applying *David Securities*, all that P bank would need to show was that the mistake caused the payment which it obviously did.

Let us now consider three complications.

(a) *Conflict of Laws*

In the actual *Chase Manhattan* case P bank and X bank were New York banks. D bank was English. Immediately one can see that the case raised possible choice of law problems. The law on choice of law for restitutionary claims is largely unexplored and unresolved and yet it is of great practical importance, given the international nature of banking and other financial transactions. In the standard Australian texts on the conflict of laws there is no mention of restitution at all, and any discussion of quasi-contract appears to be confined to claims for contribution arising out of road accidents.[39] In England the leading discussion, which has been heavily relied on by the courts, is in Dicey and Morris' *The Conflict of Laws*.[40] They suggest that the basic choice of law rule for restitution is the proper law of the obligation to make restitution. More specifically they suggest that, while the proper law of the restitutionary obligation is the proper law of the contract in so far as restitution arises in connection with a contract, the restitutionary proper law is generally the law of the country where the enrichment occurs. This can be criticised as placing excessive reliance on the choice of law rule for contract (hence arguably revealing an outdated adherence to the implied contract theory of restitution) and as producing arbitrary results where the place of enrichment is coincidental and there are other more significant factors connecting the case to a different country.

What is indisputable is that much work remains to be done, both by academics and by the courts, to produce a convincing resolution of the restitutionary choice of law dilemma.

(b) *Claim Against Agent*

What if the restitutionary claim was brought by P bank against X bank, which first received the overpayment, rather than against D

---

[39] P.E. Nygh, *Conflict of Laws in Australia* (6th edn., Butterworths, 1995); E.I. Sykes and M.C. Pryles, *Australian Private International Law* (3rd edn., Law Book Company, 1991).

[40] 12th edn. 1471 *et seq*. [See now F. Rose (ed.), *Restitution and the Conflict of Laws* (1995, Mansfield Press).]

bank? In general the answer seems clear that there is no claim against the agent as opposed to the principal. But what if, e.g. X bank knew, before it credited D's account, that P bank had paid by mistake?

In England the authorities appear to be split on that question. One view is that the bad faith of the agent can make no difference because once the money has been received for the benefit of the principal the agent drops out of the picture. The principal alone can be sued.[41] The contrary view is that the agent is subject to restitutionary liability subject to the defence that he has paid away the money to his principal in good faith in which event only the principal can be sued.[42]

Strong support for the latter view is be found in the reasoning of the High Court of Australia in *Australia & New Zealand Banking Group Ltd* v. *Westpac Banking Corporation*[43] albeit that the intermediary bank there conceded that it was liable to pay back the mistaken payment subject to being able to rely on a payment over defence. Strictly speaking the decision is therefore confined to clarifying the precise workings of the payment over defence and, in particular, laid down that there is no need for the agent to prove that the accounting to the principal was detrimental (hence divorcing the payment over defence from change of position). But it is clear that the High Court accepted the latter of the above two views as is evidenced, for example, by the following helpful summary of the law:

> "The rationale of . . . [the payment over] rule can be identified in terms of the law of agency and of notions of unjust enrichment. If money is paid to an agent on behalf of a principal and the agent received it in his capacity as such and, without notice of any irregularity in the payment, applies the money for the purpose for which it was paid to him, he has applied it in accordance with the mandate of the payer who must look to the principal for recovery."[44]

Applying that view, which seems preferable in widening the net of unjustly enriched defendants against whom plaintiffs can seek restitution, the agent bank which credits its principal's account with money that it knows to have been mistakenly paid has no defence and is liable in restitution (along with the principal) to the payer.[45]

---

[41] E.g., *Duke of Norfolk* v. *Worthy* (1808) 1 Camp. 337; *Agip (Africa) Ltd* v. *Jackson* [1990] Ch. 265 (*Per* Millett J as regards the equitable claim: upheld by the CA [1991] Ch. 547).

[42] See, e.g., *Buller* v. *Harrison* (1777) 2 Cowp. 565; *Gowers* v. *Lloyds and National Provincial Foreign Bank Ltd* [1938] 1 All ER 766.

[43] (1988) 78 ALR 157.

[44] *Ibid.*, 168.

[45] In the *Westpac* case Westpac conceded that it was liable to repay money credited to its customer's account *after notice* of the plaintiff bank's mistake.

(c) *Insolvency*

In the *Chase Manhattan* case D bank was insolvent. The action for money had and received was therefore of little use to P bank because, as a personal remedy, it would afford no priority. P bank would simply be added to the list of unsecured creditors of D bank with its entitlement to $2m being treated no differently from, e.g. claims to damages of $2m against D bank for breach of contract or a tort. The plaintiff sought to overcome this by arguing that the defendant, on receipt of the money, became a trustee of it so that, applying normal trust rules, the plaintiff would be able to assert a proprietary claim, giving priority on insolvency, over any property retained by the defendant that could be traced from the original $2m. Goulding J accepted that argument.

The difficulty is to pinpoint the basis of that trust, for it obviously is not a trust (express or implied) based on the plaintiff's intentions. One popular explanation is that the trust, whether labelled constructive or resulting, springs up by operation of law based on the principle against unjust enrichment. That is, the trust is the proprietary equivalent of the personal restitutionary remedy of an action for money had and received and is concerned, like that personal remedy, to reverse the defendant's unjust enrichment constituted by the receipt of the mistaken payment.

One policy argument that might be put against that approach is that it is not obvious that the priority afforded to the restitution claimant by recognising a trust is merited when one remembers that those who have suffered losses as victims of torts or breaches of contract are left as unsecured creditors. But perhaps a claim for unjust enrichment should rank higher than one for compensation for a wrong because an unjust enrichment, in contrast to a wrongful loss, directly affects the size of the pool of assets available for distribution.

Even if one can stomach the unjust enrichment trust as a matter of policy, one may baulk at the effect its acceptance would have on the present law. On the face of it if a mistaken payment triggers a trust so must every example of unjust enrichment, at least where money is paid that immediately enriches the defendant. For example, money paid by duress or under undue influence or by a public authority *ultra vires* must analogously be held on trust. Yet there is little, if any, support in the cases for this. Most importantly, unless one somehow cuts back the normal incidents of trusteeship,[46] it ought to follow that the

---

[46] [Ultimately this may be the best way forward. That is, one should accept that the imposition of a trust does not necessarily render the trustee a fiduciary (or, at least, a

trustee is personally strictly liable to account as a fiduciary for profits made from the payment. The consequence would appear to be that, *even if the defendant is solvent*, it will always be in a plaintiff's interests to claim a trust rather than an action for money had and received, for the latter is confined to allowing recovery of the amount paid.[47] Moreover, again applying normal trust rules, the payer would be able to avoid a change of position defence. That is, if the payee fails to return the money when the payer demands it, on the ground that he has changed his position, this will still constitute a breach of fiduciary duty for which the payer can claim an account of loss or gain; and change of position is irrelevant to a claim for loss and, according to *Lipkin Gorman*, cannot be raised as a defence to a claim for restitution for a wrong.

The startling conclusion, therefore, is that if the trust in *Chase Manhattan* rests on unjust enrichment reasoning the standard common law action for money had and received has been rendered otiose in all cases of mistaken and analogous payments and not just in cases where the payee is insolvent. It is hard to believe that that is what was intended.

One escape from this conclusion is to stick to unjust enrichment reasoning while denying that a trust was imposed *at the time of the initial receipt* in *Chase Manhattan*. On this approach, the decision would be reinterpreted as standing for the proposition that, where the defendant has been unjustly enriched by a mistaken or analogous payment, the payer is entitled to a trust concerned to reverse that unjust enrichment and affording priority on the defendant's insolvency provided he can show *at the time of his demand* that the defendant retains the original payment or its traceable product (applying equity's identification rules of tracing). The trust would attach to that retained enrichment. While a failure to comply with the demand could again trigger a fiduciary's personal liability to account for loss and gain, this approach does not emasculate the action for money had and received: that remedy would remain advantageous to a plaintiff in the usual case where it cannot be shown at the time of a claim for repayment that the payee retains the original enrichment or its traceable product.

fiduciary who is strictly liable to account for profits made): see A. Burrows, "Swaps and the Friction between Common Law and Equity" [1995] *RLR* 15, 28.]

[47] Similarly the interest awardable in a claim for an account of profits against a trustee can be compound, whereas simple interest only can be added to the common law restitutionary remedy.

However, this reinterpretation too runs into problems irrespective of the above possible policy objection to affording restitution-claimants priority on bankruptcy. Not only does it reverse the actual reasoning in *Chase Manhattan* by suggesting that a constructive trust *follows* tracing, whereas Goulding J was concerned to decide whether there was a constructive trust so as to *trigger* tracing but, subject to refinement, it also leads to the conclusion—radical by the standards of the present case law—that every example of an unjust enrichment where the defendant retains the enrichment or its traceable product at the time of demand triggers a trust.

An alternative strategy is to accept that a trust was imposed at the time of initial receipt in *Chase Manhattan* but to argue that it is not best explained by the principle against unjust enrichment. The better explanation is instead one of retention of title: just as for certain types of mistaken transfer legal title in property does not pass from transferor to transferee, so for other types of mistaken transfer legal title passes but the transferor is left with equitable title in the property. But this too runs into severe difficulties. In particular it fails to explain how one decides whether equitable title in property mistakenly transferred has passed. Moreover, it may collapse back to a reliance on unjust enrichment thinking. For while at common law it has become established through past cases that a fundamental mistake prevents legal title passing, it is difficult to see that there is any room left between a fundamental mistake and a causative mistake into which one can fit the sort of mistake needed to prevent equitable title passing. And without that gap every example of unjust enrichment by a mistaken or analogous payment would also be one in which equitable title was retained by the payor thereby emasculating the action for money had and received.

What all this indisputably shows is first, that the implications of, and justifications for, the decision in *Chase Manhattan* remain unresolved;[48] and, secondly, that a plaintiff seeking restitution of a

---

[48] In Australia, the decision has been criticised by R. Meagher, W. Gummow, and J. Lehane, *Equity Doctrines and Remedies* (3rd edn., Butterworths, 1992), para. 1402. Cf. M. Evans, *Outline of Equity and Trusts* (2nd edn., Butterworths, 1993) who justifies the decision because of the defendant's knowledge of the mistake: but Goulding J specifically denied that the defendant's knowledge of the mistake, acquired two days after the payment, had any relevance and imposed the trust from the date of receipt. [In *Westdeutsche Landesbank Girozentrale* v. *Islington London BC* [1996] 2 WLR 802, Lord Browne-Wilkinson, with whom Lords Lloyd and Slynn largely agreed, thought that Goulding J's reasoning in the *Chase Manhattan* case was incorrect, albeit that the decision might have been correct on the basis that the bank's retention of the money, when it learned of the mistake two days after receipt, may well have given rise to a constructive trust.]

mistaken payment would be well advised to plead his case both as one for money had and received and as one for the declaration of a resulting or constructive trust.

(2) *Barclays Bank Ltd* v. *W.J. Simms Son & Cooke (Southern) Ltd*[49]

Facts: P bank overlooked a stop instruction on a cheque for £24,000 drawn by its customer, X, in favour of D company for building work done.

In the actual case P bank sought restitution of the £24,000 from D company as having been paid under a mistake of fact. In allowing that claim Robert Goff J applied the causation test that, as we have seen, was subsequently approved by the High Court of Australia in *David Securities* for all types of mistake (whether fact or law).

But was it correct that a simple restitutionary claim lay against D company? Why was it is not more appropriate for P bank's restitutionary claim to lie against X?

This turns on the difficult question of whether P bank's payment to D discharged X's liability to D. If it did, D would be providing consideration for P's payment and that transaction could not therefore be nullified simply by P's unilateral mistake. Rather P's restitutionary claim would lie against X for having by mistake incontrovertibly benefited X by discharging its debt owed to D. That restitutionary claim would be enforceable either directly by an action for money paid to the defendant's (X's) use or, in a more roundabout way, through the technique of subrogation: that is, P bank would take over D's former rights and remedies against X to the extent necessary to achieve restitution of the sum paid to discharge X's debt.

Robert Goff J rejected the view that P's mistaken payment discharged X's liability to D. In so doing he followed what might be called the traditional doctrine that the payment of another's debt does not discharge that debt, without the debtor's request, unless the payer was legally compelled to make the payment.[50]

But the force of that traditional doctrine may be doubted. In terms of principle, especially given the free assignability of debts, it is hard to see why only a legally compelled payment and not, e.g. a mistaken payment, should be treated as discharging another's debt to the cred-

---

[49] [1980] QB 677.
[50] For a defence of the traditional doctrine, see J. Beatson, *The Use and Abuse of Unjust Enrichment* (Clarendon Press, 1991), 177–205.

itor provided the creditor accepts the payment as effecting a discharge. Moreover that traditional view runs contrary to some past cases. For example, the little-known banking case of *B. Liggett (Liverpool) Ltd* v. *Barclays Bank Ltd*[51] (which was cited to Robert Goff J but not referred to by him) appears to run directly contrary to the decision in *Barclays Bank Ltd* v. *W.J. Simms Son & Cooke (Southern) Ltd*.[52] In *Liggett* the defendant bank, contrary to instructions, honoured cheques drawn by its customer, the plaintiff company, that were signed by one director only. The cheques were drawn in favour of the plaintiff's creditors. In the plaintiff's action against the bank to have its account recredited, it was held by Wright J that the defendant bank was entitled in equity to take over the creditors' former remedies against the plaintiff so as to achieve restitution of the money paid discharging the plaintiff's debts.

So where a bank makes a mistaken payment that, on the face of it, goes to discharge a debt of its customer, the traditional view that the bank's restitutionary claim for mistake lies against the payee can be challenged both in principle and on authority. It is at least arguable that the more appropriate restitutionary claim lies against the customer for a mistaken discharge of its debt.

8. CONCLUSION

In 1989 Professor Laycock wrote that, "Despite its importance, restitution is a relatively neglected and underdeveloped part of the law. In the mental map of most lawyers, restitution consists largely of blank spaces with undefined borders and only scattered patches of familiar ground".[53] In this essay I have sought to meet the implied challenge in that statement and to show that the essentials of the Anglo–Australian law of restitution can now be clearly mapped. This is not to deny that there are areas, such as resulting and constructive trusts, conflict of laws, and discharge of another's debt, where the work of the restitutionary map-maker is far from complete and where a full understanding of the law of restitution remains elusive.

[51] [1928] 1 KB 48. Doubts cast by the majority of the Court of Appeal in *Re Cleadon Trust Ltd* [1939] Ch. 286 on some aspects of *Liggett* do not affect the point for which it is here relied on.
[52] [1980] 1 QB 677.
[53] "The Scope and Significance of Restitution" (1989) 67 *Texas Law Review* 1277, 1277.

4

Free Acceptance and the Law of Restitution

The first edition of Goff and Jones' *The Law of Restitution* was published in 1966. An important part of their approach to unjust enrichment was a restitutionary concept which they identified and labelled as "free acceptance". Peter Birks similarly, albeit with added refinement, made free acceptance a central pillar in his exposition of restitution's theoretical structure in *An Introduction to the Law of Restitution*. The thesis of this article is that these scholars are mistaken and that neither on principle nor authority does free acceptance have a place within the law of restitution. This is not meant to suggest, however, that the cases which Goff and Jones and Birks explain as restitutionary because of free acceptance belong outside the law of restitution. On the contrary it is believed that they can nearly all be explained as restitutionary, but on grounds other than free acceptance.

What then is free acceptance? Goff and Jones in their first edition explained the idea as follows: ". . . the defendant will not usually be regarded as having been benefited by the receipt of services or goods unless he has accepted them (or, in the case of goods, retained them) with an opportunity of rejection and with actual or presumed knowledge that they were to be paid for. For convenience we shall refer to a person who has so acted as having *freely accepted* the services or goods in question."[1] In Birks' words, "A free acceptance occurs where a recipient knows that a benefit is being offered to him non-gratuitously and where he, having the opportunity to reject, elects to accept."[2]

According to Birks' structure free acceptance is unique in showing both that there is an enrichment and that it is unjust. As what may be called an "unjust factor", it belongs alongside factors negativing

---

[1] *The Law of Restitution* (Sweet & Maxwell, 1966), 30–1. See similarly *The Law of Restitution* (4th edn., 1993), 19, 41.

[2] *An Introduction to the Law of Restitution* (Clarendon Press, 1985 and revised paperback edn. 1989).

voluntariness, such as mistake, duress and failure of consideration. But unlike them, the injustice of not giving a remedy for a benefit freely accepted focuses on the defendant's conduct and state of mind, not the plaintiff's. So, in Birks' words, where the defendant has freely accepted "he has only himself to blame for the resulting situation".[3] "The crucial difference which distinguishes free acceptance from non-voluntary transfer is that the reason for restitution is now found on the defendant's side."[4] The injustice outside non-voluntary transfer of a benefit, which free acceptance picks up, is that of refusing restitution to a disappointed risk-taker, who has conferred a benefit on the free acceptor. "This . . . is the essential point: volunteers who are disappointed risk-takers can get restitution on the basis of free acceptance."[5]

Free acceptance is also sufficient to establish that the defendant has been enriched. In many situations establishing that the defendant has been enriched presents no difficulties, for example where he has received money. Difficulties arise, however, with benefits in kind, that is services and goods, which the defendant can "subjectively devalue"[6] by stating that they have no value to him. The crucial importance of free acceptance is that it overcomes subjective devaluation. Again to quote Birks, "A defendant who has freely accepted the benefit cannot use [the subjective devaluation] argument. The reason is that, if he has freely accepted, he has *ex hypothesi* chosen to receive it, and subjective devaluation is an argument whose premiss is that where something has *not* been chosen by its recipient it cannot normally be said to have been of value to him."[7]

This then is the important role assigned by Birks to free acceptance. A similar approach is taken by Goff and Jones. In challenging this approach, I first want to attack it as a matter of principle; that is, I want to question, irrespective of authority, whether free acceptance can be sensibly regarded either as establishing that a given enrichment is unjust or as establishing that the defendant has been enriched in a situation in which the injustice is otherwise clear. Having done that, I shall then move on to a more detailed attack through the authorities.

---

[3] *Ibid.*, at 114.
[4] *Ibid.*, at 104.
[5] *Ibid.*, at 266.
[6] *Ibid.*, at 109–10.
[7] *Ibid.*, at 266. See also at 114–16.

I. THE ATTACK AS A MATTER OF PRINCIPLE

(1) *Free Acceptance as the Unjust Factor*

It is helpful to focus on the hypothetical example which Birks gives to illustrate the justice of restitution for free acceptance. "Suppose that I see a window-cleaner beginning to clean the windows of my house. I know that he will expect to be paid. So I hang back unseen till he has finished the job; then I emerge and maintain that I will not pay for work which I never ordered. It is too late, I have freely accepted the service. I had the opportunity to send him away. I chose instead to let him go on. I must pay the reasonable value of his work."[8] For Birks this provides "a clear and simple example."[9] But for the present author it was the start of the feeling that something had gone awry with the reasoning. For while (assuming, for the present, that the enrichment issue is solved) the injustice is fairly obvious if the window-cleaner had been acting non-voluntarily, for example by mistake, the crucial importance of free acceptance for Birks is that it would allow restitution to the window-cleaner even if he had been acting merely in the hope that I would pay; that is, even if the window-cleaner was a disappointed risk-taker. Yet surely on any common sense view there would be no injustice in my not paying a risk-taker. For even if I can be said to have acted shabbily, this is matched by the fact that the plaintiff was a risk-taker—without any inducement, he gambled on my willingness to pay. Why should we now want to protect him against the very risk that he undertook? In short, the plaintiff's risk-taking cancels out any shabbiness in my free acceptance. As such, free acceptance cannot be regarded in principle as an unjust factor.

It should be added that the situation would be different both where the window-cleaner was not acting voluntarily, for example if he had mistaken the number of the house, but also, and indeed most obviously, where he was acting in accordance with the terms of an express bargain with the householder. In the latter situation, he

[8] N. 2 above, 265.
[9] [Birks, "In Defence of Free Acceptance" in A. Burrows (ed.), *Essays on the Law of Restitution* (Clarendon Press, 1991), 104, 123–4 has since conceded that this description was inaccurate and that the window-cleaner was not a good case on which to concentrate attention: free acceptance would only be "unjust" if the window-cleaner would have desisted if the householder had told him that he would not be paid and if the householder had already made up his mind that he would not pay the window-cleaner. Without this combination of facts, the householder would not be "unequivocally unconscientious in not speaking out."]

would have a contractual remedy fulfilling his expectations of payment. The same would apply if the householder had induced him to clean the windows on the reasonable expectation of payment even though there was no express but merely a true implied bargain between them.[10]

(2) *Free Acceptance Establishing Enrichment*[11]

The general question of when a defendant is benefited is surprisingly complex; but in order to challenge the role of free acceptance it is necessary to give some indication straightaway of an approach to the answer.[12] It is submitted that as a matter of fact a person may be benefited either negatively—that is by being saved an expense—or positively—that is by making a gain—and that as a matter of policy one may judge the issue on a range from total subjectivity (solely through the defendant's own eyes) through to total objectivity (solely through the eyes of the reasonable man, which in this context means the market). The problem with a purely subjective approach is that one can never be sure what the defendant is thinking and, in any event, one would probably not wish to prejudice the plaintiff according to the eccentricities of the defendant. On the other hand, the problem with a purely objective approach is that it may involve a complete sacrifice of the individual's values for those of society. It would seem therefore that the best approach is one that takes a line somewhere between these two extremes.

Half of Goff and Jones' and Birks' approach to the problem of benefit sits happily with this suggestion. Hence the concept of an "incontrovertible benefit,"[13] which Birks amplifies as resting on a "no reasonable man" test,[14] is vitally important and stresses that the courts

---

[10] I.e. an offer (objectively construed) by the householder accepted by the window-cleaner's conduct.

[11] See J. Beatson, "Benefit, Reliance and the Structure of Unjust Enrichment" [1987] *Current Legal Problems* 71. His paper mounts an attack on the approach to benefit taken by Goff and Jones and Birks which is not totally dissimilar to that made in this essay. In particular he also regards free acceptance as failing to establish that the defendant has been enriched and to that extent his and my views are in agreement. However we markedly differ not only in the approach which leads us to that conclusion but also in the consequences we draw from it. Moreover he does not recognise anything akin to the "bargained for" principle of benefit put forward in this essay.

[12] For the suggested actual answer to the question see below.

[13] Goff and Jones, *The Law of Restitution* (4th edn., 1993), 22–6.

[14] N. 2 above, 116–24.

do largely take an approach between the two extremes. So, for example, the receipt of a sum of money by a defendant is regarded as a benefit because no reasonable man would deny that a sum of money benefits him. Any subjective devaluation argument by the defendant to the effect that the receipt of money is of no benefit to him is therefore ignored. Similarly a defendant who has had legally required expenses paid by the plaintiff is regarded as being benefited even though he may argue that he would not have paid those expenses. No reasonable man would make that argument. Clearly at its parameters the concept of an incontrovertible benefit is open-textured and allows a more or a less objective approach to be adopted. So, for example, necessary expenses saved can range from legally to mere factually necessary expenses.[15] Similarly positive incontrovertible gains can range from those which have been *realised* to those which are merely *realisable*.[16] But the importance of the concept should not be obscured by its open-textured nature.

However, the other half of Goff and Jones' and Birks' approach to benefit is free acceptance. Even where a defendant is not incontrovertibly benefited, they regard him as benefited where he freely accepts the plaintiff's goods or services. But why is this thought correct? The answer would appear to be that free acceptance shows that the defendant regards himself as benefited, and therefore ordering him to pay does not undermine respect for the individuality of values.[17] But the problem with this is that, even accepting that the defendant's inner wishes must be judged according to his outward conduct,[18] there is no reason why one should assume that a freely accepting defendant actually regards himself as being benefited by what the plaintiff has conferred. On the contrary a defendant is just as likely to accept what the plaintiff is conferring on him where he

---

[15] N. 2 above, at 118–21.

[16] Contrast n. 2 above, 121–4 (taking the narrower "realised" view) with Goff and Jones *The Law of Restitution* (4th edn., Butterworths, 1993), 23, 176 (taking the wider "realisable" view).

[17] [Birks n. 9 above has since clarified that he never intended that free acceptance should be taken to indicate that the recipient values the thing in question. Rather, free acceptance is unconscientious conduct which debars the defendant from exercising his usual right to appeal to the subjective devaluation argument. But by this clarification Birks tends to merge the "injustice" and "enrichment" sides of free acceptance with both ultimately resting on the same supposed injustice of the free acceptor's conduct. See also Goff and Jones, *The Law of Restitution* (4th edn., 1993), 19.]

[18] This aspect of objectivity should not be confused with that used earlier in this paragraph and in the preceding one where it refers to judging benefit by the values of the reasonable man in contrast to the values of the individual.

considers it neither beneficial nor detrimental as where he considers it beneficial.

So if we return to Birks' window-cleaning example, the fact that the householder freely accepts does not establish that he regards himself as being better off by having his windows cleaned. For even if it is a fair inference that he would have stopped the window-cleaning if he had regarded the cleaning of his windows as detrimental to him, he is acting perfectly rationally if he allows the cleaning to continue on the grounds that he is neither being benefited nor harmed. In short, he may be indifferent to the cleaning of his windows. Free acceptance cannot therefore be regarded as establishing the defendant's enrichment.

An alternative way of looking at this is to ask whether the defendant would have otherwise paid for goods or services of the kind provided by the plaintiff so that the plaintiff's intervention has now saved him incurring that expense. It is submitted that free acceptance gives no sound indication that the defendant would have otherwise been willing to pay for the goods or services provided, and hence does not establish that the defendant has been benefited by being saved expense.

2. THE ATTACK THROUGH THE AUTHORITIES

To challenge Goff and Jones' and Birks' view of free acceptance as a matter of principle can advance the argument only so far: for if the courts rely upon that notion in the law of restitution, either expressly or implicitly, one would have to concede to Goff and Jones and Birks its importance, irrespective of its defective theoretical nature. In fact, however, there is no real support in past decisions for the notion of free acceptance as these writers view it. Indeed it may come as something of a surprise to readers of their books to find out that there is no reported English case in which the term free acceptance has been used.[19] Moreover while Birks criticises some leading decisions for failing to use free acceptance reasoning—such as *Phillips* v. *Homfray*[20] on restitution following a tort and *Re Cleadon Trust Ltd.*[21] and *Owen*

---

[19] A search on Lexis threw up one unreported case, *Nemes* v. *Ata Chaglayan*, 1978 Transcript No. 1678, CA, in which free acceptance was referred to; but nothing in the decision turned on free acceptance as such.

[20] (1883) 24 Ch. D 439. Criticised in n. 2 above, 324. See also at 125. This decision can be strongly criticised for reasons that have nothing to do with free acceptance: see Burrows, *Remedies for Torts and Breach of Contract* (2nd edn., Butterworths, 1994), 290–2.

v. *Tate*[22] on restitution for discharge of another's debt—that "failure" supports the view that free acceptance is not recognised in the law of restitution.

Most importantly, however, it is submitted that none of the cases which Goff and Jones and Birks explain as restitutionary according to their notion of free acceptance need be so explained. Nor on the other hand is there any need to regard them as non-restitutionary; rather they are nearly all explicable on other restitutionary grounds. To understand this it is necessary to set out briefly a suggested scheme for the bulk of restitution.

According to this scheme (which is essentially Birks' scheme minus free acceptance) there is a basic division between unjust enrichment by subtraction and unjust enrichment by wrongdoing. The latter is concerned with restitution for torts, breach of contract or equitable wrongs, such as breach of fiduciary duty. In unjust enrichment by subtraction the main factors indicating that the enrichment is unjust are those which indicate that the benefit to the defendant was rendered non-voluntarily by the plaintiff. There are principally three such factors; mistake, compulsion, and failure of consideration. It is important to realise that failure of consideration is here being used to refer to a failure of the return that the defendant led the plaintiff reasonably to expect would be given for his rendering of the benefit to the defendant.[23] That reasonable expectation of return may have been engendered in the plaintiff according to the terms of a valid contract or of a void, unenforceable, incomplete or anticipated contract. In theory—and this is a crucial point which derives support from the reform of the common law by section 1(2) of the Law Reform (Frustrated Contracts) Act 1943—there is no good reason why the failure of consideration ever needs to be total,[24] although, in order not to undermine contracts, if a benefit has been rendered

---

[21] [1939] Ch. 286. Criticised in n. 2 above, 288–90.

[22] [1976] Q.B. 402. Criticised in n. 2 above, 311–12 and by Birks and Beatson (1976) 92 *LQR* 188.

[23] This meaning of failure of consideration is in line with the traditional "reciprocity" view of consideration and failure of consideration; see e.g. Anson, *Law of Contract* (26th edn., OUP, 1984), 78–9; *Combe* v. *Combe* [1951] 2 KB 215; *Fibrosa Case* [1943] AC 32, 48 (*per* Lord Simon). However, just as traditional views of consideration are under attack from reliance notions (e.g. in the development of promissory estoppel), so also one could sensibly extend failure of consideration to cover failure of what the defendant led the plaintiff reasonably to expect would be performed and which the plaintiff was relying upon in rendering the benefit to the defendant. Indeed it is submitted that as a matter of underlying justice this wider view is to be preferred; cf. n. 2 above, 223–6.

[24] See n. 2 above, 242–5.

under a valid contract the plaintiff should not be able to rely on failure of consideration unless the contract has been terminated. While
failure of consideration is like mistake and compulsion in being a factor negativing the plaintiff's voluntariness, it is not quite the same in
that the plaintiff has freely rendered the benefit although only on the
reasonable expectation of the defendant's return performance which
is then not forthcoming. In Birks' terminology, failure of consideration is concerned with qualification of the will, whereas mistake and
compulsion are concerned with its vitiation.

As regards the establishing of benefit, an incontrovertible benefit—using that term in a wide sense—will normally be required. So,
in the hard cases, where services have been rendered or goods transferred, the defendant can be said to have been incontrovertibly benefited either by the readily realisable (or realised) objective value of
an end product or by legally or factually necessary objective expense
saved.[25] Which of these two will be taken is a question of fact resting on which is the more realistic assessment of the defendant's position. Otherwise the most important principle[26] is that a defendant
can be regarded as negatively benefited where the plaintiff performs
what the defendant contracted or bargained[27] for, although it is
debatable whether his expense saved should be judged objectively by
the market price of the services or goods or subjectively by the contract or bargain price. The reasoning behind this "bargained-for"
principle of benefit[28] is that where the defendant has "promised" to
pay for a particular performance, the outward appearance is that he
regards that performance as beneficial or, put in an alternative way,
that he has been saved expense that he would otherwise have been
willing to incur. By the same token even if the defendant receives

---

[25] Exceptionally a defendant may be able to show that an incontrovertible benefit does
not benefit him: e.g., the payment of legally necessary expense may not benefit him if a relative was prepared to pay that expense for him gratuitously. It should also be noted that the
"at the expense of" aspect of unjust enrichment may dictate that one should take the highest common factor between the plaintiff's loss and the defendant's gain. If so, then even if
the plaintiff's claim starts with the defendant's incontrovertible benefit being the readily
realisable value of an end product, this will generally be knocked down towards the necessary expense saved.

[26] Indeed it would seem that any valuation according to this principle should override
any incontrovertible benefit valuation where both principles are made out on the same facts.

[27] The wider term bargain is necessary so as to include cases where a contract is void,
unenforceable, incomplete or anticipated.

[28] Arguably one could talk instead of a "request" principle of benefit: but it would seem
that this would not go quite far enough to establish the defendant's benefit, because request
does not necessarily indicate reciprocity (i.e. "payment" by the defendant).

only part of what he bargained for, it can be presumed that he regards himself as benefited by what he has received and that he has been saved part of the expense that he would otherwise have incurred.[29]

Having set out a scheme for restitution, we can now move to consider in more detail the main areas of the law relied on by Goff and Jones and Birks to support their notion of free acceptance. These can be conveniently divided into three: the mistaken improvement of land; services rendered or goods supplied under a contract discharged because of breach or frustration; and services rendered or goods supplied under a void, unenforceable, incomplete or anticipated contract.

(1) *The Mistaken Improvement of Land*

Both Goff and Jones and Birks[30] consider free acceptance, through the equitable doctrine of acquiescence, to play a crucial role here as establishing that the owner of the land has been benefited in a situation where, even applying Goff and Jones' wider view of the concept, there is rarely an incontrovertible benefit since the financial gain is not readily realisable.[31]

The classic exposition of the equitable doctrine of acquiescence was that of Fry J. in *Willmott* v. *Barber*.[32]

> "It has been said that the acquiescence which will deprive a man of his legal rights must amount to fraud and in my view that is an abbreviated statement of a very true proposition. A man is not to be deprived of his legal rights unless he has acted in such a way as would make it fraudulent for him to set up those rights. What, then, are the elements or requisites necessary to constitute fraud of that description?

[29] The presumption is rebuttable; for example if to complete performance would now cost the defendant as much as the original bargain (or market) price for full performance. Of course, to fall within this principle the plaintiff's performance must be in accordance with what the defendant bargained for. This idea underpins, for example, the Law Commission's recommendation in para. 2–46 of its report on *Pecuniary Restitution on Breach of Contract* (Law Com. No. 121 (1983)) that the benefit must be conferred "under the contract." So, for example, where the contract is for an end product there is no relevant part performance until part of that product has been received by the defendant—see discussion below of *Planché* v. *Colburn* (1831) 8 Bing 14.

[30] *Law of Restitution* (4th edn., 1993), 20, 167–72; *Introduction*, 279.

[31] Cf. *Law of Restitution* (4th edn., 1993), 23.

[32] (1880) 15 Ch.D 96, 105–6. See also, e.g. *Ramsden* v. *Dyson* (1886) LR 1 HL 129; *Plimmer* v. *Mayor, &c. of Wellington* (1884) 9 AC 699; *Inwards* v. *Baker* [1965] 2 QB 29; *Crabb* v. *Arun DC* [1976] Ch. 179; *Taylor Fashions Ltd* v. *Liverpool Victoria Trustees Co.* [1982] QB 133n.; *Att.-Gen. of Hong Kong* v. *Humphreys Estate (Queen's Gardens) Ltd* [1987] AC 114.

In the first place the plaintiff must have made a mistake as to his legal rights. Secondly, the plaintiff must have expended some money or must have done some act (not necessarily upon the defendant's land) on the faith of his mistaken belief. Thirdly, the defendant, the possessor of the legal right, must know of the existence of his own right which is inconsistent with the right claimed by the plaintiff. If he does not know of it he is in the same position as the plaintiff, and the doctrine of acquiescence is founded upon conduct with a knowledge of your legal rights. Fourthly, the defendant, the possessor of the legal right, must know of the plaintiff's mistaken belief of his rights. If he does not, there is nothing which calls upon him to assert his own rights. Lastly, the defendant, the possessor of the legal right, must have encouraged the plaintiff in his expenditure of money or in the other acts which he has done, either directly or by abstaining from asserting his legal right. Where all these elements exist there is a fraud of such a nature as will entitle the court to restrain the possessor of the legal right from exercising it, but, in my judgment, nothing short of this will do."

It is submitted that one half of this doctrine—and indeed the half which has been much more commonly applied—has nothing to do with mistake nor indeed with unjust enrichment; rather it is concerned with the active or passive engendering of reasonable expectations in the plaintiff and their fulfilment, and belongs within or at least alongside the law of contract.[33] But while the other half of the doctrine is concerned with restitution there is nothing in the reasoning in the cases to support the view that free acceptance here establishes the defendant's benefit. On the contrary, the courts' refusal even to advert to the existence of any problem regarding the improvement of land as a benefit may suggest that they are simply taking an objective view which ignores subjective devaluation altogether. Alternatively and in so far as the restitutionary analysis may be restricted to situations where the defendant has a financial interest only in the land (rather than living there) one can argue that the improvement in the land is an incontrovertible benefit, since for such a defendant the improvement is readily realisable in money.

But if one has both mistake and benefit irrespective of acquiescence—and hence there is unjust enrichment—why should the court

---

[33] For this division, see n. 2 above, 290–3; *Amalgamated Investment & Property Co. Ltd* v. *Texas Commerce International Bank Ltd* [1982] QB 84, 103 *per* Robert Goff J. The fact that there are really two doctrines may explain statements to the effect that all five of Fry J's requirements need not always be satisfied; see especially *Taylors Fashions Ltd* v. *Liverpool Victoria Trustees Co. Ltd* [1982] QB 133n., 143–55 (*per* Oliver J).

insist on acquiescence in the restitutionary half of the doctrine? One possible explanation is that in a fully developed law of restitution, where the types of mistake grounding restitution would rest on a simple "but for" causation test, there would indeed be no role for any form of acquiescence; but that just as the law has traditionally been wary about allowing mere unilateral mistake to give escape from a contract so here, in the mistaken improvement of land cases, it should not surprise us that the courts have wanted to restrict the recognition of unilateral mistake to the strong case where that mistake is known to the defendant. Another possible explanation is that where the defendant knows of the plaintiff's mistake, and lets him confer an objective benefit under that mistake, his acquiring of that objective benefit is so unconscionable that it cancels out any concern for the individuality of his tastes.

For Birks, however, the restitutionary half of equitable acquiescence rests on free acceptance without any need for there to have been a mistake on the improver's behalf.[34] In other words, for him free acceptance not only solves the benefit issue but is also the unjust factor. This, of course, is contrary to the classic statements of the doctrine, such as that of Fry J, which insist on a mistake by the plaintiff. Birks recognises this but purports to prove his case by reliance on *Ramsden* v. *Dyson*.[35] The plaintiffs, who were tenants at will, had built on land believing that the defendant landlords would grant them a long lease whenever they asked for it. When they did ask, however, the landlords refused to grant it. The plaintiffs sought an order that the landlords should grant the lease. The House of Lords refused their claim (Lord Kingsdown dissenting) on the ground that the evidence did not establish that the landlords knew of the tenants' "mistaken" belief and hence the requirements of *Willmott* v. *Barber* were not satisfied.

For Birks the case is important because although the majority of their Lordships used the language of mistake, what was really in issue was not a mistake but a misprediction by the plaintiffs; that is, the plaintiffs were risk-takers and were acting voluntarily. According to Birks, then, the recognition that the acquiescence doctrine could apply to such facts showed that it is synonymous with free acceptance and is not confined to restitution based on mistake.

---

[34] N. 2 above, 277–9; cf. *Law of Restitution* (4th edn., 1993), 20, 166–71, which relies on free acceptance but within a chapter entitled "Restitution in Respect of Services Rendered under a Mistake".

[35] (1886) LR 1 HL 83.

However, there are alternative explanations of the reasoning. One is that their Lordships were here dealing with the other half of the doctrine of acquiescence which is based on the defendant having engendered expectations in the plaintiff. Certainly Lord Kingsdown in his dissenting judgment saw the issue in those terms, and there is judicial support for the view that his dissent was purely in interpreting the evidence and did not represent any disagreement as to the law being applied.[36] Alternatively, one can argue that there was a true mistake in the case in that the plaintiffs mistakenly thought that the defendants had already legally (or at least morally) bound themselves to grant them the lease—an interpretation which accords with the language of mistake used by the majority.

Even if one were to accept Birks' interpretation of *Ramsden* v. *Dyson*, it is significant that there is no other improvement of land case to support it; for although Birks cites *Plimmer* v. *Mayor, &c., of Wellington*[37] and *Inwards* v. *Baker*[38] to this end,[39] it is indisputable that the courts in those cases were applying the expectation half of the acquiescence doctrine and hence relied entirely on Lord Kingsdown's dissenting judgment.

The conclusion to be reached is that the authorities on restitution for the mistaken improvement of land do not require one to recognise the notion of free acceptance.

(2) *Services Rendered or Goods Supplied under a Contract Discharged because of Breach or Frustration*

It is submitted that the unjust factor grounding restitution in this area is failure of consideration: that is, the plaintiff has not received the defendant's contractually promised performance which was the plaintiff's basis for rendering the benefit to the defendant. As regards benefit, there is sometimes an incontrovertible benefit in the form of factually necessary expenses saved. But generally it is the "bargained-for" principle of benefit that is in play.

If we look first at an innocent party being granted restitution for services conferred or goods supplied under a contract which he has treated as discharged for the other party's breach, Goff and Jones

---

[36] *Plimmer* v. *Mayor &c. of Wellington* (1884) 9 AC 699, 711.
[37] *Ibid.*
[38] [1965] 2 QB 29.
[39] N. 2 above, 278–9.

make the point that there are few relevant authorities.[40] However, a straightforward case noted by them is *De Bernardy* v. *Harding*.[41] The defendant was in control of letting seats to see the funeral procession of the Duke of Wellington. He made a contract with the plaintiff to deal with sales overseas. The plaintiff had accordingly advertised abroad and had arranged accommodation for overseas visitors. The defendant then repudiated the contract and, although the plaintiff sent applicants for tickets to him, he refused to pay the plaintiff anything. Alderson B. said, "Where one party has absolutely refused to perform, or has rendered himself incapable of performing his part of the contract, he puts it in the power of the other party either to sue for a breach of it, or to rescind the contract and sue on a *quantum meruit* for the work actually done."[42] Although the actual decision was to order a retrial, it is submitted that the quantum meruit recognised by Alderson B. was in this case fully justified according to restitutionary principles; there had been a failure of consideration and the plaintiff had carried out part of the bargained-for work, thereby saving the defendant some of the expense he would otherwise have incurred. The defendant had therefore been unjustly enriched.

A crucial question which arises once one recognises that the innocent party may have a restitutionary claim for services rendered or goods supplied is, can he wholly escape from a bad bargain by claiming restitution or is he rather restricted to the *pro rata* contract price?[43] In *Lodder* v. *Slowey*,[44] the Privy Council upheld the decision of the Court of Appeal of New Zealand that the plaintiff, who had partly completed a tunnel in accordance with a contract repudiated by the defendant, was entitled to a quantum meruit for the work done; and in expressing agreement with the lower court's approach to quantum meruit the Privy Council impliedly approved the view that the plaintiff is not restricted to the *pro rata* contract price. As Williams J said: "As the defendant has abandoned the special contract, and as the plaintiff had accepted that abandonment, what would have happened if the special contract had continued in existence is entirely irrele-

[40] *Law of Restitution* (4th edn., 1993), 425.
[41] (1853) 8 Ex 822. See *Law of Restitution* (4th edn., 1993), 425, n. 31.
[42] *Ibid.*, at 824.
[43] Even to award the plaintiff the *pro rata* contract price allows him *some* escape from a bad bargain; since the *pro rata* contract price relates only to the beneficial performance already carried out rather than to the full losing performance, it will be greater than the plaintiff's expectation loss.
[44] [1904] AC 442, affirming (1900) 20 NZLR 321.

vant."[45] This approach is also strongly supported by cases in the United States of which the best known is *Boomer* v. *Muir*.[46]

It is submitted that this whole issue turns on the nature of the defendant's benefit. If one regards the defendant as having been incontrovertibly benefited by "necessary expenses saved", there should be no restriction to the *pro rata* contract price, for this would be contradictory—if the expense saved was really necessary the defendant would have been prepared to pay at the market price rather than merely at this contract price. But if one regards the defendant as having been benefited because he has received part of what he bargained for, it may well be that the pro rata contract price should (at least[47]) form the upper limit in assessing the defendant's benefit; for to allow the plaintiff the objective market price in excess of this would be re-encounter subjective devaluation in that the defendant can validly argue that he was only willing to pay at the contractual rate.[48]

Although both Birks and Goff and Jones do at times talk of free acceptance as being important in this area,[49] it is clearly difficult to view the defendant as having freely accepted services in the usual case of the plaintiff partly completing a job, when the defendant has only agreed to pay under a contract for completion of that job.[50] Birks, recognising this, himself relies heavily on failure of consideration as the unjust factor here,[51] but in dealing with the benefit side of the unjust enrichment principle he harks back to free acceptance reasoning with his suggestion that there is a "limited acceptance" principle for establishing benefit.[52]

---

[45] (1900) 20 NZLR 321, 358.

[46] 24 P 2d 570 (1933). It is also the view taken in the (first) *Restatement of Contracts*; s. 347(1) [(second) *Restatement of Contracts*, s. 373(1);] by Williston, *Contracts* (3rd edn., Baker Voorhisd Co. Inc., 1970), ss. 1459, 1485; and by Palmer, *Law of Restitution* (Little, Brown & Co., 1978), s. 4(4).

[47] Taking an even more subjective view, it can be argued that the *pro rata* contract price should govern even where it *exceeds* the market price, i.e. where the plaintiff has made a good bargain. But since a plaintiff in this situation will be even better off with expectation damages the question is of purely academic interest.

[48] A possible counter-argument to this is that no sympathy should be shown for a contract-breaker's subjective devaluation.

[49] N. 2 above, 228–9; *Law of Restitution* (4th edn., 1993), 404–5, 409.

[50] N. 2 above, 230, 286–7.

[51] *Ibid.*, 226–34.

[52] *Ibid.*, 126–7, 232.

In addition Goff and Jones argue that a plaintiff should not be able through restitution to recover more than the *pro rata* contract price.[53] However, contrary to the approach that has been suggested above, they justify this restriction not on the grounds of the difficulty of establishing benefit beyond the contract price in the case of services or goods, but rather on the grounds that otherwise bargains would be subverted. This is startling for two main reasons. First, it is inconsistent with their approach which favours the recovery of money for total failure of consideration even where the plaintiff has made a bad bargain.[54] Secondly, it is hard to see that one is subverting the bargain, given that there is a need for the contract to be discharged before restitution can be claimed.

Finally in this area it should be noted that the much-discussed decision of *Planché* v. *Colburn*[55] is a difficult one for any restitution lawyer. The plaintiff had been contractually engaged by the defendant to write a book on costume and ancient armour for a series called *The Juvenile Library*. When the plaintiff had written part of the book the defendant abandoned the series and refused to pay the plaintiff anything even though the plaintiff was ready to complete the whole book. It was held that the plaintiff could recover a quantum meruit without tendering any part of the book. While the unjust factor of failure of consideration was present, it is hard to see that any benefit was derived by the defendant so as to ground a restitutionary remedy, for he had not received any part of the book, which was what he had promised to pay for. Goff and Jones accept this and criticise the decision accordingly,[56] whereas Birks uses the idea of "limited acceptance", which is a further and equally unwarranted step down the line from free acceptance, to justify the decision.[57] It is submitted that the case is best viewed as awarding the equivalent of contractual expectation damages and not restitution.

While continuing to focus on contracts discharged for breach, let us now switch our attention to the contract-breaker. Can he recover

---

[53] *Law of Restitution* (3rd edn., 1986), 467–8; (4th edn., 1993), 426–8. [Birks, albeit more tentatively, originally took the same line: see n. 2 above, 288. But he has since changed his mind; see "In Defence of Free Acceptance" in A. Burrows (ed.), *Essays on the Law of Restitution* (1991), 135–7.]

[54] See Beatson, n. 11 above, 85.

[55] (1831) 8 Bing 14.

[56] *Law of Restitution* (4th edn., 1993), 425–6. However, it is submitted that the reasoning given in their 2nd edn. at 378–9 is to be preferred.

[57] N. 2 above, 126–7, 132.

restitution for services rendered or goods supplied to the innocent party?

According to the reasoning so far presented, the contract-breaker's ground for restitution should be more or less symmetrical with that of the innocent party, the unjust factor being failure of consideration and the benefit being established either by showing an incontrovertible benefit (generally in the form of necessary expenses saved) or, more commonly, on the basis that the defendant has been saved expense by having received at least part of the performance bargained for. But English cases have consistently denied restitution to a contract-breaker. A leading authority is *Sumpter* v. *Hedges*,[58] where the plaintiff had contracted with the defendant to build two homes and stables on the defendant's land. The plaintiff did a good deal of the building work but later became insolvent and was unable to continue. He claimed a quantum meruit for the work done but this was denied by the Court of Appeal. This was so even though it could not be doubted that the defendant was left enriched by being saved expense in relation to the buildings.[59]

The injustice of such a result led the Law Commission in its report on *Pecuniary Restitution on Breach of Contract*[60] to recommend that the contract-breaker should have a restitutionary remedy valued objectively but subject to a ceiling of the *pro rata* contract price and subject also to the innocent party's retaining his right to counterclaim for or set off damages. This proposal, which would bring English law into line with that in the United States,[61] should be supported,[62] for an innocent party who has received part of what he bargained for can be presumed to have been negatively benefited by the contract-breaker (even if the expense saved was not necessary)[63] and that unjust factor

---

[58] [1898] 1 QB 673. See also *Boston Deep Sea Fishing and Ice Co.* v. *Ansell* (1888) 39 Ch.D 339; *Bolton* v. *Mahedeva* [1972] 1 WLR 1009; cf. *Miles* v. *Wakefield MDS* [1987] AC 539, 552–3, *per* Lord Brightman, 561, *per* Lord Templeman.

[59] The enrichment was not as great as appears at first sight in that the defendant had made substantial payments to the plaintiff; see Treitel, *Law of Contract* (9th edn.), 733.

[60] Law Com. No. 121 (1983).

[61] See (first) *Restatement of Contracts*, s. 357(1) and 93); [(second) *Restatement of Contracts*, s. 374;] *Restatement of Restitution*, s. 155; Williston, *Contracts* (3rd edn., Baker Voorhis & Co. Inc., 1970), s. 1485; Palmer, *Law of Restitution* (Little, Brown & Co., 1978), s. 5(3).

[62] Taking a more subjective view, the *pro rata* contract price would govern even where it exceeds the objective market value. But to apply this might encourage breach.

[63] But where the defendant has been incontrovertibly benefited by necessary (objective) expense saved, the *pro rata* contract price limit is justified not because it represents the defendant's benefit (see on this the analogous argument *vis-à-vis* the innocent party, above) but rather because of the desire not to encourage breach. The same policy could be equally well

is the failure of consideration. The counter-argument—that to allow restitution to a contract-breaker would encourage breach—ignores the fact that he is still liable to pay expectation damages, which ensures that the other party reaps the benefit of a good bargain.

Goff and Jones and Birks, while making some use of free acceptance here, mainly do so to explain the present limited scope of restitution for a contract-breaker.[64] In support of this they point to the fact that in *Sumpter* v. *Hedges*,[65] while denying the quantum meruit, the Court of Appeal did allow the plaintiff the value of materials left behind and used by the defendant. For both Birks and Goff and Jones this is explicable in terms of free acceptance because the defendant had an opportunity to reject the materials. But there is little in the judgments to support such reasoning, and it is submitted that the remedy given in relation to the materials is equally explicable as being the award of damages for the tort of conversion.

Moreover in supporting the calls for reform Birks and Goff and Jones naturally have to move away from free acceptance. Birks therefore relies on failure of consideration and limited acceptance,[66] while Goff and Jones, although favouring the *pro rata* contract price as the upper limit, suddenly start to place the emphasis on incontrovertible benefit.[67]

The same approach to restitution following discharge for frustration should apply as that applicable upon discharge for breach; that is, failure of consideration and receiving part of what was bargained for (or incontrovertible benefit) constitute an unjust enrichment and the *pro rata* contract price should (at least) fix the ceiling for recovery[68] (except where the benefit is incontrovertible). But the common law position, as laid down in *Cutter* v. *Powell*,[69] was that there was no restitution for services or goods. The Law Reform (Frustrated Contracts) Act 1943 section 1(3), however, has altered this and allows

achieved by relying simply on the innocent party's counterclaim for damages and placing no such artificial restriction on the contract-breaker's restitutionary claim.

[64] *Law of Restitution* (4th edn., 1993), 441–2; n. 2 above, 239.

[65] [1898] 1 QB 673.

[66] N. 2 above, 239, 240–1, 259–64. He makes no comment as to whether the *pro rata* contract price should here form the upper limit; cf. 288.

[67] *Law of Restitution* (4th edn., 1993), 446.

[68] This is the law in the United States; see (first) *Restatement of Contracts*, s. 468(3); (second) *Restatement of Contracts*, s. 377; *Restatement of Restitution*, s. 155; Williston, *Contract* (3rd edn.), s. 1977. Palmer, *Law of Restitution* (1978), s. 7(5) here favours the more subjective view that the pro rata contract price should govern even where it exceeds the objective market price. Cf. above, nn. 47 and 62.

[69] (1795) 6 TR 320.

a restitutionary remedy for a "valuable benefit" conferred other than money. While the words of section 1(3) can be straightforwardly interpreted as putting into effect the theoretical position favoured above, it is far from clear that that approach is supported by Robert Goff J's judgment in *B.P. Exploration Co. (Libya) Ltd v. Hunt (No. 2)*[70] which draws an unnecessarily sharp distinction between identifying and valuing the defendant's benefit.[71]

As regards free acceptance, this again is primarily used by Birks to explain the refusal of restitution at common law.[72] Although the notion is used more positively by Goff and Jones[73] it is hard to see how a defendant can be said to have freely accepted when he agreed to pay for services or goods only on full performance and this has not been rendered. In recognition of this Birks relies instead on failure of consideration and his notion of "limited acceptance" to justify restitution.[74] Goff and Jones again argue that the *pro rata* contract price should fix the ceiling for recovery.[75]

The conclusion to be reached is that restitution following discharge of a contract for breach or frustration is readily explicable in terms of failure of consideration and bargained for or incontrovertible benefits without resorting, as Goff and Jones and Birks do, to notions of free or limited acceptance.

(3) *Services Rendered or Goods Supplied under a Void, Unenforceable, Incomplete or Anticipated Contract*

Consistently with the approach adopted in the last section, it is submitted that the unjust factor grounding restitution in this area is failure of consideration, that is, the plaintiff has not received the defendant's promised performance which was the plaintiff's basis for rendering the benefit to the defendant. The only difference is that here the defendant's promise was not a valid contractual one. As regards benefit, this may be established either by there being an

---

[70] [1979] 1 WLR 783, esp. at 801–6; aff'd [1981] 1 WLR 232 (CA); [1982] 2 AC 352 (HL).

[71] See Dickson (1983) 34 *NILQ* 106, 115. See also Treitel's pertinent criticism that Robert Goff J paid insufficient attention to the statutory words "before the time of discharge"; *Law of Contract* (9th edn., Sweet & Maxwell, 1995), 827.

[72] N. 2 above, 230–1.

[73] *Law of Restitution* (3rd edn., 1986), 372–3, 484; (4th edn., 1993), 29, 447–8.

[74] N. 2 above, 251.

[75] *Law of Restitution* (4th edn., 1993), 459 (see also 1st edn., 336 and *B.P. Exploration Co. (Libya) Ltd v. Hunt* [1979] 1 WLR 783, 802–3, *per* Robert Goff J)).

incontrovertible benefit in the form (usually) of necessary expenses saved, or more commonly, by the defendant receiving part (or all) of what he bargained for. In contrast with this approach, and indeed with their own more muted use of free acceptance in relation to contracts discharged for breach or frustration, Goff and Jones and Birks[76] here place heavy reliance on free acceptance. In examining some of the main cases it is helpful to distinguish three types of contractual invalidity, although nothing of substance turns on this division so far as restitution is concerned.

(i) *Contracts Unenforceable for Lack of Formality*
An important case here is *Deglman* v. *Guaranty Trust Co. of Canada and Constantineau*,[77] which is a leading restitution case in Canada. The plaintiff entered into an oral agreement with his aunt by which in return for his performing various personal services for her—such as doing odd jobs, taking her out on trips and running errands— she promised to leave him a house in her will. He performed the services but she failed to leave him the house and he brought a claim against her estate. It was held that while the contract was unenforceable for lack of formality under the Statute of Frauds the plaintiff was entitled to a quantum meruit. Cartwright J said, "The deceased, having received the benefits of the full performance of the contract by the respondent, the law imposed on her, and so on her estate, the obligation to pay the fair value of the services rendered to her."[78] For Birks the decision is to be explained on the grounds of free acceptance, there being no obstacle to the application of that principle where full rather than part performance of the services has been rendered.[79]

But clearly one can also say that the unjust enrichment was constituted as follows. The plaintiff had rendered the services on the basis of a consideration that had totally failed (unjust factor) and the defendant was negatively benefited in that she was saved necessary expense (objectively valued) or, more obviously, because she had bargained

---

[76] But Birks has since conceded that, in many of these cases, because there is no initial unconscionability, the unjust factor is better viewed as failure of consideration rather than free acceptance: "In Defence of Free Acceptance" in A. Burrows (ed.), *Essays on the Law of Restitution* (OUP, 1991), 109–115.

[77] [1954] 3 DLR 785. See also *Pulbrook* v. *Lawes* (1875) 1 QBD 284 and the important Australian case of *Pavey & Matthews Pty. Ltd* v. *Paul* (1987) 162 CLR 221.

[78] *Ibid.*, at 795.

[79] N. 2 above, 287–8. [But see n. 76 above.] Goff and Jones' explanation of the restitutionary award in this case is not entirely clear; see *Laws of Restitution* (4th edn., 1993), 475.

for the plaintiff's performance of the services and had therefore been saved expense (objectively valued) up to the contract price.[80]

(ii) *Void Contracts*

Two illustrative cases here[81] are *Boulton* v. *Jones*[82] and *Craven-Ellis* v. *Canons Ltd*.[83] In the former, Jones "consumed" hose pipe ordered from Brocklehurst—with whom he had a set-off—but supplied by Boulton, who had taken over Brocklehurst's business. Boulton had no contractual right to payment because any purported contract was void for unilateral mistake as to identity. Nor was any other ground for payment (namely, restitution) recognised.

As far as restitution is concerned, Goff and Jones regard this decision as explicable in terms of free acceptance because Jones' mistake which made the contract void also undermined the inference that he had freely accepted the goods.[84] Birks would not dissent from that approach, although he leaves open the possibility that if Boulton had also been mistaken, the decision could have gone the other way on the ground that Boulton would then be relying on free acceptance solely to establish benefit, and in such a "mixed claim" acceptance need not be as free—and hence may not be nullified by mistake—as where it is being relied on to establish both injustice and enrichment.[85]

The implication of this reasoning[86] is that had Jones not "consumed" the hose pipe before he found out that the supplier was Boulton and not Brocklehurst, Boulton would have been entitled to a restitutionary quantum valebant because then the objection to free acceptance would have been removed. The strength of this reasoning is that it provides an explanation for why one judge—Channell B—did indeed leave open the question whether the decision would have been different had the demand for payment been received by Jones while he still had the goods. But there is a more obvious explanation: if Jones had known of the identity of the vendor before con-

---

[80] For discussion of whether the *pro rata* contract price should fix the ceiling for restitution see Palmer, *Law of Restitution* (1978), ss. 6.3, 6.11. See also (first) *Restatement of Contracts*, s. 355; (second), s. 375. On a more subjective view one would apply the *pro rata* contract price even where it exceeds the objective market price.

[81] [See also *Rover International Ltd* v. *Cannon Film Sales Ltd* [1989] 1 WLR 912].

[82] (1857) 27 LJ Ex. 117.

[83] [1936] 2 KB 403.

[84] *Law of Restitution* (4th edn., 1993), 488–93.

[85] N. 2 above, 115–16. See also 280.

[86] It is more explicit in Goff and Jones, *Law of Restitution* (1st edn.), at 278.

suming the goods, surely there would have been a valid contract constituted by Boulton's offer to sell and Jones' acceptance by conduct,
and Boulton would have therefore had a valid contractual claim for
the agreed price. In other words, the decision in restitution would
have been the same but the decision in contract would have differed.
Indeed in the final analysis Goff and Jones seem to concede this.[87]

However, to deny the importance of free acceptance does not
mean that no restitutionary claim should have succeeded on the facts
of *Boulton* v. *Jones*. On the contrary, given the total failure of consideration, the sole problem in establishing unjust enrichment was one
of benefit; and Jones may have been incontrovertibly benefited in
that he was saved expenses necessary to his business—i.e. he would
have had to buy the pipe elsewhere. Alternatively one can perhaps
argue that Jones was negatively enriched in that he had received the
goods he had bargained for; though this would seem to re-encounter
the problem of subjective devaluation, as Jones thought that his set-
off would pay for the goods.

In *Craven-Ellis* v. *Canons Ltd*[88] the defendant company under a
purported contract with the plaintiff agreed to pay him a certain
remuneration for work to be done. When the defendant company
refused to pay as agreed for the work done, the plaintiff brought an
action in contract or alternatively on the basis of a quantum meruit.
It was held that the plaintiff had no valid contractual claim because
the contract was void for want of authority (or alternatively on the
ground of common mistake[89]) because the directors who had made
the agreement, including the plaintiff, were not qualified to do so,
not having obtained qualification shares as required by the articles of
association. But a quantum meruit was awarded.

It is interesting that in their first edition, Goff and Jones regarded
this decision as a leading example of restitution based on free acceptance.[90] But in an influential article in 1971,[91] Birks challenged this
view on the ground that the impediment to there being a valid contract also prevented there being a free acceptance; i.e. there were no
directors qualified to "freely accept". The same objection probably
also applies to thwart any attempt to use the "bargained for" princi-

---

[87] *Law of Restitution* (4th edn., 1993), 489.

[88] [1936] 2 KB 403.

[89] If the contract is void on the ground of common mistake the plaintiff can alternatively
use his mistake as the unjust factor in a restitutionary claim.

[90] *Law of Restitution* (1st edn.), 31, 269–70, 278. See also Denning (1939) 55 *LQR* 54.

[91] "Negotiorum Gestio and the Common Law" [1971] *Current Legal Problems* 110, 120–3.
See also n. 2 above, 118–19.

ple of benefit in this context. However, in Birks' view the decision was still justified because there was an express finding that the plaintiff's services were of a kind "which, if they had not been performed by the plaintiff, they [the company] would have to get some other agent to carry out".[92] In other words there was an incontrovertible benefit in the sense of a saving of necessary business expense, and this, combined with the total failure of consideration or on Birks' analysis the plaintiff's mistaken belief that there was a valid contract, meant that there was an unjust enrichment calling for the quantum meruit award. Goff and Jones in their second edition recognised the force of this argument and *Craven Ellis* was effectively removed as an example of free acceptance.[93] It is of course the thesis of this essay that a similar but more fundamental backtrack from free acceptance reasoning must be made in all cases.

(iii) *Incomplete or Anticipated Contracts*[94]

The leading English cases discussed by Goff and Jones and Birks[95] in respect of services rendered or goods supplied under incomplete or anticipated contracts are *Way* v. *Latilla*,[96] *William Lacey (Hounslow) Ltd* v. *Davis*[97] and *British Steel Corpn* v. *Cleveland Bridge and Engineering Co. Ltd*.[98] In the first of these, the plaintiff had, at the defendant's request, obtained for him gold-mining concessions in Africa (worth about £1m). The plaintiff maintained that his services

---

[92] [1936] 2 KB 403, 412.

[93] *Law of Restitution* (2nd edn.), 17, 303–5; (4th edn.), 34, 478–82.

[94] Goff and Jones subdivide into different chapters (21 and 25) incomplete and anticipated contracts. But the distinction seems so thin that they are better treated together. A further point is that it is arguable that the boundary of contract has shifted forward and that courts today may not require the completeness insisted on in the past. If this were so then in the cases discussed in this section the plaintiff would have a valid contractual claim for protection of his expectation interest, restitution would no longer be his sole claim and there would be no need to categorise the cases as dealing with "invalid" contracts rather than breach of contract. The text, however, assumes the traditional view as to when a contract is formed and the degree of completeness required.

[95] See generally n. 2 above, 271–6, 283–5; *Law of Restitution* (4th edn., 1993), 483–7, 554–63. It is important to note that there are passages, see e.g. 557 where Goff and Jones themselves indicate that in this area free acceptance is non-restitutionary; see also Jones (1980) 18 *UW Ont.LR* 447.

[96] [1937] 3 All ER 759.

[97] [1957] 1 WLR 932.

[98] [1984] 1 All ER 504. See also *Peter Lind & Co. Ltd* v. *Mersey Docks & Harbour Bd* [1972] 2 Lloyds Rep. 234 and *Sabemo Pty. Ltd* v. *North Sydney Municipal Council* [1977] 2 NSWLR 880. For each of these cases a similar restitutionary analysis to that offered in the text can be adopted. [See also now *Regalian Properties Ltd* v. *London Docklands Development Corp* [1995] 1 WLR 212.]

had been rendered pursuant to a contract by which the defendant had agreed to give him a share in the concessions. This was rejected by the House of Lords on the ground that there had been no concluded agreement as to the amount of the share which the plaintiff was to receive. But the plaintiff was granted a quantum meruit of £5,000 in respect of the work he had done for the defendant. The House of Lords sought to justify this on the grounds of a second contract of employment between the parties, but Birks and Goff and Jones criticise this as artificial and regard the decision as restitutionary, based on free acceptance.[99] It is submitted, however, that even if one does reject the reasoning based on contract as artificial, there is no need to resort to free acceptance to explain restitution. Rather, the unjust factor can be regarded as the (total) failure of consideration, in that the plaintiff did not receive the share in the concession which he had reasonably been led to expect and which was the basis for his work; and the defendant was negatively benefited[100] (*prima facie* objectively) by the work for which he had bargained.

In *William Lacey (Hounslow) Ltd* v. *Davis*[101] the plaintiffs submitted a tender for building work and were reasonably led to believe by the defendant owners of the land that the contract would be theirs. Subsequently at the defendants' request the plaintiffs did considerable preparatory work in relation to the building, but then the contract, which would have included a term reimbursing the builders, fell through. It was held by Barry J that the plaintiffs were entitled to a restitutionary quantum meruit for the work done at the defendants' request. Comparing the instant case with *Craven-Ellis* v. *Canons Ltd*[102] he said:

"I am unable to see any valid distinction between work done which was to be paid for under the terms of a contract erroneously believed to be in existence, and work done which was to be paid for out of the proceeds of a contract which both parties erroneously believed was about to be made. In neither case was the work to be done gratuitously and, in both cases the party from whom payment was sought requested the work and obtained the benefit of it. In neither case did the parties actually intend to pay for the work otherwise than under the supposed contract, or as part of the total price which would

---

[99] N. 2 above, 272; [But see n. 76 above.] *Law of Restitution* (4th edn., 1993), 485, n. 9.
[100] Alternatively one can say that the defendant was incontrovertibly benefited by the "realisation" (subsequent sale) of the concessions: but see above, n. 25 which points out the possible impact of the "at the expense of" aspect of unjust enrichment.
[101] [1957] 1 WLR 932.
[102] [1936] 2 KB 403.

become payable when the expected contract was made. In both cases, when the beliefs of the parties were falsified, the law implied an obligation—and, in this case, I think the law should imply an obligation—to pay a reasonable price for the services which had been obtained."[103]

This passage fits very easily into the restitutionary scheme presented in this paper, with the "falsification of belief" correlating to failure of consideration (that is the failure of the expected payment through the main contract) and the "request" and "obtaining of benefit" indicating that even if not incontrovertibly benefited, the defendant had been negatively benefited by receiving part of what he had bargained for. As Birks points out, however, the reasoning is not quite so happily accommodated within a free acceptance approach: ". . . the judgment does not take any distinction between the different bases of non-contractual claims for quantum meruit. It relies heavily on *Craven-Ellis* v. *Canons Ltd* but does not say that the 'true facts' in that case were analytically different from those in *William Lacey* itself; *Craven-Ellis* was a case of non-voluntary transfer to a company unable to make a free acceptance while *William Lacey* could not be explained except on the basis of free acceptance, since the only 'mistake' which the builders made was a misprediction of the developer's future behaviour."[104] But there is no conflict at all if one regards the unjust factor in both cases as a failure of consideration.

The plaintiffs in the *British Steel* case manufactured and delivered steel nodes to the defendants following a letter of intent sent by the defendants. Robert Goff J found that there was no concluded contract between the parties (and hence no possible counterclaim for damages for late delivery) but that the plaintiffs were entitled to a quantum meruit for the reasonable value of their work, carried out at the request of the defendants and in anticipation of a contract. The judge relied on *William Lacey* v. *Davis* and it is submitted that the same "failure of consideration" and "bargained-for benefit" elements of unjust enrichment underpin his reasoning. The central passage in the judgment is as follows[105]:

"Both parties confidently expected a formal contract to eventuate. In these circumstances, to expedite performance under that anticipated contract, one requested the other to commence the contract work,

---

[103] [1957] 1 WLR 932, 939.
[104] N. 2 above, 273–4. [But see n. 76 above.]
[105] [1984] 1 All ER 504, 511.

and the other complied with that request. If thereafter, as anticipated, a contract was entered into, the work done as requested will be treated as having been performed under that contract; if, contrary to their expectation, no contract was entered into, then the performance of the work is not referable to any contract the terms of which can be ascertained, and the law simply imposes an obligation on the party who made the request to pay a reasonable sum for such work as has been done pursuant to that request, such an obligation sounding in quasi contract or, as we now say, in restitution."

Goff and Jones also mention *Jennings and Chapman Ltd* v. *Woodman, Matthews & Co.*[106] and *Brewer Street Investments Ltd* v. *Barclays Woollen Co. Ltd*[107] under restitution in respect of anticipated contracts, and these are central cases too in Birks' chapter on free acceptance. In each, a landlord had carried out alterations to his property at a potential tenant's request but the anticipated lease between them had subsequently fallen through. In the former case, payment for the landlord's work was refused, whereas it was ordered in the latter case. The majority of the Court of Appeal in each case (Somervell and Romer LJJ) appeared to use contractual expectation reasoning: and the cases can be easily reconciled on that view. For the defendant had a lawful excuse for non-performance in *Jennings and Chapman* since the landlord should have sought permission for the conversion from the head-lessee (in accordance with covenants in the head-lease); whereas there was no such excuse in *Brewer St.*—rather, negotiations for a new lease simply broke down because of disagreement between the parties concerning the right to purchase the reversion. Denning LJ, however, preferred restitutionary reasoning at least in the *Brewer Street* case. But on that approach it is harder to see how the two cases can be reconciled. In each there was on the face of it a free acceptance, but more importantly, in line with the thesis of this article, there was a total failure of consideration in that the landlord had carried out the work on the reasonable expectation of payment which was not forthcoming; and the defendant had been negatively benefited as the work bargained for had been carried out.[108] There were therefore clear grounds for restitution in each of the two cases.

The conclusion to be reached at the end of this discussion of services rendered or goods supplied under void, unenforceable, incom-

---

[106] [1952] 2 TLR 409.
[107] [1954] 1 QB 428.
[108] If ultimately the landlords themselves were benefiting from the work this should be taken into account in reducing restitution under the "at the expense of" aspect of unjust enrichment.

plete or anticipated contracts is that once again free acceptance is not needed to explain the authorities on restitution.

3. INCIDENTAL ADVANTAGE OF REMOVING FREE ACCEPTANCE

Clearly, the central importance of an attack on free acceptance is to establish whether that notion is a valid part of the law of restitution, and the conclusion that it is not means that the range of possible restitutionary claims is narrower than Goff and Jones and Birks maintain. But removal of free acceptance carries with it an incidental advantage in that the elegance—and hence comprehensibility—of the theoretical structure of the law of restitution, as most clearly expounded by Birks, is improved in at least three respects.

First, free acceptance is immediately obvious as the "odd man out" in Birks' structure; for it alone is a factor going both to injustice and enrichment (although, peculiarly, its sibling "limited acceptance" is treated as solely relevant to benefit). Moreover, within the unjust factors of autonomous unjust enrichment (leaving aside miscellaneous cases) free acceptance alone is not concerned with non-voluntary transfer. Secondly, it would seem that Birks is rather inconsistent in effectively confining his use of free acceptance to non-money benefits. Free acceptance ought to be equally relevant to the payment of money so that, for example, traditional restrictions on the recovery of mistaken payments should be irrelevant whenever the payee knew that the payor was making a mistake.[109] Thirdly, while Birks rightly explains that it must be correct for failure of consideration to be as applicable to non-money benefits as it is to money,[110] he does not consistently carry through that approach; for non-money benefits rendered under void, ineffective, incomplete or anticipated contracts are dealt with only under free acceptance and not under failure of consideration.[111] Removal of free acceptance would be one way of removing all these apparent imperfections in Birks' book.

4. A SECONDARY LINE OF ATTACK

Even for those not willing to accept the thesis of this essay and to remove free acceptance from the law of restitution, it is submitted

[109] Cf. n. 2 above, 267.
[110] *Ibid.*, 226–34.
[111] [But see n. 76 above.]

that it is necessary to recognise how controversial that notion is; for, at the end of the day, as there is more than one possible interpretation of the authorities, the case for free acceptance must rest on arguments of principle which at the very least are finely balanced. This opens up a secondary line of attack on the use of free acceptance by Goff and Jones and Birks, which runs as follows. Since free acceptance is so controversial it should only be used to justify restitution as a last resort; where possible, other less controversial justifications, like failure of consideration and a bargained-for principle of benefit, should be adopted.[112] As it has been shown that it is possible to explain all authorities on other less questionable grounds, reliance on the last resort and controversial notion of free acceptance is unwarranted.

CONCLUSION

While on the one hand there are still those who resist the view that we have a law of restitution founded on unjust enrichment,[113] the publication of *An Introduction to the Law of Restitution* represented something of a landmark; for, in building on Goff and Jones' pioneering work, Birks' book represents the most sophisticated attempt in the common law world to map out the law of restitution. However, in the crusade to convert the sceptics it is crucial that the message of restitution be as accurate, rational, elegant and comprehensible as possible. It is with that in mind that this essay has sought to challenge one central notion in the view of restitution propounded by its leading scholars, namely the notion of free acceptance.

---

[112] [For Birks' subsequent acceptance of this suggestion, see "In Defence of Free Acceptance" in A. Burrows (ed.), *Essays on the Law of Restitution* (Clarendon Press, 1991), 144–5].

[113] E.g. S. Hedley, "Unjust Enrichment as the Basis of Restitution—An Overworked Concept" (1985) 5 *Legal Studies* 56; S. Hedley, "Unjust Enrichment" [1995] 54 *CLJ* 578.

5

Restitution: Where do We Go From Here?

This essay is divided into three unequal parts. The first asks the question, where have we got to with the law of restitution? The second asks the question, how have we got here? The third reflecting the title, asks, where do we go from here?

I. WHERE HAVE WE GOT TO?

On one level, there is a very straightforward description of where we have got to. We now have a law of restitution founded on the principle against unjust enrichment, whereas 100 years ago, and indeed until the decision of the House of Lords in *Lipkin Gorman* v. *Karpnale Ltd*[1] in 1991, England had no such subject or category of law.

But what does it actually mean to say that we now have a law of restitution whereas previously we did not?

Clearly what it does not mean is that there is suddenly a whole new body of law that did not previously exist. In that sense the law of restitution is not like, for example, social security law, European Community law, or even, perhaps, administrative law. They are new because they deal with a large body of new law that did not previously exist.

Nor is the position quite the same as with, for example, family law, which has become a new subject in the latter part of the twentieth century only in the limited sense that books,[2] and subsequently law school courses, started to study all the law relating to the same *factual* subject matter, namely the family.

What it means to say that we now recognise a law of restitution, whereas previously we did not, is that we now recognise that there is a principle, namely the principle against unjust enrichment, that

---

[1] [1991] 2 AC 548.
[2] The pioneer was Peter Bromley's *Family Law* (1st edn., Buterworths, 1957).

underpins a wide body of law that was previously regarded as a
hotch-potch of different unconnected areas. Restitution is a new subject in that we now recognise that there is a body of law based not so
much on the same factual subject matter but rather on the same legal
principle. In this sense the law of restitution is as fundamental as, for
example, the law of contract or the law of tort, which are similarly,
in my view, categories of law based on underpinning principles.

In recognising the principle against unjust enrichment there were
two main barriers that had to be overcome in the law as it stood at
the start of the century.

The first was the implied contract theory. If, for example, a plaintiff paid a defendant £1,000 under a mistake of fact, his common law
remedy to recover the £1,000 was said to rest on the defendant's
implied promise to pay it back. Yet such a promise plainly did not rest
on the defendant's actual intention to repay and was a fiction which
served merely to obscure the real basis of the remedy. Yet, until the
latter part of the twentieth century, the implied contract theory held
sway. It was this fiction that accounted for the law on mistaken payments and payments made under duress, on failure of consideration,
on necessitous intervention, and on discharge of another's debt under
legal compulsion, being seen as an off-shoot of contract law—hence
the label "quasi-contract". It is also why the two classic contract
books in existence at the end of the nineteenth century—*Chitty*, the
practitioners' work first published in 1828, and *Anson*, the classic student text, first published in 1879—each had separate sections dealing
with implied contracts or quasi-contract. Despite the recognition of
an independent law of restitution, the current editions of those books
still have those sections, albeit that the editors have felt duty-bound
to change the titles of the offending chapters from quasi-contract to
restitution.[3]

The second main barrier was the division between common law
and equity. The principle against unjust enrichment underpins and
draws on areas of common law and equity. It is a principle that fuses
those historical divisions. Although the common law courts and the
Court of Chancery had been fused in the 1870s, it is not surprising
that at the turn of the century a fusion of the substantive rules of law

---

[3] The relevant ch. in *Chitty* was renamed "Restitution and Quasi-Contract" in the 23rd
edn. (Sweet & Maxwell) in 1968. Quasi-contract was entirely removed from the title in the
24th edn. in 1977. The relevant ch. in *Anson* was renamed "Restitution" in the 25th edn.
(OUP) in 1979. In the previous edn. in 1975 it had still been called "Quasi-contract". Cf.
G.C. Cheshire and C.H.S. Fifoot, *Law of Contract* (1st edn., Butterworths, 1945) in which
"Quasi-contract" is still the title of the relevant chapter in the 13th edn. in 1996.

and equity would have been thought to be a long way off. Even today the single greatest battle faced by the law of restitution is to integrate and fuse the areas of common law and equity that are based on the principle against unjust enrichment. It is a battle that has by no means been won and certainly in, for example, Australia, where the dominance of great equity lawyers such as Justice Gummow and Judge Finn is all-pervasive, and Justice Deane and Chief Justice Mason have recently retired, one fears that the battle in the short term may be lost and that unjust enrichment thinking may be confined to areas of the common law only.

But what difference does the recognition of this new subject make? Mr Hedley has recently argued that recognition of the principle against unjust enrichment, and the refinement of it by commentators, serves no useful goal.[4] Is he correct?

I would immediately concede that recognition of unjust enrichment does not mean that, in a wide range of cases, the courts will suddenly reach different decisions than before. On the contrary, as the "implied contract" theory was a fiction, deeper reasoning must always have been guiding the courts; and it is my view that the courts have throughout been applying the principle of unjust enrichment, albeit at times in an unadventurous and stunted way. This is why the law of restitution legitimately draws on case law—and indeed is largely comprised of case law—pre-*Lipkin Gorman*.

But, with respect, Mr Hedley is making a serious mistake in suggesting that recognition of unjust enrichment makes no practical difference. He is wrong for at least two reasons.

First, it is a good in its own right that the judges, the legislature and commentators use language that is accurate, simple and clear. The rule of law demands this. Fictions and obscure jargon in the law are an abomination and must be sought out and excised. The law cannot fulfil its role of guiding behaviour if fictions, like the "implied contract" theory, survive. Much of the modern writing on restitution is an attempt to explain legal concepts in precise and modern terminology. A criticism can be made that the new language of "unjust factors", "incontrovertible benefit", "free acceptance", "unjust enrichment by subtraction", "restitutionary damages" is not simple enough. But it is a bit rich when some lawyers accuse restitution

---

[4] S. Hedley, "Restitution: Contract's Twin?" (paper presented to SPTL Annual Conference, Cambridge, 1996). He has been making similar claims for over a decade. See S. Hedley, "Unjust Enrichment as the Basis of Restitution—An Overworked Concept" (1985) 5 *Legal Studies* 56; and "Unjust Enrichment" (1995) 54 *CLJ* 578.

commentators of using incomprehensible jargon. They would no
doubt prefer to stick with the language of the club, nonsensical to
outsiders: actions for money had and received to the plaintiff's use,
money paid to the defendant's use, quantum meruit, liability as a
constructive trustee, subrogation, waiver of tort, and so on. This is
the language of the late nineteenth century. It should not be the language at the turn of the twentieth century.

There is a linked footnote point here. In the shrinking world of
the global economy, and with talk of harmonising the laws of the
European Union, civil law becomes ever more important to the
development of the common law. Civil law systems have long recognised a category of law based on unjust enrichment and it would
therefore only have served to hamper meaningful dialogue—and to
undermine this opportunity to enrich our own law—if we had failed
overtly to recognise the unjust enrichment principle.

The second, and perhaps more important, reason why Mr Hedley
is wrong is that the acceptance of the unjust enrichment principle can
be expected to lead to some differences in the results of cases. While
in most cases, the judges would have got to the same result anyway,
however obscurely, clarity of concept does have practical consequences. This is an important point and I want to give six examples
of it.

(1) *Money Paid under Void Contracts*

In *Sinclair* v. *Brougham*,[5] decided by the House of Lords in 1914, a
building society acted ultra vires by carrying on a banking business.
On the winding-up of the society, one question was whether those
who had loaned money under the *ultra vires* banking facilities (the
"depositors") could recover their money in a personal restitutionary
remedy, that is, in an action for money had and received. The House
of Lords held that they could not. In reaching that decision their
Lordships were heavily influenced by the "implied contract" theory.
As an express contract to repay the loans would have been void as
being *ultra vires* the building society, so necessarily, it was argued,
must be an implied contract. And as an action for money had and
received was conceived as being based on an implied contract, the
claim failed.

[5] [1914] AC 398.

But once one recognises that the basis of the action for money had and received is unjust enrichment, not implied contract, the way is open to reach a different decision. *Prima facie* the building society was unjustly enriched by receiving the depositors' money for a purpose that could not be carried through. And there is no convincing reason why the fact that the contract of borrowing was unenforceable should mean that the building society was left unjustly enriched at the depositors' expense. So it is that, in applying unjust enrichment reasoning, the House of Lords in 1996 in *Westdeutsche Landesbank Girozentrale* v. *Islington London BC*[6] overruled *Sinclair* v. *Brougham*. Lord Browne-Wilkinson said, "The common law restitutionary claim is based not on implied contract but unjust enrichment: in the circumstances, the law imposes an obligation to repay rather than implying an entirely fictitious agreement to repay. In my judgment, your Lordships should now unequivocally and finally reject the concept that the claim for moneys had and received is based on an implied contract. I would overrule *Sinclair* v. *Brougham* on this point. It follows that . . . the depositors should have had a personal claim to recover the moneys at law based on a total failure of consideration."[7]

(2) *Change of Position*

In *Lipkin Gorman* v. *Karpnale Ltd*[8] the House of Lords accepted for the first time that it is a general defence to restitutionary claims that the defendant has changed its position. Lord Goff said, "the defence is available to a person whose position is so changed that it would be inequitable in all the circumstances to require him to make restitution, or alternatively to make restitution in full."[9] What is basically in mind is the situation where the recipient of an unjust enrichment, in good faith, spends or loses that enrichment or incurs a detriment in reliance on it. The defence responds to the fact that, while once unjustly enriched, the defendant is no longer so. Indeed one simply cannot explain this defence without recognising that the law is based on a principle against unjust enrichment.

Although there was a limited all or nothing form of change of position recognised pre-*Lipkin Gorman* in the defence of estoppel,

---

[6] [1996] 2 AC 669.
[7] *Ibid.*, at 710.
[8] [1991] 2 AC 548.
[9] *Ibid.*, at 580.

acceptance of change of position cannot but alter decisions. If we again turn to the early part of this century, in 1913 in *Baylis* v. *Bishop of London*[10] the plaintiffs had mistakenly paid to a bishop (who was acting as sequestrator for a parish on the bankruptcy of its rector) tithe rent-charges on certain property in which their leasehold interest had already expired. The bishop in good faith applied some of the money in providing for the needs of the parish and paid over the surplus to the rector's trustee in bankruptcy. It was held by the Court of Appeal that the bishop had no defence to the plaintiffs' restitutionary claim for money paid by the mistake of fact. Today the bishop would have a defence of change of position and restitution would be denied on the same facts.

(3) *Restitution of Money Paid by Mistake of Law and Restitution of Money Paid on a Partial, but not Total, Failure of Consideration*

It remains the general law that money paid under a mistake of law, rather than of fact, or for a consideration that has failed partially rather than totally, is irrecoverable.[11] While it is possible to expose the weaknesses in those bars to restitution without relying on a theory of unjust enrichment, recognition that these areas are based on the unjust enrichment principle makes it all the easier to see that those bars lack justification.

If an insurer pays £10,000 to his assured because he mistakenly believes that the policy between them is valid, it cannot make any difference to the injustice of the assured's enrichment that the insurer's mistake rests on his false belief that the assured has kept up all his premiums—a mistake of fact—or on his false belief that he is not entitled to avoid the policy for the assured's non-payment of premiums—a mistake of law.

As Dickson J said in his dissenting judgment in the Canadian case of *Hydro-Electric Commission of Nepean* v. *Ontario Hydro*,[12] which was later approved by the Supreme Court of Canada in *Air Canada* v.

[10] [1913] 1 Ch. 127.

[11] See, e.g., R. Goff and G. Jones, *The Law of Restitution* (4th edn., Sweet & Maxwell, 1993), ch. 4, 400–4; Birks, *An Introduction to the Law of Restitution* (1985, rev. paperback edn., 1989), 164–7, 242–8; A. Burrows, *The Law of Restitution* (Butterworths, 1993), 109–20, ch. 9. The Law Commission has recommended legislative abrogation of the mistake of law bar: see *Restitution: Mistakes of Law and Ultra Vires Public Authority Receipts and Payments* (1994), Law Com. No. 227.

[12] (1982) 132 DLR (3d) 193, 209.

Pacific Airlines[13] in removing the mistake of law bar in Canada: "Once a doctrine of restitution or unjust enrichment is recognised, the distinction as to mistake of law and mistake of fact becomes simply meaningless." And in the words of the majority of the High Court of Australia, led by Mason CJ, in *David Securities Property Ltd* v. *Commonwealth Bank of Australia*,[14] which abrogated the mistake of law rule in Australia, "If the ground for ordering recovery is that the defendant has been unjustly enriched, there is no justification for drawing distinctions on the basis of how the enrichment was gained, except insofar as the manner of gaining the enrichment bears upon the justice of the case."

Similarly if a bank has paid £100,000 up front to a local authority under a void interest rate swap transaction[15] can it possibly make sense to allow restitution to the bank where the local authority has made no counter-payment but to deny restitution to the bank where the local authority has made one counter-payment of £10 so that the consideration for the payment has not totally failed?[16] The injustice of the local authority's enrichment is the same in both cases and the difference between them can be easily dealt with by allowing the local authority counter-restitution of £10.

The principle against unjust enrichment provides a strong *prima facie* justification for allowing restitution for mistakes of law, as well as fact: and for allowing restitution for partial, as well as total, failure of consideration. With respect to Mr Hedley it seems to me indisputable that such glaring defects in the law can be exposed more easily—and hence can be eradicated more quickly—once one sees the law as being based on unjust enrichment.

(4) *Restitution for Ignorance and Restitution for Wrongs*

My fifth and sixth examples are again connected. These are restitution for ignorance and restitution for wrongs. Here the unjust enrichment principle has the important consequence of linking together for the first time areas of common law and equity and thereby exposing inconsistencies between them. Although the picture I am about to

---

[13] (1989) 59 DLR (4th) 161.

[14] (1992) 175 CLR 353.

[15] For this type of situation, see *Westdeutsche Landesbank Girozentrale* v. *Islington London BC* [1996] AC 669.

[16] The notion of "total failure" may be distorted to avoid this result: see, e.g., the *Westdeutsche* case [1996] AC 669, 710. Cf. *Goss* v. *Chilcott* [1996] AC 788.

paint remains controversial, I am confident that it will ultimately emerge as the way forward.

If we first take restitution for ignorance, there are a number of cases in which money has been recovered from a defendant in an action for money had and received at common law where the ground for restitution was that the plaintiff's money was transferred to the defendant without the plaintiff's knowledge; and the defendant has been held strictly liable to repay the money, subject to a change of position or *bona fide* purchase defence. A classic example is *Lipkin Gorman* v. *Karpnale Ltd* [17] itself. Cass, without the knowledge of his co-partners, had drawn on the partnership account at Lloyds Bank to pay for his gambling at the Playboy Club. The partners had thereby suffered the loss of some £220,000. The club had overall won £154,695 from the money stolen and used for gambling by Cass: that is, although the stolen money staked by Cass was a lot higher, the club had changed its position by paying out winnings to Cass thereby reducing its net gain. The solicitors succeeded before the House of Lords in being awarded £150,960 in an action for money had and received against the club (plus £3,735 damages for conversion of a banker's draft that on one occasion had been used for gambling by Cass instead of cash). Here one has strict liability applied at common law, subject to the successful partial defence of change of position and the unsuccessful, on the facts, although carefully discussed, defence of *bona fide* purchase.

This model (strict liability subject to defences) is exactly in line with the well-accepted standard case of payment by a mistake of fact, the only differences being that, first, the plaintiff's intention is vitiated not by a mistake but by a complete lack of knowledge and consent to the payments (that is, ignorance); and, secondly, that the payment is made to the defendant by a third party rather than by the plaintiff itself.

Stripped down to its bare essentials the same elements are present in the equity cases discussed conventionally under the heading of "knowing receipt and dealing". [18] Here the plaintiff's money is paid away in breach of fiduciary duty—without the plaintiff's knowledge or consent—to the defendant. In principle, applying unjust enrichment, the position ought to be that, as at common law, the defendant

---

[17] [1991] 2 AC 548.
[18] E.g. *Carl-Zeiss* v. *Herbert Smith & Co.* (*No. 2*) [1969] 2 Ch. 276; *Belmont Finance Corp.* v. *Williams Furniture Ltd* (*No. 2*) [1980] 1 All ER 393; *Re Montagu's Settlement Trusts* [1987] Ch. 264.

is strictly liable to repay the money, subject to defences such as change of position and *bona fide* purchase. And although mysteriously and irrationally hived off as being concerned with the administration of estates, this is very close to the position actually reached on the personal equitable claim in *Ministry of Health* v. *Simpson (sub. nom. Re Diplock)*.[19] Yet in the vast bulk of equity cases, the approach has been to insist on the recipient being at fault—and in some cases even dishonest—before a personal liability to account for the money received has been imposed.

We therefore have needless irrationality and inconsistency between the strict common law and the fault-based equitable approaches to what is essentially the same fact situation. The importance of recognising the unjust enrichment principle is that it enables us suddenly to see that inconsistency and to question its validity and to argue for its eradication.[20] Contrary to Mr Hedley, I do not believe that that inconsistency would have been exposed without reliance on the principle against unjust enrichment.

The same applies as regards restitution for wrongs. We have long been used to the equitable restitutionary remedy of an account of profits being awarded to strip away gains made by an equitable wrong, such as breach of fiduciary duty or breach of confidence. Yet when it comes to common law wrongs, for example, torts, we are initially surprised that the courts are sometimes concerned to strip away the wrongdoer's gains rather than compensating the victim for its loss. As late as 1988 we find the Court of Appeal in *Stoke-on-Trent CC* v. *Wass*[21] suggesting that it is outside the powers of a court below the House of Lords to award a restitutionary, rather than a compensatory, remedy for a proprietary tort. Again the unjust enrichment principle enables one to cut through the confusion and inconsistency. It reveals that through different personal remedies—that is through an action for money had and received in "waiver of tort" cases, through damages assessed according to the gains made by a tortfeasor rather than the loss to the victim, and even through an account of profits awarded for intellectual property torts—there are examples of the courts awarding restitution for torts as they have been standardly doing for equitable wrongs.[22] Indeed the real dilemma is not so much

---

[19] [1951] AC 251.

[20] The inconsistency was first exposed by P. Birks, "Misdirected Funds: Restitution from the Recipient" [1989] *LMCLQ* 296.

[21] [1988] 1 WLR 1406.

[22] See, e.g., Goff and Jones, n. 11 above, ch. 38; Birks, n. 11 above, ch. X; Burrows, n. 1 above, ch. 14.

whether restitution is a possible remedial measure for a tort but whether restitution should be effected by a proprietary rather than a personal remedy as the equitable wrong cases, such as *Boardman* v. *Phipps*[23] and *Attorney General for Hong Kong* v. *Reid*[24] would suggest.

As with restitution for ignorance, the essential point is that the recognition of the principle against unjust enrichment has for the first time exposed the inconsistency (or, at least, the initial apparent inconsistency) between the treatment in common law and equity of what, stripped down to essentials, is the same phenomenon. The way has been paved for these like cases of gains made by wrongdoing to be treated alike in the future.

2. HOW HAVE WE GOT HERE?

Here I ask, what influences have brought about the recognition and present shape of the law of restitution? I divide this into two sections. The first looks at the critical events in the growth of restitution in the twentieth century and the most influential individuals involved; and the second looks at the general philosophies and ideas in society that have shaped the law.

(1) *Events and People*

This is a story which largely involves an interplay between Harvard, Oxford and Cambridge. I would argue that there have been four key events in the growth of restitution in this century, involving five main players.

The first was the publication in 1937 of the US *Restatement of Restitution* by the American Law Institute. The Chief Reporters for that *Restatement*, and the first two individuals I wish to name, were the Harvard Professors Austin Scott and Warren Seavey: the former, a specialist in trusts and equity; the latter a common lawyer, whose other main interest was torts. Pooling their talents, they were able to pull together the operation of the unjust enrichment principle in common law and equity. And for better or for worse, it was they who christened the subject "Restitution".[25]

---

[23] [1967] 2 AC 46.
[24] [1994] 1 AC 324.
[25] See W. Seavey and A. Scott, "Restitution" (1938) 54 *LQR* 29.

It is of interest and significance to appreciate the *raison d'être* and working methods of the American Law Institute.

First, the *raison d'être*. The preface to the *Restatement of Restitution* includes the following passage: "The Institute recognises that the ever increasing volume of the decisions of the courts, establishing new rules or precedents, and the numerous instances in which the decisions are irreconcilable, taken in connection with the growing complication of economic and other conditions of modern life, are increasing the law's uncertainty and lack of clarity. It also recognises that this will force the abandonment of our common law system of expressing and developing law through judicial application of existing rules to new fact combinations and the adoption in its place of rigid legislative codes, unless a new factor promoting certainty and clarity can be found. The careful restatement of our common law by the legal profession as represented in the Institute is an attempt to supply this needed factor."

The working methods of the American Law Institute in relation to the *Restatement of Restitution* were as follows. The Institute at the time (and still today) comprised a large body of senior judges, practitioners and academics. An executive committee of thirty-three drawn from those ranks then chose two reporters (both academics), aided by an advisory committee (largely academics), to draw up the *Restatement*. We are told that the work took approximately three years, that the advisory committee held twenty-eight conferences lasting three to four days each, and that the Council put forward a tentative draft at the annual meetings of the Institute in 1935 and 1936. The point I wish to emphasise is that this is a superb working methodology. Academic lawyers had primary responsibility for the drafting but their draft was then scrutinised and commented on, not only by other academics but also by judges and practitioners. The process exemplified the academic and practising branches of the legal profession working together to a common goal.

The second key event was the publication in 1966 of Goff and Jones' *The Law of Restitution* (now in its fourth edition, published in 1993). This was to do for England what the *Restatement* did for the United States. The third and fourth individuals I want to mention therefore are Robert Goff and Gareth Jones. There are three points of interest here. First, we again have the combination of the common lawyer, Robert Goff, and the equity lawyer, Gareth Jones. Secondly, when the work was started both were academics, the former a don at Lincoln College, Oxford, the latter at Cambridge, although by the time the work was finished Robert Goff had left academia for the Bar. Thirdly, it is perhaps of some relevance that, while I know not where Robert Goff's interest in the subject started, Gareth Jones studied at Harvard under Professors Austin Scott and Warren Seavey.

The third critical event was the publication in 1985 of Peter Birks' *An Introduction to the Law of Restitution*. If Goff and Jones was a masterly bringing together of the raw English material, it was Birks who rigorously exposed its structures and underlying themes in a way that fired the imagination of students, fellow-academics, and judges alike. So Peter Birks is my fifth main player.

The fourth and crowning key event was the recognition of unjust enrichment by the House of Lords, led by Lord Goff, in *Lipkin Gorman* in 1991. So Robert Goff comes in again here, but now in his role as judge rather than as author. I would also like to mention in passing his other earlier important judgments, which paved the way for *Lipkin Gorman*, in, for example, *Barclays Bank Ltd* v. *W.J. Simms*,[26] *BP (Exploration) Co. Libya Ltd* v. *Hunt (No. 2)*,[27] and *Attorney General* v. *Guardian Newspapers Ltd (No. 2)*[28]; and his rousing speech, following *Lipkin Gorman*, in *Woolwich Equitable Building Society* v. *Inland Revenue Commissioners*,[29] in which it was held, following Peter Birks' thesis,[30] that a payment demanded *ultra vires* by a public authority is recoverable as of right without any need to show mistake or duress.

(2) *Philosophies and Ideas*

I now want to examine the general philosophies and ideas in society that have shaped the law of restitution since the end of the nineteenth century.

At least until the 1880s,[31] the ruling political philosophy was still one of laissez-faire individualism. The law of obligations reflected this. The law of contract was pre-eminent as a source of obligation. Imposed obligations through the law of tort and, as we would now say, the law of restitution were relatively restricted. And, even where obligations were imposed on the basis of unjust enrichment, this was

[26] [1980] QB 677.
[27] [1979] 1 WLR 783.
[28] [1990] 1 AC 109.
[29] [1993] AC 70.
[30] P. Birks, "Restitution from the Executive: A Tercentenary Footnote to the Bill of Rights" in P. Finn (ed.), *Essays on Restitution* (Law Book Co., 1990), ch. 6.
[31] See P. Atiyah, *The Rise and Fall of the Freedom of Contract* (Clarendon Press, 1979), 587.

forced into the mould of voluntarily-undertaken obligations either by being seen as an adjunct to contract—through the quasi-contract implied contract fiction—or by being seen as an adjunct to intention-based or express trusts, through the language of constructive trusts.

In line with the gradual dilution of laissez-faire individualism and the growth of the welfare state during the twentieth century, there has been an increase in the imposed obligations of tort and restitution. So much so that by the end of this century, tort and restitution can be regarded as equal partners with contract as a source of obligation. As the quantity of imposed obligations has increased, so the artificiality of regarding them as voluntarily undertaken has been heightened, leading inevitably to the shattering of the implied contract theory. It is also possible to argue (although this is a much more difficult matter[32]) that an analogous development was Lord Browne-Wilkinson's suggestion in the *Westdeutsche Landesbank Girozentrale* case in 1996[33] that the law might develop the constructive trust as a restitutionary remedial device wholly divorced from the intention-based express trust.

It can be seen from this that tort and restitution have a close affinity with each other as imposed, rather than voluntarily-undertaken, obligations. There is a further parallel that I want to draw. At the turn of the century, the tort of negligence was not identified as such. One rather had a range of individual instances of liability for negligence. It took Lord Atkin to draw them together into a tort of negligence based on the neighbourhood principle—the duty to use reasonable care not to harm one's neighbour—in 1932 in *Donoghue* v. *Stevenson*.[34] The tort of negligence continued to develop incrementally, underpinned by Lord Atkin's principle, until the late 1970s when Lord Wilberforce in *Anns* v. *Merton London Borough Council*[35] thought that the time had come to abandon incrementalism and to move instead to a *prima facie* or generalised negligence principle, restricted only by clearly articulated policy constraints. We know that ten years later in *Murphy* v. *Brentwood DC*[36] the House of Lords abandoned Lord Wilberforce's scheme and reverted to incrementalism for fear that otherwise the scope of the tort of negligence would be too far-reaching. One can see parallel trends and tensions in the law of

[32] See Burrows, n. 11 above, 39.
[33] [1996] AC 669, 716.
[34] [1932] AC 562.
[35] [1978] AC 728.
[36] [1991] 1 AC 398.

restitution. One can say that for much of this century it developed as a mass of individual instances of liability until finally, as per Lord Atkin, it was drawn together by Goff and Jones and by the House of Lords in *Lipkin Gorman* into a law of restitution based on the unjust enrichment principle. The equivalent to Lord Wilberforce's *general* principle approach was Goff and Jones' call, in the second and third editions of their work,[37] for there to be a generalised right to restitution, wherever there is an unjust enrichment, qualified only by clearly articulated policy constraints. But, as with the tort of negligence, this idea has not found favour. Incrementalism remains the name of the game at the end of the twentieth century and, in line with the demise of *Anns* v. *Merton*, Goff and Jones in their fourth edition in 1993 have abandoned all reference to a generalised right to restitution.

I want to finish this second part of this essay by making some comments on the role of law schools in the development of restitution and, more generally, on what law schools can learn from the development of the law of restitution. The recognition of the law of restitution in the last third of the twentieth century can be regarded as a triumph for a close working relationship between academia and the judiciary. Just as the two bodies came together in the work of the American Law Institute, so in this country the two have worked together to mould and create new law. If we focus on the interests and activities of the now numerous academic "restitution-lawyers" involved in this collaborative enterprise, we can see that, while academics, they nevertheless regard their role as being to grapple with, and unravel, difficult practical problems; we see that they are concerned to analyse carefully the latest reported decisions; that they regard precision in analysis and language to be essential; that they seek to influence the judiciary and aspire to, and can expect to, be cited in judgments; that they regard the primary purpose of their work as being to ensure consistency and rationality in decision-making, based on shared political and moral values in society, rather than the introduction of new social policies; and that they tend to have close contact with practitioners, especially at the Bar.

And yet in many law schools today—especially in the United States and Australia but, perhaps, increasingly here—we find that this type of academic lawyer is derided as a "black-letter lawyer" or a "formalist", or a "rule fetishist". The praise is often lavished on those

---

[37] See n. 11 above (2nd edn., 1978), 23–5; (3rd edn., 1993), 15, 29–30.

who stand outside the enterprise, who analyse the law from an economic or feminist or philosophical perspective, and who tend to dismiss case analysis and all practitioners' works as far too boring and straightforward for them.

I do not seek for one moment to deny the fascination and significance of jurisprudence, law and economics, law and literature, and the like. I have long been fascinated by them myself. Without question they have a role to play in a modern law school. But to regard those studies as "what proper legal academics should be doing" seems to me unacceptable. How on any true scale of values can one regard theorising about, say, philosophy as somehow more worthy and more of an intellectual challenge than the (academic) lawyer's task of shaping practical decisions affecting the workings of society in general.

In this respect I have been intrigued by the on-going debate in the United States sparked by Harry T Edwards' 1992 article in the *Michigan Law Review* entitled, "The Growing Disjunction between Legal Education and the Legal Profession".[38] In that article, Edwards criticises the "law and something else" movements; he calls for legal academics to concentrate on "practical scholarship" that can be of direct use to judges, legislatures and practitioners, rather than "impractical scholarship" which has no direct relevance to decision-making; he calls for theory to be woven into arguments that affect practical decisions rather than theory being exposed for its own sake; and he articulates the view that, for example, the economic analysis or philosophical analysis of law should be carried out by those who are first-rate economists and first-rate philosophers rather than by first-rate lawyers who are second-rate economists and second-rate philosophers and are in danger of ending up being jacks-of-all trades and masters of none. In short, the article is a call for law to be treated essentially as an autonomous discipline. While not denying the insights that other disciplines can offer—and the value therefore of studying those subjects at law school—the primary concentration in

---

[38] (1992) 91 *Mich. LR* 34. See also R Zimmermann, "Savigny's Legacy History, Comparative Law, and the Emergency of a European Legal Science" (1996) 112 *LQR* 576; John H. Langbein, "Scholarly and Professional Objectives in Legal Education: American Trends and English Comparisons" in *Pressing Problems in the Law, Volume 2, What are Law Schools For?* P. Birks (ed.), (Clarendon Press, 1996), 1–7. Edwards' article stimulated 18 responses in a symposium in the (1993) 91 *Mich. LR*, of which perhaps the most important was R. Posner, "The Deprofessionalisation of Legal Teaching and Scholarship" (1993) 91 *Mich. LR* 1921. See generally William Twining, *Blackstone's Tower: The English Law School*, Hamlyn Lectures 1994, ch. 6.

law schools and in legal scholarship should, in Edwards' view, be on practical decision-making and not on deep theory.

If one wanted an example of the sort of scholarship of which Edwards would approve, then one could do no better than to point to the bulk of English scholarship on the law of restitution over the last thirty years. Indeed it is a sad fact, and directly supports Edwards' criticism of the position in his homeland, that in the United States equivalent scholarship on the law of restitution has virtually died a death. While in this country Goff and Jones and Birks have inspired a large number of books and articles and indeed the subject's own law review, George Palmer's excellent four-volume treatise on restitution in the United States, published in 1978, has had comparatively little impact. A course on restitution or unjust enrichment is not to be found in any of the major law schools in the United States and a student learns his or her restitution, if at all, in remedies courses. In line with this the American Law Institute has shelved a second *Restatement of Restitution* (although I understand that Professor Andrew Kull of Emory University is attempting to persuade the Institute to take it up again).

But on this side of the Atlantic such is the practical utility of English scholarship on restitution that in 1997—in sharp contrast of course to 1897—few judges deciding a restitution case, or practitioners arguing a restitution case, would think it sensible to proceed without knowing what the restitution scholars have to say. Long may this close and productive working relationship between academics and practitioners continue.

3. WHERE DO WE GO FROM HERE?

So I come to the third and final part of this essay, the future. Where do we go from here? Gazing into my crystal ball, I would anticipate six significant developments in the next few decades.

First, I believe that defences, in particular change of position, will play an increasingly important role in the development of the law of restitution. Until recently, the courts have tended to restrict the ambit of restitution by limiting the grounds for restitution. In particular, we have seen above the artificial restrictions imposed on restitution for mistakes and for failure of consideration.[39] But the new

---

[39] See 104–5 above.

strategy is likely to be to cast off old restrictions on the grounds for restitution and to rely instead on defences to control the ambit of the unjust enrichment principle. A clear signal that this will be the way forward was given by Lord Goff in *Lipkin Gorman* where he said that one beneficial effect of recognising the defence of change of position was that "it will enable a more generous approach to be taken to the recognition of the right to restitution, in the knowledge that the defence is, in appropriate cases, available".[40]

Secondly, I think that we will see a continued assimilation of common law and equitable rules on restitution. To use Jack Beatson's phrase,[41] "integrating equity" is the law of restitution's "unfinished business". Relating back to the examples given earlier,[42] I would expect to see strict liability subject to defences, such as change of position and *bona fide* purchase, taking over "knowing receipt and dealing". I would expect personal restitutionary remedies for wrongs, stripping away gains made by wrongdoers, to become widely accepted in respect of torts as well as equitable wrongs. And I would expect the other great area where English law at present irrationally divides common law and equitable rules, namely tracing, to be reformed so that, for example, the apparent common law rule that one cannot trace into a mixed fund will be emasculated.[43]

Thirdly, I anticipate that within the near future there will be a solution to the continuing mystery of the relationship between property law and unjust enrichment. This is obviously not an appropriate essay for me to attempt to solve that mystery but I would like to make three observations that may of assistance.

The first is that, while in the past, I thought it helpful to treat a proprietary remedy given because the plaintiff owned particular property before and after it was received by the defendant as restitutionary, based on an unjust factor of "the retention of property belonging to the plaintiff",[44] I now accept that it is more helpful to draw a clear distinction between that case (which Goff and Jones call a "pure proprietary claim" and civil lawyers would call a *vindicatio* claim) and other cases where the proprietary remedy is given because the law is creating a new proprietary right in response to the defendant's unjust enrichment at the plaintiff's expense (what Goff and

[40] [1991] 2 AC 548, 581.

[41] *The Use and Abuse of Unjust Enrichment* (Clarendon Press, 1991), 244.

[42] See 105–8 above.

[43] See, in particular, the observations of Millett LJ in *Trustee of the Property of F.C. Jones v. Jones* [1996] 3 WLR 703.

[44] N. 11 above, ch. 13.

Jones call a "restitutionary proprietary claim"[45]). An important consequence of recognising this distinction is that change of position ought to be a defence to a proprietary restitutionary claim but not to a pure proprietary claim (for example, a delivery up of one's property).

The second observation is that, as the work of Peter Birks and Lionel Smith has emphasised,[46] one needs to distinguish between the process of tracing and the decision whether to award a personal or proprietary restitutionary remedy. I would argue that tracing is a technique that goes to the "at the expense of" element of subtractive unjust enrichment. That is, a plaintiff will need to rely on the technique of tracing where establishing that the defendant's enrichment was "subtracted from" the plaintiff is problematic because of a change in the form of the property subtracted and/or because the property in question has been received by the defendant from a third party rather than directly from the plaintiff. While, no doubt, tracing is normally invoked by a plaintiff with the aim of obtaining a proprietary restitutionary remedy over property retained by the defendant, tracing may also be invoked with the aim of seeking a personal restitutionary remedy (for example, an award of money had and received or an equitable accounting) in respect of property *received* by the defendant where property has reached the defendant from a third party (so that establishing that the enrichment was subtracted from the plaintiff is problematic) as, for example, in *Lipkin Gorman* itself.

The third observation is that any attempt to confine the unjust enrichment principle to the law of obligations, by denying that proprietary (as opposed to personal) remedies are ever restitutionary, flies in the face of a wide range of situations where, in my view, the law already creates new proprietary rights in response to unjust enrichment. Examples include constructive trusts imposed on gains made by equitable wrongs (as in *Boardman* v. *Phipps*,[47] and *Attorney General for Hong Kong* v. *Reid*[48]); some examples of subrogation (for example, as provided for in section 5 of the Mercantile Law Amendment Act 1856, and as illustrated in the cases of *Boscawen* v. *Bajwa*,[49] and *Lord*

---

[45] N. 11 (4th edn.), 73–4.

[46] P. Birks, "Mixing and Tracing: Property and Restitution" (1992) 45(2) *CLP* 69; L.D. Smith, *The Law of Tracing* (Clarendon Press, 1997). See also Millett LJ's observations in *Boscawen* v. *Bajwa* [1996] 1 WLR 328.

[47] For discussion of this, see P. Birks, "Unjust Enrichment—a Reply to Mr Hedley" (1985) 5 *Legal Studies* 67, 68–9.

[48] [1994] 1 AC 324.

[49] [1996] 1 WLR 328.

Napier v. *Hunter*[50]); equitable liens that have been imposed on land because it has been mistakenly improved[51]; the rescission of an executed contract which has revested the proprietary rights to goods or land transferred under the contract (as in, for example, *Car and Universal Finance Company Ltd* v. *Caldwell*[52]); and equitable proprietary remedies awarded following equitable tracing,[53] where it is important to see that it is fictional to say that one's entitlement to the property is based on one's pre-existing equitable ownership of it. That is, if one is entitled to trace from a pig to a horse to a car one cannot say, without invoking fiction, that one is entitled to proprietary restitution of the car because one already owns it. The truth is that one's ownership of the pig which has been substituted by the car entitles one to claim for the first time ownership of the car because the owner of the car is unjustly enriched at one's expense (the tracing rules being invoked to show that the subtraction of one's pig has become the defendant's enrichment in the form of the car). On the other hand (running contrary to the above examples), after *Westdeutsche Landesbank* we now know that a defendant who is unjustly enriched by a mistaken payment or a payment under a void contract is normally susceptible to only a personal and not a proprietary restitutionary remedy. It has to be conceded, it seems to me, that this picture of the law as to when unjust enrichment will and will not trigger new proprietary rights lacks all coherence. The judges must and, I am sure will, move the law, with the assistance of academics, to a more coherent position on this most difficult of issues.

Fourthly, I expect legislation to have a greater impact on the law of restitution than hitherto. My recent work on a cases and materials book on restitution with Ewan McKendrick has made it startlingly apparent to me just how limited has been the role of statute in this sphere. One hardly gets beyond the Law Reform (Frustrated Contracts) Act 1943, the Civil Liability (Contribution) Act 1978, the Minors' Contracts Act 1987 and a few minor sections in the Torts (Wrongful Interference with Goods Act) 1977 and intellectual property statutes. Yet, as Dean Calabresi has emphasised, we are in the age of the statutes.[54] Certainly

[50] [1993] AC 713.

[51] *Unity Joint Stock Mutual Banking Assoc* v. *King* (1858) 25 Beav. 72; *Cooper* v. *Phibbs* (1867) LR 2 HL 149.

[52] [1965] 1 QB 525.

[53] See e.g., *Re Hallett's Estate* (1880) 13 Ch D 696; *Re Diplock* [1948] Ch. 465.

[54] D. Calabresi, *A Common Law for the Age of the Statutes* (Harvard UP, 1982). See also J. Beatson, "Has the Common Law A Future?" (Inaugural lecture, 29 Apr. 1996, Cambridge University Press).

within three of the projects with which I am concerned at the Law Commission—namely, limitation periods, non-compensatory damages and illegal transactions—it is essential that we deal legislatively with aspects of restitution.[55] And I am optimistic that the Law Commission's legislative recommendations abrogating the mistake of law bar will be enacted in the near future.[56] I would expect that the nonsense of the decision in *Friends Provident Life Office* v. *Hillier Parker May & Rowden*,[57] where existing wording designed for compensation in the Civil Liability (Contribution) Act 1978 was forced to fit restitution, will increasingly be rendered unnecessary as the legislature, following on *Lipkin Gorman*, and with the assistance of the Law Commission, comes to terms with the language and ideas of the law of restitution.

Fifthly, I expect to see comparative European law having an increased influence over the English law of restitution. This expectation is a reflection of, first, the increased recognition by our judiciary of comparative material; and, secondly, of the fact that the UK's membership of the European Union has brought us closer to European thinking. Certainly in the area of unjust enrichment there is an enormous amount that we can learn from, for example, German law. Perhaps as with Olé Lando and Hugh Beale's *The Principles of European Contract Law*,[58] we will see in the future a publication entitled "Principles of European Unjust Enrichment Law". In this respect Dr Eric Clive's superb Scottish Code of Unjust Enrichment Law produced in 1996 for the Scottish Law Commission may be of great significance.[59]

Finally, for better or worse, I think academic literature on restitution will tend to become more theoretical and to move further away from Harry Edwards' "practical scholarship". Kit Barker, in an excellent recent review article of English literature on restitution entitled "Unjust enrichment: Containing the Beast",[60] writes that we should now "look more closely at [the subject's] internal 'philosophical foundations' or 'ground-theory'. If there is a general flaw in the recent literature, it is the failure to excavate this deeper level of enquiry. Authors tend to engage in lively arguments about what the

---

[55] See 169–71, 179–81, 191–5 below.
[56] *Restitution: Mistakes of Law and Ultra Vires Public Authority Receipts and Payments* (1994) Law Com. No. 227, Part I.
[57] [1996] 2 WLR 123.
[58] Part 1: Performance, Non-Performance and Remedies (Martinus Nijhoff, 1995).
[59] *Scottish Law Commission Draft Rules on Unjustified Enrichment and Commentary* (Appendix to Scot. Law Com. Discussion Paper No. 99) (HMSO Scotland, 1996).
[60] (1995) 15 *OJLS* 457.

beast should look like. . . . They have tended to fight shy of the logically prior (and governing) question of why it exists."[61]

I agree that there is scope for more theory but the challenge facing Kit Barker, and others, who have embarked on the same enterprise, is to ensure that their theories link directly and intelligibly to practical decision-making. The danger of the next generation of restitution-scholars crossing the line from practical to impractical scholarship—and thereby losing the influence we have over decision-makers in the area—is very great indeed.[62]

This leads me to leave you with a question that has long troubled me. Does my predicted trend towards deeper theory indicate that the practical legal academic has a limited role? Put another way, does a particular field become so saturated with practical scholarship that one has to move to deeper theoretical analysis to say anything original? If we take Contract as an example, is the explosion in deep theoretical analysis, the United States style of scholarship, inevitable?

It is true that, once Goff and Jones or Birks has been written, one cannot write another "path-breaking" book in the same style. My own firm view, however, is that the law is so rich that at any one time there are numerous path-breaking articles and books of practical legal scholarship that cry out to be written. At this moment in time unjust enrichment is still far from saturated but, even if it were, there are other areas where the possibilities seem endless, most especially I would suggest in the field of commercial law (one thinks for example of our poor understanding of the law on guarantees or assignment or agency). The work of the practical legal scholar is never complete. As lawyers, while there may be a need for us to switch specialist horses, there is no need for us to abandon our subject in order to find opportunities for intellectually challenging, creative, and path-breaking work. At the end of the twentieth century the work of the practical legal scholar—and our working relationship with the judiciary—is too important to society for us to sell out to the departments of philosophy, history or economics. If there are no heirs to Scott and Seavey in the United States, I am confident that in England there will be heirs aplenty to Robert Goff, Gareth Jones, and Peter Birks.

---

[61] *Ibid.*, at 463.

[62] I recognise that views may differ as to where the line should be drawn between practical and impractical scholarship and that the distinction is one of degree rather than of kind.

6

In Defence of Tort

For the last thirty years or so, the English tort system of compensating personal injuries has been subject to attack. The best-known critic has been Patrick Atiyah. His *Accidents Compensation and the Law*[1] subjected the tort system to detailed and vigorous criticism. More recently, after more than a decade of silence, Atiyah has taken up the theme again in *The Damages Lottery*.[2] Several other commentators have put forward similar ideas, both here and elsewhere in the common law world.[3] In this article, I shall attempt to defend tort against its critics and to show that it continues to play a valuable role—and one worth retaining—in modern society.

2. THE CENTRAL ATTACK ON TORT

The central argument put by opponents of the tort system can be expressed in the following way:

> (i) Although tort fixes individual defendants with liability, those individuals rarely pay the damages themselves. Rather, the damages are largely paid by liability insurers.

[1] (1st edn., Weidenfeld & Nicholson, 1970). The latest edition, the 5th by Peter Cane, was published in 1993 by Butterworths.

[2] (Hart Publishing, 1997). See also P.S. Atiyah, "Personal Injuries in the Twenty-First Century: Thinking the Unthinkable" in P. Birks (ed.), *Wrongs and Remedies in the Twenty-First Century* (Claendon Press, 1996), 1–46.

[3] See, e.g., T. Ison, *The Forensic Lottery* (Staples Press, 1967); J. O'Connell and B. Kelly, *The Blame Game* (Lexington Books, 1987); P. Bell and J. O'Connell, *Accidental Justice* (Yale UP, 1997). See also B. Hepple, "Negligence: The Search for Coherence" (1997) 50 *CLP* 69, 84–6, 93 agreeing with much of Atiyah's thinking, albeit not his latest "leave it to the free market" proposal. Atiyah in "American Tort Law in Crisis" (1987) 7 *OJLS* 279, 291 acknowledges that the first edition of *Accidents Compensation and the Law* was extensively influenced by the writings of Professor Fleming James of Yale. See, e.g., F. James, "Accident Liability Reconsidered: The Impact of Liability Insurance" (1948) 57 *Yale LJ* 549.

(ii) It follows from (i) that damages are being financed by most members of society through the insurance premiums that most people pay.

(iii) The tort system should therefore be viewed as a type of taxation-based social welfare system financed by most people in society.

(iv) Yet, in contrast to taxation-based social welfare, tort compensates very few injured persons, picks out those to be compensated on the invalid basis of how the injury was brought about, rather than on the basis of need, and compensates only at huge administrative expense. The statistics Atiyah puts forward here are that about one in ten accident victims receive compensation through the tort system[4] and that for each £1 of compensation 80p is spent in costs.[5]

(v) The tort system should therefore be scrapped and the costs saved used either to finance an extension of the social welfare system (this was Atiyah's 1970's position[6]); or to give people more money in their pockets with individuals being left to choose whether to take out personal accident insurance protection (this is essentially Atiyah's 1990's position).[7]

One should note immediately that, while the logic of steps (i)–(iv) has remained consistent, the conclusion to be drawn on (v) shows Atiyah adopting a radically different position in the 1990s, from that adopted in the 1970s. This can be portrayed as Atiyah abandoning liberal "left-wing" thinking in favour of a "right-wing" "Thatcherite" approach. Atiyah would no doubt prefer to see it as facing up to the realities of the late twentieth century, when any political party worth its salt can see that social welfare must be stringently cut back not extended.

One must have concerns, however, about Atiyah's willingness to argue so vehemently for such radically different conclusions in such a relatively short space of time. Critics would say that, had

---

[4] *The Damages Lottery* (Hart Publishing, 1997), 178. Atiyah also refers to the statistic of about 1 ½% of all the ill and injured receiving damages: see 100, 144.

[5] *Ibid.*, 153, 179. The Pearson Royal Commission on Civil Liability and Compensation for Personal Injury (1978) estimated that, during 1971–6, £200m was paid in damages at an administrative cost of £175m.

[6] In *Accidents, Compensation and the Law* (1st edn.), n. 1 above, esp. ch. 19.

[7] In *The Damages Lottery*, n. 2 above, ch. 8. But he suggests that basic first party road accident insurance should probably be compulsory: see 187.

policy-makers applied his arguments in the 1970s, we would have abolished the tort system and instead had in place a wide-ranging social welfare scheme for the benefit of the injured. Yet only fifteen years later those policy-makers would have been condemned by Atiyah for creating a misconceived new system which should be abolished. Those concerned with legislative reform may be forgiven for thinking that such a willingness to "switch horses" means that one must not take Atiyah's views too seriously. Fascinating, beautifully expressed and brilliantly argued as they are, they may be the stuff of classrooms and academic conferences and not for the real world. Indeed—and this is a point that I have directly put to Patrick Atiyah in open seminar discussion—he is in danger of shaping the common law according to short-term political goals. To my way of thinking, for the common law to react according to the political fad of the moment would be to contradict its very essence: contract, tort and restitution rest on fundamental long-term values that, while evolving and adapting to new conditions over the course of time, and while influenced by long-term policies, should be immune from short-term party politics.

3. THE CENTRAL DEFENCE

My central defence of the tort system rests on it being a system of individual responsibility. It pins responsibility for compensating another on an individual because of what the individual has, or has not, done. It has a very different rationale from a social welfare system, which is a system of community responsibility and responds to the needs of the injured, ill, disabled or otherwise disadvantaged in society, irrespective of whether those needs have been caused by the particular conduct of an individual. There is therefore a contrast between two distinct ideas: individual responsibility triggered by one's conduct; and community responsibility based on the needs of the disadvantaged. Both have a role to play. They can happily co-exist. There is no need for the former to be swallowed up by, or abandoned in favour of, the latter.[8]

A central flaw in the argument put by critics of tort is to assume that because individual defendants rarely pay the damages themselves, tort cannot stand up as a system of individual responsibility. The

---

[8] See L. Klar, "New Zealand's Accident Compensation Scheme: A Tort Lawyer's Perspective" (1983) 33 *UTLJ* 80.

assumption is that individual responsibility entails that the individual pays. In *The Damages Lottery* Atiyah repeats the point that "the defendant does not pay the damages" no fewer than sixteen times.

But whether the defendant pays the damages himself or herself is not of central importance. What is important is that the defendant is made legally responsible for ensuring that the plaintiff is paid compensation. It is the pinning of that legal responsibility on the defendant that is at the heart of the tort system. The fact that the defendant discharges that liability through insurance, or that someone else pays the damages on behalf of the defendant is not significant. Tort does not say, "the defendant must pay" but rather "the defendant must ensure that payment is made".

That pinning of legal responsibility to ensure compensation on a defendant rests on basic morality or justice. It responds to there being a particularly strong case for compensating injury (or illness) where that injury has been caused by another's conduct, especially where that conduct was blameworthy. While, as against other individuals, we have to bear the risk of natural misfortune—that is, we cannot validly attach responsibility to others for our own bad luck—there is no reason why we should have to bear the risk of another's harmful conduct, particularly where that conduct was blameworthy.

Atiyah begins *The Damages Lottery* with a true newspaper story of a 5-year-old girl who was taken to hospital with a severe attack of meningitis. The doctors saved her life, but in order to do so, they had to amputate both her legs. Atiyah writes, as if an indictment of the system, "She had no chance of obtaining damages from anybody because her injuries were nobody's fault. It was just bad luck[9]". It is clear that, assuming parents of similar wealth, the *needs* of that girl and of a girl whose legs had been amputated because a driver negligently crashed into her are identical. Ideally a social welfare system responding to needs ought not to treat the two girls differently: that is, the different causes of the amputations should be irrelevant on a needs-based approach. But this is not to deny that the girl whose legs have been amputated because of another's negligent driving has a right to compensation that the girl who was the victim of a natural illness does not have. It is a right not against the state but against the negligent driver. It is a right that responds specifically to the difference between bad luck, the risk of which we must bear, and another's harmful conduct which, especially if blameworthy, we should not have to bear.

---

[9] N. 2 above, 1.

A person injured by another's wrongful conduct has a right to compensation—derived from basic morality or justice—that a person injured as a consequence of natural misfortune simply does not have.

The moral validity of tort as against a needs-based welfare system is further illustrated by the treatment of self-inflicted injuries. Under the tort system a person who injures himself has no right to compensation: but under a needs-based welfare system he has an equal entitlement to compensation with any other injured person (even if his injuries have been *deliberately* self-inflicted). Commenting on New Zealand's accident compensation scheme, which since 1974 has replaced tort claims for personal injury caused by accidents,[10] Richard Mahoney writes the following: "observers of the scheme will have to confront the elementary moral question raised by a compensation system which treats the self-inflicted injuries of the fool, the drunk or the daredevil equally with the injuries of the innocent victim who may have suffered at their hands. Taking the extreme example, the thug who [injures himself when he] headbutts a passer-by will . . . receive compensation equal to that of the victim if the injuries and financial circumstances of the two parties are the same. The scheme's highly touted . . . goal of efficiency . . . hardly seems a sufficient justification for this sort of result[11]".

The pinning of responsibility to ensure compensation on a defendant is not only morally valid but carries with it at least two significant subsidiary advantages as against social welfare (or first party personal accident insurance).

First, it is likely, at least in some circumstances, to deter wrongful conduct. Although it may be true that the deterrence effect of the tort system is less strong where the defendant does not himself or herself pay the damages, the pinning of responsibility to ensure compensation on the defendant—especially where the conduct is declared to be blameworthy—surely has some deterrent effect. Nobody likes having their conduct declared to be negligent. This is,

[10] The Accident Compensation Act 1972 came into force on 1 Apr. 1974. This implemented the recommendations of the Royal Commission of Inquiry, *Compensation for Personal Injury in New Zealand* (1967), chaired by Woodhouse J. Amendments to the 1972 Act were consolidated in the Accident Compensation Act 1982. The 1982 Act has been replaced, and radically altered, by the Accident Rehabilitation and Compensation Insurance Act 1992. See S. Todd (ed.), *Law of Torts in New Zealand* (2nd edn., Brooker's, 1997), ch. 2; R. Miller, "An Analysis and Critique of the 1992 Changes to New Zealand's Accident Compensation Scheme" (1992) 5 *Cant LR* 1.

[11] R. Mahoney, "Trouble in Paradise: New Zealand's Accident Compensation Scheme" in S. McLean (ed.), *Law Reform and Medical Injury Litigation* (Dartmouth, 1995), 31, 33.

perhaps, especially true of professional defendants whose reputation—even if only amongst colleagues—might be detrimentally affected by a finding of negligence. This seems to be borne out by the fact that many professionals strenuously seek to deny negligence even though there may be no adverse financial consequences for them of having legal responsibility pinned on them. Moves towards "defensive medicine" and defensive practices by other professionals similarly appear to indicate that the present law does have some deterrent effect. Of course, it is difficult definitively to prove that tort deters because it is always possible to argue that a person would have acted in the same way for other reasons (for example, many professionals by their very character and training would seek to exercise reasonable care in performing their services irrespective of any legal obligation). But it seems fair to claim that, at least in some circumstances, pinning responsibility on a person to ensure compensation because of his or her wrongful conduct is a deterrent even though the defendant is insured and is not going to have to pay the damages. And if that claim is thought fair, it can be extended to say more generally that tort helps to maintain (and indeed to improve) general standards of safety in society.

One should add that in some circumstances there is a financial detriment to the insured defendant of being found liable in the form of increased insurance premiums or the loss of no-claims bonuses.[12]

Secondly, pinning responsibility to ensure compensation on a defendant may help to establish the true facts of a particular accident. This may in turn be of benefit both to the public at large (who, for example, are made aware of the dangers of certain products) and to the immediate victims and their families. One commonly hears victims asserting that the motivation for their legal claim is not so much the obtaining of compensation but establishing the truth of what happened. In this respect, tort fulfils an "ombudsman" role that a social welfare (or first party insurance) system does not.

The tort system, based as it is on individual responsibility, is therefore fundamentally distinct from needs-based welfare. It not only applies basic morality, but carries with it the subsidiary advantages of deterrence and public accountability. Those features apply irrespective of whether the defendant pays the damages or not.

---

[12] But in some areas (e.g. employers' liability insurance) insurers show little inclination to embark on a more flexible fixing of premiums according to the accident record of defendants: see P. Cane, *Atiyah's Accidents, Compensation and the Law* (5th edn., Butterworths, 1993), 369–74.

It follows that it is misleading for critics of tort to treat it, and assess it, as if it were a type of taxation-based welfare system. If one judges the success of tort by asking how well it meets the needs of the injured and ill in society, it will fare badly precisely because it is not a needs-based system. But if one recognises it for what it is—a system of individual responsibility—it has important advantages (especially in applying basic moral values) that would be lost under a welfare, or first party insurance, system.

4. THE SCOPE OF THE TORT ATTACK: WHERE DOES IT STOP?

A major problem with the arguments advanced by the critics of tort is that the precise subject-matter under attack is never made entirely clear.

If we first of all confine ourselves to tort, is it the whole of tort or only parts of it that are under attack? While the main focus is clearly on negligently caused personal injury and death, what about intentionally caused personal injury (through the tort of trespass to the person)? What about strict liability causing personal injury (through, for example, the tort of breach of statutory duty or the Consumer Protection Act 1987)? And is the attack also intended to knock out negligently, or intentionally, caused property damage or pure economic loss? What about the torts of defamation and nuisance?

It is not obvious that the critics of tort have properly considered this issue. Certainly a good deal of attention is devoted to trying to show the moral incoherence and needless expense of establishing fault. Yet in describing the essential features of the tort system, it is not necessary to identify that system with a standard of reasonable care. I have studiously avoided so doing in my description of the moral validity of tort above. If critics of tort were simply criticising the normal fault standard in tort the criticism could, arguably, be deflected by advocating a move to strict liability. Arguably, a strict liability tort system can be defended as having a moral basis, namely that one ought not to harm others by one's activities (even if one has taken all reasonable care to avoid such harm).[13]

If, as appears to be the case, the primary criticism being made is that tort makes no sense unless the defendant pays the damages—and he does not—that criticism would extend to all areas of tort, for it can

---

[13] See, e.g., R. Epstein, *A Theory of Strict Liability* (CATO Institute, 1980); A. Honoré, "Responsibility and Luck" (1988) 104 *LQR* 530.

be said of all torts that it will be rare for a defendant to pay damages from his or her own pocket.

The fuzziness of focus is well-illustrated by the experience in New Zealand. The Woodhouse Report looked entirely at personal injury and death caused by fault. Yet when the comprehensive accident compensation scheme was introduced it covered intentional personal injury as well so that claims for compensation for trespass to the person in tort were, on the face of it, abolished.

The same lack of clarity is to be found in *The Damages Lottery*.[14] Atiyah writes, "In general this book is not concerned with . . . intentional torts, and certainly no proposal will be found here to abolish or reduce the liability of a person who commits an intentional tort. But there are some cases which do raise issues with intentional torts which are really identical to issues which arise with negligence. These cases concern the liability of employers or others for the actions of a wrongdoer. When, for instance, a policeman uses excessive force in arresting someone (and thereby commits a tort) the police authority will be liable for the damages, just as much as the policeman himself. This kind of liability—which is actually the liability of the public in the last resort—is very much the concern of this book, and raises problems in no way different from the liability of police officers for negligence. But apart from that this book is not concerned with intentional torts which do not give rise to anything like the volume of claims and litigation which negligence does."[15]

But what is it that links the police or employer intentional torts with negligence, yet does not link other intentional torts with negligence?

Yet if one were to abolish only some torts one would be in danger of not treating like cases alike, particularly as it is now clear that a non-tort system of compensation is unlikely to be able to offer the same "full" compensation aspired to by tort. For example, can one tolerate a system where a person injured in a car crash receives full compensation (through the tort system) for damage to his car but receives only say 80 per cent of full compensation through a state welfare scheme for the personal injuries suffered? Can it be just for a person to continue to receive full compensation for pecuniary and non-pecuniary loss caused by the tort of defamation or nuisance

---

[14] See also Ison, n. 3 above, ch. 6, who tentatively suggests abolishing at least some liability for property damage (and for breach of contract) but regards negligently caused pure economic loss as "a separate social problem" beyond the scope of his book.

[15] N. 2 above, 7.

whereas a person who is negligently (or intentionally) personally injured has to make do with less than full compensation?

Richard Mahoney makes the same point in criticising the New Zealand accident compensation scheme. He writes, "the scheme makes no attempt to bar litigation for *property* claims. They can continue as before. Thus, in the typical case of a car accident, litigation over broken bones is impossible yet a full-fledged lawsuit to attempt to recover the costs of repairing the car is perfectly acceptable. To highlight the continued availability of property suits, [I shall later make] reference to a case illustrating the disastrous civil consequences which resulted to a defendant who, by negligently spraying weeds, ruined some of the plaintiff corporation's roses. No claim, however, could have been made in a law suit (nor . . . under the scheme) had the spray merely crippled or killed the plaintiff's workers and created similar losses of profits. Can anyone support such an anomaly?"[16]

Is it a fair civil justice system if a person is entitled to recover proportionately more for less serious harm caused by the same conduct? Indeed it is ironic that, while tort critics have sought to expose what they regard as the incoherence of treating injury victims differently according to whether the injury was caused by another's fault or not, the examples above indicate that the system they favour seems more obviously riddled with anomalies.

Similarly, one wonders whether by focusing on abolishing tort for personal injuries, tort-critics are guilty of inverting true priorities. Given, as we have said, that the same basic criticisms made can be extended to all areas of tort, why applying their views would it not make more sense to argue that, in the first instance, all torts *not concerned with personal injury* should be abolished? The costs saved could fund a state welfare scheme for those, for example, whose reputations have been damaged or, perhaps more appealingly, diverted to provide better state welfare for the ill and disabled. Critics need to explain why they have focused their attack on the most serious harm compensated through tort (personal injury) rather than the less serious harms compensated through tort (non-personal injury).

And why stop at tort? If one is criticising the tort system on the basis that defendants do not themselves pay the damages and that its costs are very high, why is the whole system of civil wrongs (and indeed aspects of the law on unjust enrichment) not subjected to the same attack? Take damages for breach of contract. These will almost

[16] Mahoney, n. 11 above, 31, 34.

always be paid for through liability insurance or through increasing the costs of goods and services. So why are tort critics not also directing their fire at compensation through the contract system? Indeed in some cases of personal injury (for example, contracts for the carriage of passengers) concurrent liability in contract and tort is commonplace so that it would seem particularly odd to call for abolition only of the tort claim.

In fact, although hardly brought to the fore, tort critics have shown some awareness of the difficulties of their position in relation to contract. Certainly the New Zealand accident compensation scheme abolishes all common law actions for accidental personal injury (including contractual claims) even though in the Woodhouse report there is not a single overt mention of contract. Similarly, although he did not mention this in *Accidents Compensation and the Law*, Atiyah in *The Damages Lottery* does devote a few pages to contract. He says: "Contractual cases are generally outside the scope of this book, but . . . there are some claims for damages for negligence which are classified as breaches of contract, and raise issues very similar (if not identical) to those which arise in other negligence actions."[17] He goes on to give two illustrations: death owing to breach of a contractual duty of care by a tour operator and the loss of films sent for developing. In relation to both examples, he argues that it would be preferable to abolish the right to sue for breach of contract. Holiday-makers and those who want films developed should instead have to take out first party insurance for compensation. So as regards the latter example he writes, "claims like this are usually quite contrary to consumer interests, because consumers will only end up paying more for their purchases. If these risks were covered by first party insurance rather than legal liability and third party insurance, then those who have specially valuable films to protect could be left to buy special first party policies, while these who do not, could save themselves the extra expense."[18]

But as with Atiyah's treatment of intentional torts, one is left asking why all or most of contract is not seen as raising similar issues.

All this tends to show that the attacks made on the tort system for personal injuries cannot sensibly be "ring-fenced". Critics must face up to the alarming fact that their criticisms are, as a matter of logic, applicable to most, if not all, civil rights to compensation (and could even be extended to criticise all civil remedies). In essence, it is civil

[17] N. 2 above, 134.
[18] *Ibid.*, 137.

justice that is on trial here, not tort alone. In commenting on the
New Zealand system, Richard Mahoney is again directly on point.
He writes, "Why should not *all* civil litigation be banned and
replaced by administrative systems which magically do away with
waste, delay and uncertainty? The same criticisms made of personal
injury litigation could be levelled at all types of litigation, yet the civil
lawsuit remains a common feature of New Zealand's legal system.
Thus, even if it is true that litigation is costly, uncertain and time con-
suming, it apparently remains a satisfactory avenue for redressing the
wrongs of the victims of a contract breach, a defamatory statement or
a poorly designed building (or a negligently damaged car)."[19]

5. WHAT SHOULD BE THE WAY FORWARD?

One wonders what Atiyah's 1970s supporters make of his 1990s
reincarnation. With all sides of the political spectrum making clear
that expansion of state welfare is not an realistic option, are the "wel-
farists" forced, like Atiyah, to turn their backs on justice and to advo-
cate a "look-after yourself through first party insurance" approach?
Or do they stay in the wilderness for the foreseeable future, hoping
for the day when community responsibility, through wide-ranging
social welfare, is back on the agenda?

My hope is that they may be persuaded that, while abolition of tort
is unacceptable, there are worthwhile reforms to tort that can be
made.

First, and foremost, the expense and delay of the present civil litigation system is an outrage. Critics of the tort system suggest that
costs and delay cannot be significantly improved so long as the fault-
based system remains.[20] In my view, that is needlessly pessimistic.
Lord Woolf's proposed procedural reforms,[21] including an encouragement of alternative dispute resolution,[22] are likely to reduce the
present costs of obtaining compensation. While the administration of
justice is unlikely ever to be cheap—not least because disputes over
rights are likely to involve the expensive skills of lawyers—present
costs in obtaining compensation are too high.

---

[19] Mahoney, n. 11 above, 31, 34.
[20] Atiyah, n. 2 above, 126, 152. See also Ison, n. 2 above, 30, 78.
[21] Lord Woolf, *Access to Justice: Final Report to the Lord Chancellor on the Civil Justice System in England and Wales* (HMSO, 1996).
[22] *Ibid.*, Recommendations 35, 39–41, 191, 295, 302, 303.

Secondly, it is arguable that collateral benefits—that is compensation received by tort victims from third parties (other than tort damages)—ought to be more widely deductible from damages than under the present law.[23] While English law has largely moved to deducting social security benefits and sick pay, disability pensions and first party accident insurance are not deductible. Yet, particularly given the costs of tort compensation, there may be thought to be no sufficiently convincing reason why those who are already fully compensated through other sources should be able to recover "double compensation" by being able to cumulate collateral benefits with tort damages. Retaining the tort system is one thing. Ignoring other systems of compensation is another matter altogether.

It might be thought that to deduct collateral benefits, such as personal accident insurance, would be unacceptable because, in a situation where a tort claim could be brought, the person who has had the foresight to take out insurance ends up no better off than the person who has chosen not to insure. But the counter-argument is that the insured person has peace of mind in knowing that he will be compensated and is guaranteed early payment of compensation. And, of course, he is also entitled to compensation in situations where there is no overlap with the tort system.

Thirdly, there is a good case for encouraging the taking out of first-party insurance to cover the pecuniary and non-pecuniary losses of injury and illness. If more people were covered by personal accident or illness insurance policies, the expensive tort system would tend to be relied on less often: this would especially be so if the collateral insurance benefit were deducted (and if insurers were to continue not to have subrogation rights under non-indemnity insurance). While the tort system of individual responsibility would remain intact, encouragement would be given to individuals to make their own provision for injury and illness which could take precedence in the event of an overlap with tort. Of course, in many situations—and this ought to be a primary selling feature of personal accident or illness insurance—the injured or ill would be covered by insurance where there would be no possibility of compensation under the tort system; for example, where a person is injured in an accident that is no-one's fault or is the victim of a natural disease. Rationally, anyone who is seriously concerned about future illness or injury, and who would not

---

[23] The issues are explored in *Damages for Personal Injury: Collateral Benefits*, Law Commission Consultation Paper No. 147 (1997). See 186–8 below.

wish to rely on social security, should take out some form of personal accident or illness insurance, for the simple reason that relatively few of those who are injured or ill can recover tort
compensation. But while compulsory first-party insurance for all
risks in life would presumably be prohibitively expensive—and, in
any event, seems objectionable in principle as too great an interference with individual autonomy—there is good reason, in order to
make more efficient use of resources, why the state should encourage the voluntary taking out of first party insurance. Such encouragement might be fostered by a national advertising campaign and
by giving insurance companies financial incentives to develop and
sell first party insurance.

Given his strong preference for first-party insurance, Atiyah would
presumably find this third suggested reform unobjectionable. But, for
him, it would be of little value provided the tort system continues to
exist. In contrast, I have argued that replacing the tort system is unacceptable. If one were instead to reform the law on the deduction of
collateral benefits, and to encourage first-party insurance, the position would be that, where such insurance has been taken out and
covers the same loss as tort damages, a victim would normally have
no need, or incentive, to resort to tort litigation.

It is, therefore, my belief that tort critics should be thinking more
carefully about reforms that stop short of abolishing much, or all, of
the tort system. In this respect, I have some sympathy with the "early
offer" plan proposed in the United States by Professor Jeffrey
O'Connell (albeit that I cannot ultimately agree with it). A promi-
nent and long-standing critic of the tort system, O'Connell has put
forward numerous suggestions for reforming tort, most notably various types of "no-fault" road accident compensation scheme. But his
most recently suggested "early offer" plan is of particular interest
because it operates within the tort system. He explains his proposal as
follows: "any defendant in a personal injury claim is given the option
of offering to a claimant within 180 days after a claim is made peri-
odic payment of the claimant's net economic loss. . . . Such payment
will cover any medical expenses, including rehabilitation, and wage
loss, beyond any collateral sources already payable to the claimant,
plus a reasonable hourly fee for the claimant's lawyer. A defendant in
a tort suit promptly offering to pay these amounts to the claimant
forecloses further pursuit of a tort claim. In other words, the claimant
is forced to accept such an offer . . . offers could be refused, however,
and a normal tort claim pursued, when the defendant's misconduct

was intentional or wanton proved by clear and convincing evidence".[24]

O'Connell argues that defendants would have an interest in making such an early offer because they would avoid paying damages for non-pecuniary loss, if they were to be found liable for negligence. On the other hand, plaintiffs would be benefited by such a plan in that they would avoid having to prove negligence. Underpinning allowing such a trade-off is a subtle combination of at least four policy-choices by O'Connell; first, that it would be advantageous in saving costs to avoid litigation especially involving proof of fault; secondly, that of the plaintiff's losses it is easier to quantify and justify damages for pecuniary loss than for non-pecuniary loss; thirdly, that it is not easy to decide whether the basis of liability in tort should be strict or fault-based; fourthly, that deliberate or reckless infliction of personal injury is altogether more serious than mere negligence.

O'Connell writes, "The essence of this . . . proposal is the opportunity for many injured persons to obtain relatively fast payment for their economic losses, while being able to make use of the full tort apparatus in egregious cases. Incentives—but not requirements—are built in to encourage early resolution of tort disputes. The [plan] thereby attacks, *within the tort system itself*, the grievously high costs of resolving tort disputes. The worst nightmares of uncertain, delayed compensation for injured people are dramatically reduced. Much of the tort system's deterrence is retained: the party paying the bill is the party responsible for the injury. In those instances in which the defendant behaviour is clearly unreasonable, the full threat of tort damages remains as a disincentive to such behaviour. The plan thus permits some of tort law's strengths to function—forcing those arguably at fault to bear substantial burdens for injuries inflicted".[25]

Ultimately, however, it is hard to see why plaintiffs who can clearly establish fault should lose their existing rights to compensation, particularly where non-pecuniary loss is the major element of loss. It is also unclear what would happen if, having made such an early offer, the defendant subsequently refuses to pay some of the plaintiff's net economic losses or (*bona fide*) disputes the amount of such losses. Moreover, O'Connell's plan is directed towards the specific problem in the United States of large and unpredictable awards

---

[24] J. O'Connell, "The McConnell Tort Reform Bill" (1996) *Michigan Law and Policy Review* 111, 116. See also J. O'Connell and B. Kelly, *The Blame Game* (Lexington Books, 1987), 130–5.

[25] *Ibid.*, at 117 (O'Connell's emphasis).

for pain and suffering. There is no equivalent problem in England where non-pecuniary loss awards are, as with all damages, nearly always assessed by judges not juries, and where such awards are relatively easy to predict and, if anything, are too low rather than too high.[26]

Although I have given some thought as to how the details of O'Connell's plan could be reworked to avoid such deficiencies, it is not easy to see how this could be achieved. Nevertheless the main point for the purposes of this essay is that adoption of the "early offer" plan would be far preferable to Atiyah's "look-after-yourself-through-insurance" proposal. O'Connell's plan shows that even the most committed of tort critics can be interested in developing reform proposals that do not involve abolishing tort.

6. CONCLUSION

The debate about the merits of the tort system will not go away. For lawyers and policy-makers the issues raised represent a fascinating challenge that goes to the very heart of our civil justice system. In England Patrick Atiyah has been the central figure leading the fight for reform of tort. His abolition proposals of the 1970s did not find favour. His 1990s proposals for scrapping personal injury tort claims and leaving victims to self-insure are even less likely to be well-received. In this essay, I have sought to defend the tort system, against its critics, as a system of individual responsibility. This is not to deny that changes are required. I have looked at possible reforms. But those reforms do not involve scrapping the tort system. Alongside contract and restitution, tort should and, I believe, will remain a fundamental feature of our law of obligations in the twenty-first century.

[26] See 183–4 below.

7

Legislative Reform of Remedies for Breach of Contract

I. INTRODUCTION

The English and Scottish Law Commissions have a close working relationship. Indeed some projects are, formally, joint projects of both Commissions and recommend legislative reforms for both sides of the Border.

The stimulus for this essay was the Scottish Law Commission's desire to identify any areas of the Scottish law on remedies for breach of contract that are ripe for legislative reform or clarification. As an English Law Commissioner, I have found it of great interest and help to pay close attention to the work of law reform bodies in other jurisdictions. I therefore thought that it would be of general interest—as well as being of some specific assistance to the Scottish Law Commission—to examine those areas of remedies for breach of contract that are, or have been, the subject of review by the English Law Commission. These are, in the order in which I deal with them[1]: exemplary, restitutionary, and mental distress damages for breach of contract; contributory negligence as a defence to breach of contract;

---

[1] In addition to the projects discussed in this essay the Law Commission was the guiding force behind the Law of Property (Miscellaneous Provisions) Act 1989, s. 3 abolishing the anachronistic rule in *Bain* v. *Fothergill* (1874) LR 7 HL 158: see Law Com. No. 166. The Law Commission has also produced a Report on *Pecuniary Restitution on Breach of Contract*, Law Com. No. 121: but in my view that work deals with the autonomous law of restitution and is not concerned with remedies for breach of contract (see below at 140–1). For similar reasons I shall also not be discussing the Civil Liability (Contribution) Act 1978 which implemented *Law of Contract: Report on Contribution* (Law Com. No. 79, 1977). I shall also not be discussing the Common Law Team of the Law Commission's work on joint and several liability, which is directed at all causes of action (including breach of contract): see 174–9 below. One should also note that in its early days the Law Commission worked on the whole law of contract with the intention of codifying it. A draft code was drawn up by Harvey McGregor QC and has relatively recently been published: see H. McGregor, *Contract Code drawn up on behalf of the English Law Commission* (Giuffré Editore and Sweet & Maxwell, 1993) dealing with remedies at 87–166.

interest on late payment of contractual debts; damages in contracts for the benefit of third parties; penalty clauses; and limitation periods.

Before proceeding any further I should explain that, perhaps oddly for a Law Commissioner, I am not a great fan of legislative reform of the non-criminal common law. I have too much faith in the judiciary, and too much love of the deductive technique of common law development to wish to see the law frozen by widespread legislative intervention. In my view legislative reform of the law of obligations ought normally to be confined to situations where the law is either already based on statute (e.g. the law on limitation periods or the Fatal Accidents Act 1976) or where the common law has plainly taken a wrong turn so that, short of waiting for an enlightened decision of the House of Lords, there is no other way of getting the law back on the right track (e.g. the law on restitution of payments under a mistake of law or on contracts for the benefit of third parties). In particular, I am far from convinced that it is sensible for there to be a legislative codification of areas of the law like contract, tort or restitution. The role of clarifying and rationalising—and hence codifying—wide areas of the common law is, in my view, generally best left to individual academics through the writing of books, or to learned bodies, such as the American Law Institute, through the publication of non-binding *"Restatements"*. Non-binding codes are invaluable. Binding codes are dangerous. This point is all the more pertinent now that we see an increasing willingness on behalf of the English judiciary (I cannot speak for Scottish judges) to take account of academic writings. The prospects of outstanding academic work—or a non-binding code—being ignored by the appellate courts are fast diminishing. In my opinion a binding code would tend to destroy that new working relationship.

2. THE STRUCTURE OF THE ENGLISH LAW ON JUDICIAL REMEDIES FOR BREACH OF CONTRACT

I would like first to give the flavour of the structure of the English law on judicial remedies for breach of contract by identifying a number of issues at differing levels of generality. This will also serve the purpose of putting into context several of the reform issues that I shall be examining in detail.

At a high level of generality, one can say that there are six main purposes that might be pursued by judicial remedies for breach of contract: compensation, specific enforcement, prevention, declaring rights, restitution and punishment. Of these six, English law pursues the first four but not the last two. A question of importance here, therefore, is whether English law should award restitutionary and/or punitive damages for breach of contract. I shall come back to this later.

Another question at this level is whether a plaintiff has a free choice between claiming specific enforcement or compensation. In English law the answer is "no". The enforcement of positive obligations (other than payments already owed) through the remedy of specific performance is secondary to compensation; i.e. a plaintiff is only entitled to specific performance (and then subject to further bars, such as "no specific performance of contracts for personal service") where compensatory damages would be inadequate.[2] In essence this boils down to an insistence that a plaintiff is not entitled to specific performance where he or she could reasonably mitigate some or all of his or her loss. This, as I have always understood it, contrasts with the position in civilian jurisdictions, such as Scotland, where specific implement is the primary remedy, although I suspect that the difference is not as clear-cut as it is often alleged to be. One also notes, in this respect, the contrast between enforcement through specific performance and enforcement of payments already owed through the separate remedy of an award of an agreed sum (sometimes referred to as an action in debt). In respect of the latter there is no insistence that damages first be shown to be inadequate i.e. a plaintiff is entitled to the award of an agreed sum whether or not he or she could reasonably have mitigated some or all of its loss from non-performance.[3] Having said that, the sharpness of the contrast is blunted by dicta and decisions to the effect that a plaintiff loses the entitlement to the award of an agreed sum where its failure to mitigate would be "*wholly unreasonable*".[4]

If one then moves down the scale of generality to focus on compensation (i.e. compensatory damages) as the primary remedial purpose, a further series of questions arises. The first concerns the aim of the compensation; should it be to put the plaintiff into as good a

---

[2] See A. Burrows, *Remedies for Torts and Breach of Contract* (2nd edn., Butterworths, 1994) ch. 8.

[3] The leading case remains *White & Carter (Councils) Ltd* v. *McGregor* [1962] AC 413.

[4] See, e.g., *The Odenfeld* [1978] 2 Lloyd's Rep. 357; *Clea Shipping Corpn.* v. *Bulk Oil International Ltd* [1984] 1 All ER 129. See also Lord Reid's reference to where the plaintiff has "no legitimate interest" in the performance of the contract in the *White & Carter* case itself: [1962] AC 413, 431.

position as if the contract had been performed; or into as good a position as if no contract had been made. In other words, should one be protecting the plaintiff's expectation or reliance interest?[5] The answer given by English law is that the aim should be to protect the plaintiff's expectation interest. Nevertheless, a plaintiff can opt to frame his claim as one for protection of his reliance interest and thereby throw onto the defendant the burden of proving that the claim exceeds the plaintiff's expectation interest.[6] Put another way, a plaintiff cannot escape from a proven bad bargain by claiming protection of his reliance interest. This is correct in principle precisely because it is the breaking of a promise, disappointing the plaintiff's expectations, that renders the defendant's conduct wrongful. This contrasts with damages for tortious misrepresentation where the aim is to protect the plaintiff's reliance interest because the very objection is that the defendant ought not to have induced the plaintiff to rely on an untrue statement.[7]

Having opted for the expectation measure of compensation, three further issues arise. The first is whether, when the two differ (typically in contracts for work on one's land) a plaintiff is free to choose between an assessment of the expectation measure according to "difference in value" (i.e. the difference in the plaintiff's financial position with and without the contracted-for performance) and an assessment of the expectation measure according to the "cost of care" (i.e. what it would cost the plaintiff to complete or rectify the defective performance). I shall return to this later when I examine the important recent decision of the House of Lords in *Ruxley Electronics and Construction Ltd* v. *Forsyth*.[8]

The second—and a woefully unexplored issue in the context of damages for breach of contract—is how does the law deal with compensating advantages or, as they are often misleadingly termed, "collateral benefits"? I shall tangentially touch on this later when discussing contracts for the benefit of third parties.

[5] This terminology derives from L. Fuller and W.R. Perdue, "The Reliance Interest in Contract Damages" (1936–7) 46 *Yale LJ* 52 and 373.
[6] *C. & P. Haulage* v. *Middleton* [1983] 3 All ER 94; *CCC Films (London)* v. *Impact Quadrant Films Ltd* [1984] 3 All ER 298. See also the important but difficult Australian case of *Commonwealth of Australia* v. *Amann Aviation Pty. Ltd* (1991) 66 ALJR 123.
[7] See A. Burrows, *Remedies for Torts and Breach of Contract* (2nd edn., Butterworths, 1994) 172–6.
[8] [1995] 3 All ER 268.

The third issue is what are the principles and rules limiting compensatory damages?; i.e. in what respects does English law not fully protect the plaintiff's expectation interest? There are at least six limiting concepts, each of them spawning its own voluminous case law on where the precise limits are being drawn. The six are: remoteness, intervening cause,[9] the duty to mitigate, contributory negligence, and where the "loss" comprises either mental distress or the loss of an existing reputation.[10] I shall be returning to mental distress, contributory negligence and remoteness in due course.

In diagram form, the structure of English judicial remedies may be represented as follows:

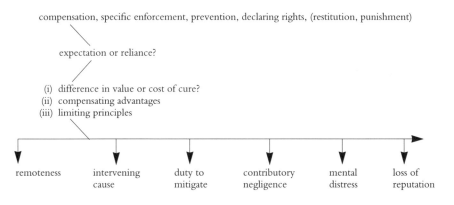

compensation, specific enforcement, prevention, declaring rights, (restitution, punishment)

expectation or reliance?

(i) difference in value or cost of cure?
(ii) compensating advantages
(iii) limiting principles

| remoteness | intervening cause | duty to mitigate | contributory negligence | mental distress | loss of reputation |

3. EXEMPLARY, RESTITUTIONARY, AND MENTAL DISTRESS DAMAGES FOR BREACH OF CONTRACT

In December 1997 the Law Commission published its Report on *Aggravated, Exemplary and Restitutionary Damages*,[11] following a consultation paper in 1994, and a short supplementary consultation paper in 1995 seeking views on three main options for the reform of

---

[9] For an interesting fairly recent decision on this principle, see *Galoo Ltd* v. *Bright Grahame Murray* [1994] 1 WLR 1360 in which the Court of Appeal held that an auditor's breach of contract in negligently auditing the plaintiff companies' accounts was not the effective cause of their trading losses and insolvency.

[10] Even where the loss of reputation comprises a pecuniary loss the courts generally deny damages in contract on the basis that this is the effect of *Addis* v. *Gramophone Co. Ltd* [1909] AC 488; see, e.g., the disappointing decision of the Court of Appeal in *O'Laoire* v. *Jackel International Ltd (No. 2)* [1991] ICR 718. For criticism of this restrictive approach, see Burrows, n. 7 above, 221–5. See now the enlightened House of Lords decision in *Malik* v. *Bank of Credit and Commerce International SA* [1997] 3 WLR 95.

[11] Law Com No. 247 (1997). See 169–71 below.

exemplary (i.e. punitive) damages. It should be stressed immediately that the main focus of this work is on torts and not breach of contract. Here, however, I shall concentrate on breach of contract.

(i) *Exemplary Damages*

Dealing first with exemplary damages, the standard position in English law is that, whatever the position in tort, no exemplary damages can be awarded for breach of contract. The leading authority is *Addis* v. *Gramophone Co. Ltd*[12] in which, following the harsh and humiliating wrongful dismissal of the plaintiff, the House of Lords refused to award any damages (including it should be noted mental distress damages) for the manner in which he had been dismissed. Rather, the damages were to cover only the plaintiff's pecuniary loss.

The main issue with which the Law Commission's work is concerned is whether the law on exemplary damages *for torts* as laid down in *Rookes* v. *Barnard*[13] should be reformed. As a reflection of the views of most consultees to the main consultation paper, we clarified in the supplementary consultation paper and confirmed in the Report, that we would not be recommending the expansion of exemplary damages to claims for breach of contract.[14] I suspect that this will meet with approval North of the border for, as I understand it, exemplary damages are not available in Scottish law.

(ii) *Restitutionary Damages*

It is perhaps less obvious what should be done about restitutionary damages for breach of contract. In general the position, as with exemplary damages, is that restitution cannot be awarded for a breach of contract. This needs a little explanation. The question is whether a remedy should be given requiring the defendant to disgorge gains made by a breach of contract. Restitutionary remedies, such as the recovery of money had and received and a quantum meruit, which an innocent party can claim once he or she has validly terminated a contract for breach, are better viewed as remedies within the autonomous law of restitution based on reversing an unjust enrich-

---

[12] [1909] AC 488. See also, e.g., *Perera* v. *Vandiyar* [1953] 1 WLR 672.
[13] [1964] AC 1129.
[14] See the Report, Law Com. 247, 1997, paras. 5.71–5.73.

ment by subtraction; they are not remedies *for* the wrong of breach of contract.[15] This explains why it is no restriction on the recovery of money paid in an action for money had and received that the defendant had made a good bargain. Say, for example, the plaintiff contracts to buy a car from the defendant for £900 and pays £100 in advance; the defendant fails to deliver the car: the market price is £700: the plaintiff can recover £100 in an action for money had and received.[16] This cannot be sensibly explained if the recovery is regarded as a restitutionary remedy *for* the breach of contract: for the breach cannot be regarded as a cause of the defendant's gain, since if there had been no breach, the defendant would still have made that gain from the contract. In contrast the law is readily explicable if one regards such restitutionary remedies as falling within autonomous unjust enrichment by subtraction rather than unjust enrichment by wrongs; for if the basis is not breach of contract, but rather an invalidation of the shift of wealth from the plaintiff to the defendant, there is no necessary reason why the value of the defendant's contractual counter-performance should be regarded as relevant.

So confining ourselves to restitution *for* breach of contract, it can readily be seen that in general English law does not award restitution. In *Tito* v. *Waddell* (*No. 2*),[17] where the defendants broke their covenant to replant an island in the Pacific after mining operations, Sir Robert Megarry VC thought it irrelevant to consider the expense the defendants had saved themselves. He said, "It is fundamental to all questions of damages that they are to compensate the plaintiff for his loss or injury by putting him as nearly as possible in the same position as he would have been in had he not suffered the wrong. The question is not one of making the defendant disgorge what he has saved by committing the wrong, but one of compensating the plaintiff".[18]

So in that case it was irrelevant that the defendants had saved themselves considerable expense by not replanting Ocean Island as they had covenanted to do. The plaintiff's loss was alone considered relevant, and as the islanders no longer intended to replant the island, and were therefore not entitled to the cost of cure, a small sum of damages for the trivial difference in the value of the land was awarded

---

[15] P. Birks, *An Introduction to the Law of Restitution* (Clarendon Press, 1985) 334; Burrows, n. 7 above, 307–8. See also 22–4 above.

[16] *Wilkinson* v. *Lloyd* (1845) 7 QB 27; *Ebrahim Dawood Ltd* v. *Heath* (*Est. 1927*) *Ltd* [1961] 2 Lloyd's Rep. 512.

[17] [1977] Ch. 106.

[18] *Ibid*. at 332.

(i.e. the difference between the value it would have had if replanted and its present value).[19]

Again in the leading case of *Surrey CC* v. *Bredero Homes Ltd*[20] the Court of Appeal refused to award restitutionary damages for a breach of contract, whether assessed according to the full profits made by the breach by the contract-breaker or according to the expense saved by the contract-breaker in not seeking a release from its contractual undertaking. The plaintiff councils had sold two adjoining parcels of land to the defendant for the development of a housing estate. The defendant covenanted to develop the land in accordance with the scheme approved by the plaintiffs. In breach of that covenant it built more houses on the site than under the approved scheme thereby making extra profit. Although aware of the breach, the plaintiffs did not seek an injunction or specific performance but waited until the defendant had sold all the houses on the estate and then sought damages. Nominal damages only were awarded on the ground that the plaintiffs had suffered no loss and restitutionary damages were inappropriate because this was an action for ordinary common law damages for breach of contract: it did not involve either a tort or an invasion of proprietary rights or equitable damages.

The reference to proprietary rights and equitable damages reflects the fact that in the earlier case of *Wrotham Park Estate Co. Ltd* v. *Parkside Homes Ltd*[21] Brightman J did award damages, that are best rationalised as restitutionary,[22] for breach of a restrictive covenant preventing the building of houses that was enforceable in equity by the plaintiffs.

It is further noteworthy that where a breach of contract also constitutes the tort of trespass (as in *Penarth Dock Engineering Co. Ltd* v. *Pounds*[23]), or a breach of confidence (as in *A.-G.* v. *Guardian Newspapers Ltd* (*No. 2*) (*"Spycatcher"*)[24]) or a breach of fiduciary duty

---

[19] An interim sum, which it was argued the plaintiffs would have accepted for releasing the defendants from their obligation, was also rejected, *ibid.* at 319.

[20] [1993] 3 All ER 705. See on this case: R. O'Dair, "Remedies for Breach of Contract: A Wrong Turn" [1993] *RLR* 31; A. Burrows, "No Restitutionary Damages for Breach of Contract" [1993] *LMCLQ* 453; P. Birks, "Profits of Breach of Contract" (1993) 109 *LQR* 518; S. Smith, "Of Remedies and Restrictive Covenants" (1994) *JCL* 164.

[21] [1974] 1 WLR 798.

[22] The restitutionary interpretation is strongly supported by Steyn LJ in *Surrey CC* v. *Bredero Homes Ltd* [1993] 3 All ER 705, 714. But the contrary view, favouring a compensatory analysis (based on loss of bargaining opportunity) has been taken by the Court of Appeal in *Jaggard* v. *Sawyer* [1995] 1 WLR 269 in awarding compensatory damages for trespass and breach of a restrictive covenant.

[23] [1963] 1 Lloyd's Rep. 359.

[24] [1988] 3 All ER 545.

(as in *Reading* v. *A.-G.*[25]) restitution may be awarded for those other causes of action, in the latter two cases through the award of an account of profits.[26]

It would seem, therefore, that, while restitution may be available where a breach of contract also constitutes a proprietary wrong (whether breach of a restrictive covenant or a tort) or an equitable wrong, restitution is not available for a pure breach of contract.[27] And that denial is, of course, supported in Scotland by the well-known case of *Teacher* v. *Calder.*[28]

If we turn to academic thinking as to what the law ought to be, we find a myriad of different views, including the following:

—the Goff and Jones radically wide view that restitution should essentially be available wherever a gain has been made that would not have been made but for the breach of contract;[29]
—the central Birksian "moralistic" view that restitution should be available where the breach of contract was cynical;[30]
—the view that restitution should be available where damages are inadequate;[31]
—the Beatson approach that restitution is a form of "monetised specific performance" so that it should be available where specific performance (or an injunction) would have been awarded;[32]

[25] [1951] AC 507.

[26] Or even through the imposition of a constructive trust, following the controversial decision in *A.-G. for Hong Kong* v. *Reid* [1994] 1 AC 324. See on that case, R.A. Pearce, "Personal and Proprietary Claims against Bribees" [1994] *LMCLQ* 189; D. Crilley, "A Case of Proprietary Overkill" [1994] *RLR* 57.

[27] [But this restrictive approach has been thrown into doubt by the dicta of the Court of Appeal in *Attorney-General* v. *Blake*, [1998] 1 All ER 833. favouring restitutionary damages for breach of contract in at least two situations: "skimped performance" (i.e. where the defendant fails to provide the full extent of the services contracted for) or where the defendant has obtained his profit by doing the very thing he contracted not to do. The Court of Appeal (Lord Woolf MR, Millett and Mummery LJJ) said, "it appears to us that the general rule that damages for breach of contract are compensatory can safely be maintained without denying the availability of restitutionary damages in exceptional cases."]

[28] (1899) 1 F 39.

[29] R. Goff and G. Jones, *The Law of Restitution* (4th edn., Sweet & Maxwell, 1993), 414–17; G. Jones, "The Recovery of Benefits Gained from a Breach of Contract" (1983) 99 *LQR* 443.

[30] Birks, n. 15 above, 334; "Restitutionary Damages for Breach of Contract: *Snepp* and the Fusion of Law and Equity" [1987] *LMCLQ* 421.

[31] P.D. Maddaugh and J.D. McCamus, *The Law of Restitution* (Canada Law Book, 1990), 436–8. See also R. O'Dair, "Restitutionary Damages for Breach of Contract and the Theory of Efficient Breach: Some Reflections" (1993) 46(2) *CLP* 113.

[32] *The Use and Abuse of Unjust Enrichment* (Clarendon Press, 1991), 17. See also S.M. Waddams in Burrows (ed.), *Essays on the Law of Restitution* (Clarendon Press, 1991), 208–12.

—the view that restitution should never be available for breach of contract *per se*. Jackman, for example, has argued that while restitution is justified as a means of protecting the "facilitative institution" of private property, it is not needed to protect the facilitative institution of contract because expectation damages already do that.[33] Denying restitution for breach of contract is also the approach associated with those who consider that contract should, and does, promote economic efficiency: it is more economically efficient to allow breach of contract than to deter it as restitution would *prima facie* do.[34]

Nowadays, having argued for a mid-position that, on reflection, I think is probably flawed,[35] I am unsure what the best way forward is on this complex issue.

When it comes to restitution for torts there appears to be more of a consensus that restitutionary damages are sometimes justified. In particular there appears to be a widely shared view that where a tort is committed in deliberate disregard of the plaintiff's rights, the defendant ought not to be allowed to keep the ill-gotten gains. This is reflected in the law on some of the intellectual property torts[36] and may also be said to be the true justification of the second category of exemplary damages recognised in *Rookes* v. *Barnard*. On the other hand, a number of cases also suggest that there is a good case for restitutionary damages, irrespective of whether a tort is committed cynically, where the tort in question involves an infringement of the plaintiff's proprietary rights, e.g. trespass to land.[37]

What is one to make of all this from the perspective of statutory law reform?

If one was an ardent believer in legislation one might wish to enter the fray and to resolve the uncertainty by laying down definitively when restitution is available for a tort and whether and, if so, when restitution is available for a breach of contract. As a legislation sceptic, I favour the opposite approach. Given that the idea of restitution

[33] "Restitution for Wrongs" [1989] *CLJ* 302.

[34] For this general theory, see R.A. Posner, *Economic Analysis of Law* (3rd edn., Little, Brown & Co., 1986), 107.

[35] I.e. that the law could legitimately award restitution, depriving the defendant of the expense saved by breach, but should not strip away (other) profits made by breach: see A. Burrows, *Remedies for Torts and Breach of Contract* (1st edn., Butterworths, 1987), 273 and for why flawed see the second edn. at 310.

[36] See, e.g., *Edelsten* v. *Edelsten* (1863) 1 De GJ & SM 185 (infringement of trade mark).

[37] The most important case on restitution for the tort of trespass is now *Ministry of Defence* v. *Ashman* [1993] 40 EG 144.

for wrongs has only recently been analysed and understood by academics, and as the law's development on this front is similarly in its infancy, I think it would be premature to imagine that legislation is a better way to proceed than incremental development by the judiciary. This is particularly so in the realm of breach of contract where, as we have seen, a law reformer cannot turn to a settled academic consensus for assistance. So, in general, my own view is that we should leave this area to the courts, in the expectation that the judges will derive some assistance, in deciding the cases before them, from the academic writings.[38]

A final point of interest is whether one could consistently abhor exemplary damages while accepting restitutionary damages. I think one could. The objection to exemplary damages is essentially that they duplicate the criminal law, the essence of which is punishment. In contrast one cannot say that the essence of the criminal law is restitution. Again, although both restitutionary and exemplary damages represent a windfall to the plaintiff, there is the difference that, if restitution is not awarded, the wrongdoer will himself or herself be left with a windfall, whereas punishment is applicable irrespective of any windfall to the defendant.

(iii) *Damages for Mental Distress*

An initial question is whether it makes sense to say, as is often said, that while damages for mental distress can sometimes be awarded for breach of contract, aggravated damages can never be awarded for breach of contract? I would argue that this does not make much sense. Aggravated damages are available for some wrongs where a plaintiff's damages for mental distress/injured feelings/insult etc. are increased because of the exceptional conduct of the defendant, either at the time of the wrong or even subsequent to it. But such damages should be seen as a sub-category of mental distress damages and, if mental distress damages are available at all, it is absurd to ignore the heightened mental distress caused by the defendant's conduct in respect of some wrongs but not in respect of others. I would therefore suggest that the best way forward is, first, to recognise that

---

[38] See *Aggravated, Exemplary and Restitutionary Damages*, Law Com. No. 247, 1997, paras. 3.38–3.57 recommending that legislative reforms on restitutionary damages should be confined to those necessary as a consequence of our proposed reforms on punitive damages. See also 171 below.

aggravated damages are a category of mental distress damages;
secondly, to abandon the label "aggravated damages"; and thirdly, to
recognise that wherever mental distress damages are available for a
tort or breach of contract the extent of the compensatable mental distress may be heightened (or diminished) by the defendant's conduct
at the time of the wrong or subsequently.

The situations in which one can recover damages for mental distress for breach of contract have stabilised in recent years in England.
It is now clear that they are recoverable in two situations only. First
and most important is where the predominant object of the contract,
from the plaintiff's point of view, was to obtain mental satisfaction,
whether enjoyment or relief from distress. The ruined holiday cases,
such as *Jarvis* v. *Swan's Tours*[39] and *Jackson* v. *Horizon Holidays*[40] most
obviously fall within this. So does *Heywood* v. *Wellers*,[41] where the
defendant solicitors, in breach of their contractual duty of care, had
failed to gain an injunction to stop molestation of the plaintiff by her
former boyfriend; and so does the influential Scottish case of *Diesen*
v. *Samson*[42] in which mental distress damages were awarded for the
defender's breach of contract in failing to appear at a wedding to take
photographs.

One should also add here the award for lost amenity of £2,500
awarded to Mr Forsyth in *Ruxley Electronics and Construction Ltd* v.
Forsyth.[43] Mr Forsyth had contracted to have a swimming pool built
in his garden with a depth at the deep end of 7′6″. When built the
pool was in fact only 6′9″ at the deep end. Nevertheless it was still
perfectly safe for diving into so that the difference in resale value of
the property was not affected by the admitted breach of contract. To
increase the depth of the pool to the agreed depth would cost
£21,560 (nearly a third of the total price of the pool). Overturning
the Court of Appeal, the House of Lords refused to award Mr Forsyth
the cost of cure of £21,560; that would be unreasonable, given the
contrast with the nil difference in value and, particularly importantly,

---

[39] [1973] QB 233.

[40] [1975] 1 WLR 1468. See also *Hunt* v. *Hourmont* [1983] CLY 983; and for unreported
Court of Appeal decisions, see (1983) 80 LS Gaz. 1429.

[41] [1976] QB 446. See also *McLeish* v. *Amoo-Gottfield & Co.* (1993) 137 Sol. Jo. LB 204.
Cf. *Dickinson* v. *Jones Alexander & Co.* [1990] Fam. Law 137 (which is controversial because
the wife's mental distress consequent on the negligent handling of her financial claims surely
fell outside this first category).

[42] 1971 SLT 49. See also *Reed* v. *Madon* [1989] 2 All ER 432 (contract of exclusive burial
rights).

[43] [1995] 3 All ER 268.

given the first instance judge's finding that Mr Forsyth had no intention to use the damages to rebuild the pool. This approach was in accordance with a line of English authorities stressing the importance—in deciding between a cost of cure and a significantly lower difference in value—of whether the plaintiff intended to effect the cure.[44] But rather than awarding Mr Forsyth no damages at all for the breach the House of Lords upheld the first instance judge's award of damages of £2,500 for loss of pleasure; and this is best rationalised as flowing from the fact that the plaintiff's primary object in specifying the particular depth for the pool was mental satisfaction.

A second situation in which mental distress damages can be awarded for breach of contract is where the plaintiff's mental distress is directly consequent on physical inconvenience caused by the defendant's breach of contract. Hence in *Perry* v. *Sidney Phillips & Son*[45] and *Watts* v. *Morrow*,[46] mental distress damages for the distress and inconvenience of living in poor accommodation, purchased as a result of negligent surveys, were awarded against surveyors for breach of contract.

In the latter case, Bingham LJ neatly summarised the general position in contract as follows: "A contract-breaker is not in general liable for any distress, frustration, anxiety, displeasure, vexation, tension or aggravation which his breach of contract may cause to the innocent party. The rule is not, I think, founded on the assumption that such reactions are not foreseeable, which they surely are or may be, but on considerations of policy. But the rule is not absolute. Where the very object of a contract is to provide pleasure, relaxation, peace of mind or freedom from molestation, damages will be awarded if the fruit of the contract is not provided or if the contrary result is procured instead. If the law did not cater for this exceptional category of case it would be defective. A contract to survey the condition of a house for a prospective purchaser does not, however, fall within this exceptional category. In cases not falling within this exceptional category, damages are in my view recoverable for physical inconvenience and

---

[44] See, e.g., *Tito* v. *Waddell (No. 2)* [1977] Ch. 106; *Radford* v. *De Froberville* [1977] 1 WLR 1262; *Dean* v. *Ainley* [1987] 3 All ER 748 (although the contrary view was taken by Kerr LJ in that case). These cases are also consistent with *Sealace Shipping Co. Ltd* v. *Oceanvoice Ltd, The Alecos M* [1991] 1 Lloyd's Rep. 120, CA.

[45] [1982] 1 WLR 1297. See also *McCall* v. *Abelesz* [1976] QB 585; *Buckley* v. *Lane Herdman & Co.* [1977] CLY 3143; *Calabar Properties* v. *Stitcher* [1984] 3 All ER 759; *Lubren* v. *London Borough of Lambeth* (1988) 20 HLR 165; *Cross* v. *David Martin & Mortimer* [1989] 1 EGLR 154; *Bigg* v. *Howard Son & Gooch* [1990] 1 EGLR 173.

[46] [1991] 1 WLR 1421.

discomfort caused by the breach and mental suffering directly related to that inconvenience and discomfort".[47]

In terms of policy and principle it has to be doubted whether the restriction to just the two exceptional categories should be maintained.[48] For while the first exceptional category perhaps presents the strongest claim for such relief since mental distress damages there reflect the "consumer surplus"[49] (namely the particular value to the plaintiff of the contractual performance over and above its objective market value), the compensatory principle dictates that mental distress caused by the breach of contract should always be compensated, subject to the usual limiting principles like remoteness. After all, the confusion between exemplary and mental distress damages has been clearly exposed in cases like *Rookes* v. *Barnard*[50] and, while assessing damages is difficult for mental distress, it is no more difficult than for other non-pecuniary losses. Similarly, the fact that mental distress is difficult to prove should not deter the courts, since if the plaintiff cannot establish that she has suffered mental distress that is not *de minimis*, she should recover no damages. Certainly in many other jurisdictions there has been a greater willingness to award mental distress damages.[51] Finally it should be realised that even if mental distress damages were freely available, it would not be correct to imagine that they would figure in almost every contractual damages claim, for often the plaintiff is not a human person, but is, for example, a company which is incapable of experiencing mental distress.[52]

Again while I would not favour legislation which would lay down precisely when mental distress damages in contract are available I think there is a case for minimal legislation to sort out the confusion caused by the "aggravated damages" label.[53]

[47] [1991] 1 WLR at 1445.

[48] The general bar on damages for mental distress is taken to have been laid down in *Addis* v. *Gramophone Co. Ltd* [1909] AC 488. The New Zealand Law Commission recommended reform of *Addis* in Report No. 18; *Aspects of Damages: Employment Contracts and the Rule in Addis v. Gramophone Co.* (1991).

[49] D. Harris, A.I. Ogus and J. Phillips, "Contract Remedies and the Consumer Surplus" (1979) 95 *LQR* 581.

[50] [1964] AC 1129.

[51] For Canadian cases, see S.M. Waddams, *The Law of Damages* (2nd edn., Canada Law Book Co., 1991), paras. 3.1310–3.1450. For the USA, see *Second Restatement of Contracts*, s. 353. And for New Zealand, see the excellent decision of Thomas J in *Rowlands* v. *Collow* [1992] 1 NZLR 178.

[52] *Contra* is *Messenger Newspapers Group Ltd* v. *National Graphical Association* [1984] IRLR 397.

[53] See Report, Law Com. No. 247, 1997, paras. 2.39–2.43. See 171 below.

4. CONTRIBUTORY NEGLIGENCE AS A DEFENCE TO BREACH OF CONTRACT

This is an area in which over the past ten years—and in entirely separate projects—both the English and the Scottish Law Commission have completed work.[54] Yet, although each Commission has arrived at similar recommendations for reform, neither of the relevant draft bills (or parts of bills) has yet been implemented.

The question at issue is this; if a plaintiff has been partly at fault for his own loss can, and should, damages for the defendant's breach of contract be reduced?

It is important to stress that contributory negligence leads to a reduction of damages, proportionate to the parties' respective fault, in contrast, for example, to the duty to mitigate and intervening cause which are all or nothing restrictions. The contributory negligence defence is entirely contained in the Law Reform (Contributory Negligence) Act 1945 and, while it is clear that the defence applies to nearly all torts and, in particular, to the most important tort of negligence, it is now clear that, subject to where there is concurrent liability with tort, it does not apply to breach of contract.

In accordance with the leading cases of *Forsikringsaktieselskapet Vesta* v. *Butcher*[55] and *Barclays Bank plc* v. *Fairclough Building Ltd*[56] cases are divided into three categories.

> A category 1 case is where the defendant has been in breach of a strict contractual duty;
> A category 2 case is where the defendant has been in breach of contractual duty of care;
> A category 3 case is where the defendant has been in breach of contractual duty of care and is also liable in the tort of negligence.

According to *Vesta* v. *Butcher* (although, strictly speaking the discussion was only *obiter dicta*) it is in a category 3 case only that contributory negligence can apply to breach of contract. In *Barclays Bank Ltd* v. *Fairclough Building Ltd*, while the Court of Appeal accepted that contributory negligence was applicable in a category 3 case, the main

---

[54] *Contributory Negligence as a Defence in Contract* (1993) Law Com. No. 219 (proposing a Contributory Negligence Bill); *Report on Civil Liability—Contribution* (1988) Scot. Law Com. No. 115 (proposing a Contribution in Damages (Scotland) Bill, Part II of which would deal with Contributory Negligence).
[55] [1989] AC 852 (CA), aff'd. on a different point [1989] AC 880 (HL).
[56] [1994] 3 WLR 1057.

point of the decision was that it is not applicable in a category 1 case: nothing was said about a category 2 case.

This state of affairs is patently unsatisfactory. It stems from the fact that the definition of fault in the 1945 Act is geared towards tort, not contract.[57] It cannot be rational for the question whether contributory negligence is applicable in contract to turn on whether the defendant is also liable for the tort of negligence. Indeed it encourages an odd reversal of roles, in that a blameworthy plaintiff will be better off, as regards contributory negligence, if it can establish that the defendant was merely liable for breach of a contractual duty of care (or the breach of a strict contractual duty) and was not also liable for the tort of negligence. In other words, as far as contributory negligence is concerned, the plaintiff will be trying to show that the defendant was not also liable in the tort of negligence, while the defendant will be trying to show that he was also liable in the tort of negligence.

Although one might argue that in pure principle contributory negligence ought to apply to all three categories of breach,[58] both the Law Commission and the Scottish Law Commission steered clear of that and recommended the uncontroversial reform of extending contributory negligence to breach of a contractual duty of care (i.e. to category 2).

Now it is true that, since the House of Lords' acceptance of concurrent liability in *Henderson* v. *Merrett Syndicates Ltd*,[59] and the confirmation in that and other cases[60] that the recovery of pure economic loss in the tort of negligence is still alive, there is little, if any prospect, of a case falling within category 2 but outside category 3. The fact remains that the present approach is needlessly contorted. The reversal of roles ought not to be necessary; and the ebbing and flowing of the tort of negligence should not be affecting the ambit of contributory negligence in contract. If, as we believe it to be, the Law Commission's remit is to make the law simpler and fairer, it must be sensible to amend the 1945 Act to make it clear that contributory

---

[57] "Fault" is defined in s. 4 of the Act as: "negligence, breach of statutory duty or other act or omission which gives rise to a liability in tort or would, apart from this Act, give rise to the defence of contributory negligence."

[58] See A. Burrows, *Remedies for Torts and Breach of Contract* (2nd edn., Butterworths, 1994), 80–7. This is also the position adopted in O. Lando and H. Beale, *Principles of European Contract Law* (Martinus Nijhoff, 1995), Art. 4.504.

[59] [1994] 3 WLR 761. See essay 2 above.

[60] See, esp., *White* v. *Jones* [1995] 2 WLR 187.

negligence should apply to reduce damages for the breach of a contractual duty of care.

5. INTEREST ON LATE PAYMENT OF CONTRACTUAL DEBTS

Leaving aside where there is a contract term dealing with the payment of interest, the law in England (in early 1998) on interest on agreed sums can be stated as follows:

(i) Following *London, Chatham & Dover Rly. Co.* v. *South Eastern Rly.*[61] and its confirmation in *President of India* v. *La Pintada Compania Navigavion SA*[62] no damages can be awarded at common law for the loss of the general use of the money during a delay before the agreed sum is paid i.e. loss of interest cannot be compensated by an award of damages. This contrasts with any "special loss" that has been suffered by the failure to pay the agreed sum: for example, in *Wadsworth* v. *Lydall*,[63] after the defendant failed to pay all the agreed sum, the plaintiff had to take out a mortgage loan in order to finance a contract to purchase some land and also incurred legal costs. He was awarded damages for the "costs" of the mortgage (i.e. the interest paid on the loan) and for his legal costs.

(ii) By section 35A of the Supreme Court Act 1981, a court has a discretion to award simple (not compound[64]) interest on agreed sums (from the date of the cause of action until the date of the judgment or payment) but there is no such discretion where the agreed sum was paid *before proceedings to recover it had begun*.

In 1978 in its Report on Interest[65] the Law Commission proposed legislation whereby, subject to contracting out, a creditor should have an automatic right to interest on an unpaid contractual debt. In cases where the date for payment was fixed by the contract, interest would run from that date. Where no such date had been fixed, interest should begin to run twenty-eight days after service on the debtor of a notice demanding payment.

This reform can be supported on a number of grounds:

---

[61] [1893] AC 429.

[62] [1985] AC 104.

[63] [1981] 1 WLR 598.

[64] This is an anomaly which the Law Commission probably should examine: see 199–201 below.

[65] Law Com. No. 88. Various other law reform bodies have looked at this issue: see most recently, for example, the New Zealand Law Commission's Report No. 28, *Aspects of Damages: The Award of Interest on Money Claims* (1994).

(i) It is correct in principle that a plaintiff should be compensated for its loss caused by the late payment of money.
(ii) Giving a right to interest, encourages prompt payment.
(iii) Late payments tend to increase prices to the detriment of everyone.
(iv) In nearly every country in Europe, a creditor has an automatic right to interest on an overdue debt.[66]

These arguments render the case for implementing the Law Commission's recommendations, or something similar, a very strong one. Yet those central proposals were initially rejected. The reasons for rejection given by the Government (in particular DTI) in 1980[67] included the following:

(i) Strong borrowers would remain able to resist paying interest (e.g. by contracting out, or by insisting on long credit periods, or simply by not paying). In contrast consumers would not.
(ii) The scheme would add to the antagonism that already frequently exists in commercial transactions.
(iii) There would be an unwarranted increase in paperwork for businesses.
(iv) There was wide resistance in the business-world to the proposals.

The issue resurfaced in November 1993 when the DTI published a Consultative Document *Late Payment of Commercial Debt*. Of the 360 replies received to that document, there was a small majority (55 per cent) in favour of a statutory right to interest, although many of these expressed qualified support.[68]

However, in its White Paper on "Competitiveness"[69] the Conservative Government again decided against legislation on the central issue, preferring instead measures such as (i) requiring public companies to state their payment policies in their directors' reports; (ii) helping small businesses to improve their credit management by

---

[66] See also the Recommendation of the Commission of the European Communities dated 30 Nov. 1994. This is also supported by the *Principles of European Contract Law*, Art. 4.507; the *UNIDROIT Principles of International Commercial Contracts*, Art. 7.4.9; the Uniform Law of International Sales 1964, Art. 83 and the Vienna Convention on the International Sale of Goods 1980, Art. 78.

[67] As discussed with the Law Commission at a meeting in Nov. 1980.

[68] See the Government's White Paper on Competitiveness.

[69] May 1994.

work with business links, trade associations and others; and (iii) requiring government departments to endorse the principles of the CBI Prompt Payers Code, and to state in their annual reports whether they have observed the code. Nevertheless, the Government did not close its mind entirely on legislation. Rather, it committed itself to reviewing the case again in 1996.

Matters moved on with the election of the Labour Government in May 1997 with a commitment to legislate on a statutory right to interest. A DTI consultation paper, *A Statutory Right to Claim Interest on Late Payment of Commercial Debt*, was published in July 1997. The Late Payment of Commercial Debts (Interest) Bill was introduced in the House of Lords on 10 December 1997.[70]

6. DAMAGES IN CONTRACTS FOR THE BENEFIT OF THIRD PARTIES

We had to consider this issue in our work on *Privity of Contract: Contracts for the Benefit of Third Parties*.[71]

One of the options we considered, and rejected, is to reform the law on privity not by allowing a third party to sue but rather by allowing the contracting party to recover the third party's loss. This is not an adequate method of reform, *inter alia*, because the promisee may be unwilling or unable to enforce the contract. But a further question then arises: alongside the central reform, allowing a third party in certain circumstances to sue, should there be legislative reform of a promisee's remedies in a contract for a third party's benefit?

Under present law the promisee can in some circumstances enforce the promise for the benefit of the third party. The promisee may be able to obtain an order of specific performance (as in *Beswick* v. *Beswick*[72]) or, if the promisor's breach causes loss to the promisee, may obtain substantial damages (as in *Jackson* v. *Horizon Holidays*,[73] as explained in *Woodar Investment Development Ltd* v. *Wimpey Construction UK Ltd*[74]). If, however, the breach does not cause the promisee any loss and the case is not an appropriate one for specific

---

[70] The consequent Act seems likely to be passed before the Summer recess of 1998. The Bill gives creditors an automatic right to simple interest after thirty days on unpaid commercial debts.

[71] Consultation Paper No. 121 (1991). The Report, Law Com. No. 242, was published on 31 July 1996: see 166–8 below.

[72] [1968] AC 58.

[73] [1975] 1 WLR 1468.

[74] [1980] 1 WLR 277.

performance, there will be a difficulty. Normally, the promisee can recover only for his or her own loss, and this may mean that he or she will get only nominal damages even if there has been a substantial loss to the third party. The traditional view is also that the promisee will normally be unable to bring an action in debt to enforce payment to him or her of sums due to the third party under the contract, since those sums were by definition not due to the promisee.[75]

In recent years there have been important construction contract cases on this question of a promisee's remedies in a contract for a third party's benefit.

In *Linden Gardens Trust Ltd* v. *Lenesta Sludge Disposals Ltd*[76] the question arose as to the damages which could be recovered by a company (the "employer") which had contracted for work on its property (the removal of asbestos) but had then, before breach of the works contract, sold the property to a third party (to whom the employer had made an invalid assignment of its contractual rights). The House of Lords held that the employer could recover substantial damages— the cost of curing the defects in the work—despite the fact that it no longer had a proprietary interest in the property by the time of the breach and despite the fact that the cost of the repair had been borne by the assignee and not by the employer. The reasoning of the majority of their Lordships was that the employer could recover the third party's (the assignee's) loss on an application of the exceptional principle applicable to a changed ownership of property established by *Dunlop* v. *Lambert*[77] and *The Albazero*.[78] In *The Albazero* Lord Diplock explained the principle as follows: "In a commercial contract concerning goods where it is in the contemplation of the parties that the proprietary interests in the goods may be transferred from one owner to another after the contract has been entered into and before the breach which causes loss or damage to the goods, an original party to the contract, if such be the intention of them both, is to be treated in law as having entered into the contract for the benefit of all persons who have or may acquire an interest in the goods before they are lost or damaged, and is entitled to recover by way of damages for breach

---

[75] See *Chitty on Contracts* (27th edn., 1994), para. 18–030, and *Coulls* v. *Bagot's Executor and Trustee Co. Ltd* [1967] ALR 385, 411. *Quaere* whether the promisee can bring an action for sums due to the third party if the sums are to be paid direct to the third party rather than to the promisee: see Burrows, n. 2 above, 317.

[76] [1994] 1 AC 85.

[77] (1839) 6 Cl. & F 600.

[78] [1977] AC 774.

of contract the actual loss sustained by those for whose benefit the contract is entered into".[79] The only modification required for the application of this principle to *Linden Gardens* was that the property in question was land and buildings not goods. Note however that Lord Browne-Wilkinson in *Linden Gardens* confined the exception to cases where the third party had no direct right of action.

But Lord Griffiths decided *Linden Gardens* on a much wider basis. He took the controversial view—albeit it was a view with which the other Law Lords were sympathetic—that the employer had itself suffered a loss (measured by the cost of repairs) by reason of the breach of contract, in that it did not receive the bargain for which it had contracted: whether the employer did, or did not, have a proprietary interest in the subject matter of the contract at the date of breach was irrelevant. Nor did it matter to Lord Griffiths that it was the assignee, and not the employer, who had ultimately borne the cost of repairs for, according to Lord Griffiths, "The law regards who actually paid for the work necessary as a result of the defendant's breach of contract as a matter which is *res inter alios acta* so far as the defendant is concerned".[80]

All this raises certain difficulties:

(1) Applying either the majority view or Lord Griffiths' view, is the contracting party bound to pay over the damages recovered to the third party?

(2) If Lord Griffiths' view is correct, does it not lead to the position whereby, if the third party has the legal right to sue, as is sometimes the case in Scotland under the *ius quaesitum tertio*, the defendant is bound to pay substantial damages to both the contracting party and the third party?

(3) Does not Lord Griffiths' view—that it is *res inter alios acta* to determine who ultimately bears the cost of the cure—undermine the law on compensating advantages (mitigation in fact) in contract?

A second important case was *Darlington BC* v. *Wiltshier Northern Ltd.*[81] Darlington BC wished to build a recreational centre on its land, but needed to avoid contravening restrictions on local authority borrowing. Thus an arrangement was reached whereby Morgan Grenfell (Local Authority Services) Ltd ("Morgan Grenfell")

---

[79] *Ibid.*, at 847.
[80] [1994] 1 AC 85, 98.
[81] [1995] 1 WLR 68.

contracted with Wiltshier Northern Ltd ("Wiltshier") for the latter
to build the recreational centre on Darlington BC's land. The council then entered into a covenant agreement with Morgan Grenfell
which provided, *inter alia*, that Morgan Grenfell would pay Wiltshier
all sums falling due under the building contract, that the council
would reimburse these monies, and that Morgan Grenfell were not
liable to the council for building defects. It also provided that, on
request, Morgan Grenfell would assign any rights against Wiltshier to
Darlington BC. The rights were duly assigned pursuant to the
covenant agreement. The council alleged that Wiltshier's construction work was defective. The Court of Appeal had to decide whether
Darlington BC, as the assignee of Morgan Grenfell's rights under the
construction contract, could recover substantial damages for the cost
of repairs that it had incurred. This in turn depended on whether
Morgan Grenfell could have claimed substantial damages. The Court
of Appeal, by extending the principle in *Linden Gardens* v. *Lenesta
Sludge Disposals Ltd*, held that Morgan Grenfell, and hence
Darlington BC, were entitled to substantial damages.

The principle of *Linden Gardens* required extension because, in
contrast to the facts of *Linden Gardens* and Lord Diplock's formulation of the principle in *The Albazero*, the original contracting party
(Morgan Grenfell) had never had a proprietary interest in the property. It was not therefore a case of the owner at the time of contract
transferring ownership before breach. Nevertheless Steyn LJ was able
to describe the extension required as a "very conservative and limited" one.[82] In effect the principle becomes that wherever there is the
breach of a contract for work on property causing loss to a third party
who is an owner of that property, and it was known or contemplated
by the parties that a third party was, or would become, owner of the
property and that owner has no direct right to sue for breach of contract, the original contracting party, who has the right to sue, can
recover substantial damages as representing the owner's loss.[83]

[82] [1995] 1 WLR 68, 80.

[83] [The principle has been generalised still further by the Court of Appeal in *Alfred
McAlpine Construction Ltd* v. *Panatown Ltd*, *The Times*, 11 Feb. 1998. It was there held that,
at least in a building contract case, a contracting party (the promisee) has the right to recover
a third party's loss where the parties to the contract intended or contemplated that it should
have that right. The promisee is then liable to account for those damages to the third party.
A contract between the third party and the promisor does not displace the promisee's right
to damages unless that is what the parties (to the main contract) intended. So on the facts it
was held that the employer had the right to recover the owner's loss as damages from the
building contractor; and the duty of care deed between the owner and the building contractor was not intended (by the employer and building contractor) to displace that right.]

It should also be noted that Steyn LJ (but not Dillon LJ or Waite LJ) expressed support for Lord Griffiths' wider view, albeit that he did not agree with Lord Griffiths that there was any need to show an intention to carry out the repairs by someone. On this qualification, however, Steyn LJ's view has subsequently been rejected (albeit without direct reference) by the approach of the House of Lords in the *Ruxley* case, in which, as we have seen, the plaintiff's intention to effect repairs was considered a crucial ingredient in deciding whether it was reasonable for the plaintiff to claim the cost of repairs when higher than the difference in value.

It would be tempting to dismiss all these problems as stemming from the English adherence to the doctrine of privity of contract; and it might be thought that they do not arise in Scotland, where a *ius quaesitum tertio* is recognised, and that they would have no application in England if the doctrine of privity were reformed. This would be misleading and inaccurate. Even if the *Linden Gardens/Darlington* principle does not apply if the third party itself has the right to sue, the *ius quaesitum tertio*, as recognised in Scotland, and our proposed reform of privity would not always enable a contemplated subsequent owner to sue for breach of a contract for work on the property. For example, on the facts of *Linden Gardens* itself, I would be surprised to learn that the subsequent owner (the assignee) falls within the Scottish *ius quaesitum tertio*; and it would also not be able to sue under our proposed reform.

Even more central to damages generally is Lord Griffiths' approach, which appears to be as applicable to standard two-party contracts as to those which we can loosely class as contracts for the benefit of third parties. The precise width of Lord Griffiths' approach is not entirely clear: is it confined to damages for the cost of repairs; does it extend to all contracts for services; or, at its widest, does it extend to all contracts and to all claims for damages? On the one hand, one can see that if a third party *gratuitously* pays for the cost of repairs, that should not stop a plaintiff, who has contracted for those works, from recovering the cost of repairs in damages from the contract-breaker.[84] On the other hand, we know from scores of cases— most notably *British Westinghouse* v. *Underground Electric Rly. Co. of London Ltd*[85]—that if the plaintiff mitigates its loss it cannot then

---

[84] This is in line with the general approach in tort to non-deduction of gratuitously rendered compensating advantages: see, e.g., *Redpath* v. *Belfast & County Down Rly.* [1947] NI 167; *Donnelly* v. *Joyce* [1974] QB 454.

[85] [1912] AC 673.

claim damages for the difference in value between the defendant's promised and actual performance. And I would have thought that where, following defective building work, an owner sells off the land at full value, or where as a commercial matter a third party pays for the cost of repairs, those "compensating advantages" should be taken into account as eliminating the plaintiff's loss.

As regards our work on privity, we have taken the view that one cannot hope to solve these damages difficulties at a legislative stroke. We therefore propose that the law on a promisee's remedies under a contract for the benefit of a third party should be left to the common law.[86] On the other hand, the possibility of substantial damages being recovered by both the contracting party and the third party must be dealt with in the legislation.[87]

7. PENALTY CLAUSES

In 1975 in its Working Paper No. 61 on *Penalty Clauses and Forfeiture of Monies Paid*, the Law Commission considered that:

(1) The law on penalty clauses is basically satisfactory and does not require radical amendment, although views were sought, for example, on what the position should be where the plaintiff's actual loss exceeds the penalty.

(2) The law on penalty clauses should be extended to analogous clauses where there is a sum payable on an event other than breach.

(3) The same approach to relief against forfeiture of a deposit or part payment should be applied as is applied to penalty clauses, i.e. the question to be asked should be whether the amount of the deposit or part payment represented a genuine pre-estimate of the loss likely to be occasioned by a breach of contract.

Unfortunately the Law Commission did not address what seems to me to be the central puzzle about penalty clauses: namely, why should they be void if the parties to the contract are of equal bargaining power. Normally one does not knock down terms of a contract that have been freely entered into between commercial parties, unless the contract is illegal or otherwise contrary to public policy. Can it really be said that penalty clauses are analogous to illegal trans-

[86] See Report No. 242, paras. 5.12–5.17.
[87] See Report No. 242, paras. 11.1–11.4, 11.16–11.21; Draft Bill, cl. 5.

actions? Certainly since the publication of the Law Commission's working paper, much of the academic writing on this topic has been devoted to showing what a good thing penalty clauses are.[88]

Most unusually, the Law Commission did not proceed to a report in this area. The explanation for this is not entirely clear. Consultation showed support for the Law Commission's provisional recommendations on penalty clauses and sums payable on an event other than breach, although there was more of a split of views on the forfeiture proposal. Initially the delay in moving to a report was put down to the need to wait for the conclusion of work in this area by the Council of Europe[89] and then UNCITRAL.[90] I suspect therefore changes in personnel at the Law Commission, the emergence of other more pressing priorities, and perhaps the feeling that the working paper was out of line with European thinking led to inaction. My own view is that the working paper is now so dated—and in my opinion flawed in not addressing the essential dilemma—that one would need to start with a new Consultation Paper if one were to resurrect work in this area.[91]

8. LIMITATION PERIODS

Item 3 of our Sixth Programme of Law Reform is headed "limitation periods".[92] This is a very wide project which goes far beyond just breach of contract. Nevertheless within it we focus on such questions as: should the scheme of the Latent Damage Act 1986, with its discoverability starting point, be extended beyond tort to include breach of contract, and should one retain a different limitation period for contracts made by deed (twelve years) rather than contracts supported

[88] See e.g. C.J. Goetz and R.E. Scott, "Liquidated Damages and the Just Compensation Principle" (1977) 77 *Columbia LR* 554–94; P.R. Kaplan, "A Critique of the Penalty Limitation on Liquidated Damages" (1977) 50 *Southern California LR* 1055–90; G.A. Muir, "Stipulations for the Payment of Agreed Sums" (1985) 10 *Sydney LR* 503–27; T.A. Downes, "Rethinking Penalty Clauses" in P. Birks (ed.), *Wrongs and Remedies in the Twenty-First Century* (Clarendon Press, 1996).

[89] The Council of Europe published a report on penalty clauses in 1976 recommending harmonisation on the basis that all penalty clauses be valid but with a wide-ranging judicial power to change the amount of the penalty.

[90] UNCITRAL published *Uniform Rules on Liquidated Damages and Penalty Clauses* in 1983.

[91] [The Scottish Law Commission published a discussion paper, *Penalty Clauses*, Discussion Paper No. 103 in Dec. 1997.]

[92] Consultation Paper No. 151, *Limitation of Actions*, was published on 6 Jan. 1998. See 179–81 below.

by consideration (six years)? I shall not dwell on this further here, not least because the Scottish Law Commission has fairly recently carried out extensive work on limitation of actions, including for breach of contract.[93]

9. REMOTENESS

I would like to finish by something of an indulgence. An area that has long intrigued me is remoteness of damage in contract and its relationship to remoteness in tort. In this respect the House of Lords' decision in the Scottish case of *Balfour Beatty Construction (Scotland) Ltd* v. *Scottish Power Plc*[94] is an interesting one. The pursuers were the main contractors for the construction of the Edinburgh City by-pass. In order to carry out the work they installed a concrete batching plant and entered into an agreement with the defenders (the South of Scotland Electricity Board) for a temporary supply of electricity to the plant. During a critical moment in the construction of a concrete aqueduct—i.e. at a time when concrete had to be poured with no more than a gap of thirty minutes between the pour from each lorry—the electricity supply failed. As a consequence the concrete last poured hardened, which meant that, unless demolished and reconstructed, there was a risk that the aqueduct would not be watertight. The pursuers sought to recover the cost of the demolition and reconstruction from the defendants. The House of Lords held that they could not recover that loss because it was too remote.

The classic remoteness cases of *Hadley* v. *Baxendale*[95] and *Koufos* v. *C. Czarnikow Ltd, The Heron II*[96] were applied and it was decided that the crucial question was whether the demolition and reconstruction of the aqueduct consequent upon the failure of the power supply was within the defendant's contemplation as likely to occur with a "very substantial degree of probability". In answering that question in the negative their Lordships thought that the defenders, at the time of entering the contract, could not have been expected to know the technical details of concrete construction. They had no

---

[93] *Report on Prescription and Limitation of Actions* (*Latent Damage and other Related Issues*), Scot Law Com. No. 122 (1989). This Report has not yet been implemented.

[94] 1994 SLT 807 (HL); *The Times*, 23 Mar. 1994. See H. MacQueen, "Remoteness and Breach of Contract" [1996] *Jur. Rev.* 295.

[95] (1854) 9 Exch. 341.

[96] [1969] 1 AC 350.

reason to be aware of the importance of time in the hardening process, nor of the consequences of adding freshly poured concrete to that which had already hardened; nor did they have reason to expect that concrete would be required for the construction of a watertight aqueduct.

All this may on the face of it seem straightforward. The difficulties arise when one throws into the ring cases that have had to, or thought it important to, deal with remoteness in tort alongside remoteness in contract. The most notorious is *Parsons* v. *Uttley Ingham & Co. Ltd*,[97] in which the question at issue was whether the supplier of a defective pig hopper should be held liable in contract for the loss of 254 pigs that had died from a rare intestinal disease after eating nuts that had gone mouldy in the hopper. The Court of Appeal decided that the loss of the pigs was not too remote, but they found this difficult to reconcile with the traditional *Hadley* v. *Baxendale* approach. The majority therefore resorted to saying that the crucial question was whether the type of loss, not the extent or precise nature of the loss, was important; and that as illness of pigs and death of pigs was the same type of loss and the former was reasonably contemplatable, the death of the 254 pigs was not too remote. The majority also went out of their way to try to equate the remoteness test in contract and tort, Scarman LJ saying, ". . . the law must be such that in a factual situation where all have the same actual or imputed knowledge . . . the amount of damages recoverable does not depend on whether, as a matter of legal classification, the plaintiff's cause of action is breach of contract or tort".[98]

More recently this attempt to elide the tests in contract and tort has been taken up by Sir Thomas Bingham MR in dicta in the negligent valuation case of *Banque Bruxelles Lambert SA* v. *Eagle Star Insurance Co. Ltd*.[99] He said, "It is trite law that a plaintiff may not recover damages which are held to be too remote from the breach of duty of which he complains. Somewhat different language has been used to define the test in contract and tort, but the essence of the test is the same in each case. The test is whether, at the date of the contract or tort, damage of the kind for which the plaintiff claims compensation was a reasonably foreseeable consequence of the breach of contract or tortious conduct of which the plaintiff complains. If the kind of

---

[97] [1978] QB 791.
[98] *Ibid.*, at 807.
[99] [1995] 2 All ER 769, 841. The decision of the Court of Appeal in this case was overturned by the House of Lords: [1997] AC 191: see 209–11 below.

damage was reasonably foreseeable it is immaterial that the extent of the damage was not."

Again in *Brown* v. *KMR Services Ltd*[100] one of the questions in claims by underwriting Names at Lloyds against their members' agents for breach of contract (and negligence) was whether the losses were too remote, in that the magnitude of the financial disasters that struck and the consequent scale of the losses was unforeseeable/uncontemplatable. The Court of Appeal held that the loss was not too remote because it was the type and not the extent of the loss that needed to be foreseen or contemplated: here the relevant type of loss was underwriting loss and that was clearly foreseeable. *Parsons* v. *Uttley Ingham* and Sir Thomas Bingham's dicta in *Banque Bruxelles* were both cited with approval.

In the light of *Brown*—and albeit that in *Balfour Beatty* the question whether *Parsons* was correctly decided was explicitly left open—it now seems clear (although, on one view, it was never in doubt) that the remoteness test in contract focuses on the type of loss in question and not the specific loss that occurred. In other words, there is no longer any real dispute but that the majority in *Parsons* did correctly state and apply the law. The issue now is not whether the emphasis on the type of loss is appropriate, but rather on how the courts should be dividing up types of loss in contract claims.

If, as *Parsons* and *Brown* indicate, the courts are taking a broad view of types of loss, it may well be that the well-known distinction drawn in *Victoria Laundry (Windsor) Ltd* v. *Newman Industries Ltd*[101] between recoverable loss of ordinary profits and irrecoverable loss of exceptional profits can no longer stand. And in any remoteness case it would appear that a crucial question is whether there was any broader category of loss, which was reasonably contemplatable, to which one can link the actual loss suffered by the plaintiff. Applying this to the *Balfour Beatty* case it is hard to see that there was a contemplatable broader category of loss to which the demolition and construction of the aqueduct could be linked. At first blush one might have thought that such a broader category might be "loss of profit owing to a delay in construction work caused by the electricity failure"; but on the facts, it would appear that there was no such delay or loss of profit. On the facts the loss could not be stated any more broadly than that of "repair work to concrete 'damaged' because of the interruption in the pouring"; and on their Lordships' findings, as the defenders did

---

[100] [1995] 4 All ER 598.
[101] [1949] 2 KB 528.

not know of the intricacies of concrete construction work, they could not have reasonably contemplated that the electricity failure would lead to any "damage" to the concrete construction.

10. CONCLUSION

In this essay, I have sought (with the exception of the last section on remoteness) to explore those aspects of remedies for breach of contract that the English Law Commission has thought worthy of examination. I had intended to include a further substantial section on aspects that, resources permitting, the English Law Commission *ought* to be looking at in the future, but, in truth, I could hardly identify any.[102] This is not because the English law on remedies for breach is perfect—although I do think it works pretty well—but rather because, where there are defects, they seem to me to be soluble, and best solved, by the courts rather than by legislation. This brings me back to where I started; one's strategy towards legislative law reform. For a committed codifier, particularly with the catalyst provided by moves towards a European Civil Code, remedies for breach perhaps represent an attractive and manageable chunk of the law of contract with which to start the process of codification. But the English Law Commission abandoned the codifying strategy for contract in 1973 in favour of pursuing particular problem areas. And in the 1990s it seems to me that, despite European initiatives and despite our statutory duty to consider codification,[103] the political will to support a codification of contract is now non-existent south of the border.

---

[102] But the courts' general inability to award compound interest probably should be examined by the Law Commission: see n. 64 above and 199–201 below. Confusion as to how one should assess contractual (or tortious) damages for negligent valuation has been caused by *Banque Bruxelles Lambert SA* v. *Eagle Star Insurance Co. Ltd* [1997] AC 191: see 209–11 below.

[103] Law Commissions Act 1965, s. 3(1).

8

Improving Contract and Tort:
The View from the Law Commission

I. INTRODUCTION[1]

By section 3(1) of the Law Commissions Act 1965, it is the duty of the English Law Commission to "keep under review all the law . . . with a view to its systematic development and reform, including in particular the codification of such law, the elimination of anomalies, the repeal of obsolete and unnecessary enactments, the reduction of the number of separate enactments and generally the simplification and modernisation of the law . . .". This means that Law Commissioners constantly have in mind, and frequently seek views on, what reforms are needed to the areas of law within their responsibility. As head of the common law team at the Law Commission, my principal focus of attention is on what is wrong with contract and tort. However, there is a distinction between, on the one hand, recognising that a particular area of the law is unfair or uncertain or out-of-date or wastes costs, or any combination of these, and, on the other hand, the Law Commission being willing to take on that area as a project. Not only must it be relatively clear that any necessary reform is more appropriately brought about by legislation than by development through the courts (and within the area of contract and tort this is a very significant constraining factor[2]) but also Government will want to be satisfied that reform is of sufficient practical importance.

---

[1] The views expressed in this essay are mine alone and, unless made clear to the contrary, do not represent the views, provisional or otherwise, of the Law Commission. The title of this essay refers to my own opinions viewed *from* my seat in the Law Commission and must not be confused with the view *of* the Law Commission.

[2] Contrast, e.g., criminal law or family law where the bulk of the law is already statutory and it can therefore more readily be assumed that legislation is the appropriate vehicle for reform.

Of course, what constitutes sufficient practical importance is open to different interpretations. But as all the Law Commission's projects must be approved by a minister (usually the Lord Chancellor) and as the Law Commission is, in any event, reliant on governmental support if its recommendations are to be implemented, it would be foolish to pursue projects that are of more theoretical, than practical, importance. However, this point must not be exaggerated. The Law Commission is an independent body charged with systematic law reform. It should not be judged or treated as if it were an adjunct to a government department concerned with pursuing policy-driven, politically-urgent, reforms. There should be a place in almost any Government's legislative programme for carefully conceived, independent, systematic law reforms even though the advantages of simpler, fairer, cheaper and more modern laws can often only be sold politically as reaping indirect and long-term advantages.

The Law Commission's Annual Report for 1996 sets out in broad terms the criteria that are applied in selecting, or agreeing to take on, projects:

> "The Commission initiates or accepts a law reform project according to its assessment of the relevant considerations, the most significant of which are the importance of the issues, the availability of resources in terms of both expertise and funding and the suitability of the issues to be dealt with by the Commission".[3]

This essay is divided into three main sections. The first looks at the Law Commission's recently completed contract and tort projects where our recommendations have not yet been implemented and are now in the Government's hands. The second looks at the Law Commission's on-going contract and tort projects.[4] The third looks

---

[3] *Thirty-first Annual Report*, Law Com. No. 244 (1996), Appendix A.

[4] Until the end of 1998, the Law Commission is working under its Sixth Programme of Law Reform, Law Com. No. 234 (1995). I do not in this essay consider the projects on Partnership Law or on the Third Parties (Rights Against Insurers) Act 1930, which are being carried out by the Company and Commercial Law team at the Law Commission and are joint projects with the Scottish Law Commission. In respect of the latter project, see *Third Parties (Rights Against Insurers) Act 1930*, Law Commission Consultation Paper No. 152, Scottish Law Commission Discussion Paper No. 104 (1998). Where an insured becomes insolvent, a person (the third party) who has a claim against the insured is entitled under the 1930 Act to proceed against the insurer (i.e. the insured's rights against the liability insurer are by law transferred to the third party). The Act indirectly, therefore, gives a form of "priority" to those who have claims against the insolvent debtor which the debtor was insured against. This means, for example, that personal injury victims can expect to receive compensation despite the insolvency of the legal wrongdoer. Unfortunately certain problems have arisen in connection with the operation of the Act: for example, at what stage should

at some possible future projects. Taken together, it is hoped that these three sections will give the reader a novel perspective on what is wrong with the present substantive law of contract and tort and how matters could be improved for the future.

2. RECENTLY COMPLETED PROJECTS

Before proceeding, I would like to clarify my preferred approach to the details of legislative reform. In the previous essay, I indicated that, in the context of considering topics for legislative reform of civil law, I am not a great supporter of legislative intervention.[5] In my opinion, statutory intervention in relation to contract and tort is essentially justified only where the area is already based on statute or where the common law has plainly taken a wrong turn which cannot be reversed short of waiting for an enlightened decision of the House of Lords. In approaching the details of reform, my approach is similar. Hence, as shall become clear, the completed work on privity of contract, on aggravated exemplary and restitutionary damages, and on liability for psychiatric illness tends to favour minimalist legislation which builds on—and gels in with—the common law tradition.

(1) *Privity of Contract*

The privity of contract doctrine has long been subjected to criticism. In our Report[6] we make recommendations for reforming that part of the doctrine which lays down that a contract cannot be enforced by

the insured's rights be transferred to the third party (under the present law, the third party may have to restore a dissolved company to the register, in order to establish its liability, before the 1930 Act can "bite")?; at what stage should the insurer have a duty to disclose information?; and what defences should be open to the insurer?

⁵ See 136 above.

⁶ *Privity of Contract: Contracts for the Benefit of Third Parties*, Law Com. No. 242 (1996). For comment on the report see, e.g., A. Burrows, "Reforming Privity of Contract: Law Commission Report No. 242" [1996] *LMCLQ* 467; A. Tettenborn, "Third Party Contracts—Pragmatism from the Law Commission" [1996] *JBL* 602; FMB Reynolds, "Privity of Contract" (1997) 113 *LQR* 53; N. Andrews, "Reform of the Privity Rule in English Contract Law: The Law Commission's Report No. 242" [1997] *CLJ* 25; J. Adams, D. Beyleveld and R. Brownsword, "Privity of Contract—the Benefits and Burdens of Law Reform" (1997) 60 *MLR* 238; S. Girvan, "The Law Commission's Draft Contracts (Rights of Third Parties) Bill and the Carriage of Goods by Sea" [1997] *LMCLQ* 541; S. Smith, "Contracts for the Benefit of Third Parties: in Defence of the Third-Party Rule" (1997) 17 *OJLS* 643.

a person who is not a party to the contract. Our proposals will mean, for example, that subsequent purchasers or tenants of buildings can be given rights to enforce an architect's or builder's contractual obligations without the cost, complexity and inconvenience of a large number of separate contracts; that an employer can take out medical expenses insurance for its employees without there being doubts whether the employees can enforce the policy against the insurance company; that a life insurance policy taken out for one's stepchild or cohabitee is enforceable (subject to a term to the contrary) by that named beneficiary[7]; and that a contractual clause limiting or excluding the liability to the promisor of a third party (for example, the promisee's subsidiary company or sub-contractor or employee) will be straightforwardly enforceable by that third party.[8]

The arguments for reform are well-rehearsed. They include that the privity rule thwarts the intentions of the original contracting parties that the third party should be benefited; that it causes injustice to the third party who has a reasonable expectation of having the legal right to enforce the contract; that it often produces the perverse result that the person (the third party) who has suffered the loss (of the intended benefit) cannot sue, while a person (the promisee) who has suffered no loss can sue; that even if a promisee can obtain a satisfactory remedy for the third party, the promisee may not be able, or wish, to sue; that the law has developed many exceptions to privity which, even though wide-ranging, have not resolved all the problems; and that the rule has been abrogated throughout much of the common law world (including the United States, New Zealand, and parts of Australia) and is out of line with the legal systems of most Member States of the European Union.

A much more difficult issue than whether the law needs legislative reform is what the detailed content of that reform should be. In particular, one has to strike the right balance between certainty and flexibility. We found the central question, "When should a third party have the right to enforce a contract?" particularly difficult to answer. Ultimately we proposed a two-limbed test of enforceability as follows:

> "A third party shall have the right to enforce a contractual provision where that right is given to him by an express term of the contract (the

[7] The Married Women's Property Act 1882 extends only to spouses and children.

[8] See on the enforcement of such a clause by a third party, cases such as *New Zealand Shipping Co. Ltd* v. *A.M. Satterthwaite & Co. Ltd* (*The Eurymedon*) [1975] AC 154; *Norwich City Council* v. *Harvey* [1989] 1 WLR 828; *The Mahkutai* [1996] 3 WLR 1.

'first limb'); a third party shall also have the right to enforce a contractual provision where that provision purports to confer a benefit on the third party who is expressly identified as a beneficiary of that provision, by name, class or description (the 'second limb'); but there shall be no right of enforceability under the second limb where on the proper construction of the contract it appears that the contracting parties did not intend the third party to have that right."[9]

The second limb therefore constitutes a rebuttable presumption of an intention to confer legal rights on a third party where the contract purports to benefit an expressly identified third party. It is this rebuttable presumption that provides the essential balance between a high degree of certainty and the flexibility necessary for the courts to deal fairly with a huge range of different situations.

Other proposals would allow the contracting parties to vary or cancel the contract without the third party's consent but not (subject to an express provision to the contrary in the contract) once the third party has relied on, or accepted, the contract.[10] Defences that would have been available to the promisor had the promisee been suing to enforce the contract would also be available as defences to the third party's action.[11] A promisee would retain its rights to sue on the contract even though enforceable by the third party.[12] And existing statutory and common law exceptions to the privity doctrine would be preserved.[13]

Our hope was that this set of proposals would be regarded as moderate and clear and would gain the wide support needed for implementation. In particular, we steered clear of pursuing a consumer-protectionist approach which, in some situations, would guarantee third parties, who are consumers, rights to enforce contracts, irrespective of the intentions of the contracting parties. Under our proposals contracting parties can be assured that they can control (by express exclusion if necessary) the conferring of rights under the contract on third parties.

---

[9] Report No. 242, para. 7.6.
[10] Report No. 242, paras. 9.26, 9.40.
[11] Report No. 242, para. 10.12.
[12] Report No. 242, para. 11.4.
[13] Report No. 242, para. 12.2.

(2) *Aggravated, Exemplary and Restitutionary Damages*

Damages for a civil wrong are normally concerned to compensate the plaintiff's loss. But this is not always so. Sometimes damages are awarded to punish the defendant (traditionally termed "exemplary damages", although "punitive damages" seems a clearer label); and sometimes they are awarded to strip the gains the defendant has made by the wrong (so-called "restitutionary damages"). The present law on punitive damages is in a particularly unsatisfactory state and was the major focus of this project.[14]

As laid down by the House of Lords in *Rookes* v. *Barnard*,[15] punitive damages, unless expressly authorised by statute, can be awarded in only two categories of case. First, where there has been oppressive and unconstitutional wrongdoing by a servant of government; and, secondly, where the defendant has committed the wrong cynically calculating that it would be profitable so to do. The Court of Appeal in *AB* v. *South West Water Services Ltd*[16] added a second restriction: even if a case falls within the above two categories, punitive damages can only be awarded if they had been awarded for that particular wrong pre-1964 (that is, before *Rookes* v. *Barnard* was decided).

The present law is plainly irrational. Wrongs developed since 1964 (for example, sex and race discrimination) cannot trigger punitive damages: and wrongs recognised pre-1964 cannot do so if one cannot trace a reported case (perhaps because of the accidents of law reporting) in which punitive damages were awarded for that wrong. Nor can the two categories be rationally defended. Why should a private store detective who maliciously falsely imprisons an alleged shoplifter be immune from punitive damages when a police officer, who does exactly the same, is not? Why should it make all the difference as regards the availability of punitive damages, whether a person who attacked an old lady was paid to do so or not?

But while it is widely accepted that reform is needed, our consultation exercise revealed very different views on the path reform should take. One view is that rationalisation demands the abolition of punitive damages, leaving punishment as the sole preserve of the criminal law. The other main view, and the one we ultimately found persuasive, is to preserve punitive damages while putting them on a clear, principled and tightly-controlled, basis. Consultees impressed

[14] *Aggravated, Exemplary and Restitutionary Damages*, Law Com. No. 247 (1997).
[15] [1964] AC 1129.
[16] [1993] QB 507.

upon us that to remove punitive damages would be to take away, for no good reason, a weapon in the judicial armoury that can be useful in fighting a wide range of outrageous wrongful conduct, including fraud, police misconduct, infringement of health and safety standards, environmental pollution, and sex and race discrimination. We have therefore recommended that punitive damages should be available for any civil wrong (other than breach of contract) where the defendant has outrageously and deliberately disregarded the plaintiff's rights.[17]

On the other hand, we are most anxious to ensure that punitive damages are kept as a last resort remedy. Hence we have recommended that they should not be awarded where another available remedy (for example, compensatory or restitutionary damages) is adequate punishment[18]; and that they should not usually be awarded where the wrongdoer has been convicted of a criminal offence for the same conduct.[19] Furthermore to ensure that there is no real risk of English law treading the United States path of easily available, and exorbitant, punitive awards, it is central to our proposed reforms that the availability and amount of punitive damages should be a matter for the judges and, even where the civil trial is otherwise by jury, should never be decided by a jury.[20]

Our proposal to retain punitive damages required us to sort out a number of further issues. For example, in order not to punish the defendant excessively for the same conduct, we have recommended that, where there are multiple plaintiffs, only the plaintiffs in the first successful action should be entitled to punitive damages ("the first past the post takes all" principle).[21] In respect of multiple defendants, our recommendation is that, rather than applying joint or joint and several liability—which could involve the courts overpunishing a joint defendant or, alternatively, refusing to award punitive damages for fear of overpunishing a joint defendant—liability to pay punitive damages should be "several" only.[22] That is, each defendant's liability to pay punitive damages should be separately examined in the light of that defendant's conduct. We have recommended that vicar-

---

[17] Report No. 247, paras. 5.44, 5.46–5.77. For civil wrongs arising under an Act, punitive damages must not be awarded unless consistent with the policy of that Act.

[18] Report No. 247, paras. 5.44, 5.99–5.102.

[19] Report No. 247, paras. 5.44, 5.103–5.115.

[20] Report No. 247, paras. 5.44, 5.81–5.98.

[21] Report No. 247, paras. 5.159–5.185.

[22] Report No. 247, paras. 5.186–5.208.

ious liability can apply to punitive damages[23]; and that it should not be contrary to public policy to insure against a liability to pay punitive damages.[24] Further, we favour a diametrically opposite approach to the present law on the survival of claims to punitive damages, so that the claim survives in favour of the deceased plaintiff's estate but does not survive against the deceased defendant's estate.[25]

Our approach to restitutionary damages is essentially one of minimal legislative interference, leaving the courts to develop the law on when such damages should be available. However, some legislative reform is necessary as a direct consequence of our proposals on punitive damages. In particular, we want to ensure that the courts can award the less extreme remedy of restitutionary damages, in preference to punitive damages, rather than being left with no mid-position between compensation and punishment. We have therefore recommended that, irrespective of any other power to award restitution, restitutionary damages should be available to remove a benefit gained by any civil wrong (other than breach of contract) where that wrong has been committed with an outrageous and deliberate disregard of the plaintiff's rights.[26] In order to avoid a different decision being reached on the same test of availability by judge and jury, we have also proposed that, where punitive and restitutionary damages are in issue in the same trial by jury, the decision as to the availability of restitutionary damages should be for the judge not the jury.[27]

A final problem is that in English law punitive damages have often been confused with "aggravated damages". Despite the best efforts of Lord Devlin in *Rookes* v. *Barnard*[28] to remove any confusion by clarifying that aggravated damages are to compensate the plaintiff's outrage and upset at the defendant's conduct, and not to punish the defendant, some features of the law, and some statements of judges, continue to exhibit that confusion. We aim to cut through the confusion once and for all by a legislative provision that "aggravated damages" (and we hope that label will disappear) are to compensate the plaintiff's mental distress and must not be awarded with the intention of punishing the defendant.[29]

---

[23] Report No. 247, paras. 5.209–5.230.

[24] Report No. 247, paras. 5.234–5.273.

[25] Report No. 247, paras. 5.274–5.278.

[26] Report No. 247, paras. 3.48–3.53. For restitution for breach of contract, see 140–5 above.

[27] Report No. 247, paras. 3.54–3.56. See also 170 above.

[28] [1964] AC 1129.

[29] Report No. 247, paras. 2.39–2.43.

(3) *Liability for Psychiatric Illness*

The law on liability in the tort of negligence for psychiatric illness (or, as lawyers have traditionally termed it, "nervous shock") has been described as "the area where the silliest rules now exist and where criticism is almost universal".[30] Popular interest in this area has been heightened by the widespread media attention given to the litigation following the disaster at the Hillsborough football stadium in 1989. Ninety-six spectators died and over 400 were injured as a result of crushing when fans were permitted to enter a terrace that was already full. Claims for psychiatric illness were brought against the Chief Constable of South Yorkshire Police by relatives of those killed or injured in the disaster and by police officers who attended at the scene. While most of the officers were held entitled to recover damages,[31] nearly all the actions of the relatives of the dead or injured were unsuccessful.[32]

Our recommendations for reform concentrate on the main situation where the present rules cause injustice.[33] As laid down by the House of Lords in *Alcock* v. *Chief Constable of South Yorkshire Police*,[34] a person who foreseeably suffers a recognised psychiatric illness as a result of the death, injury or imperilment of another, caused by the defendant's negligence, cannot recover damages from the defendant unless he or she can establish the requisite degree of proximity in terms of: (i) the class of persons whose claims should be recognised (and this is essentially confined to those who have a close tie of love and affection to the person injured or killed or who are rescuers); (ii) the closeness of the plaintiff to the accident in time and space; and (iii) the means by which the shock is caused (that is, the requirement of perception through one's own unaided senses, rather than hearing of the accident from another or seeing it on television). Applying these restrictions, the claims of all but one of the plaintiffs in the *Alcock* case failed. They were either not present at the disaster or its immediate aftermath but rather saw it on television or heard of it from friends or on the radio; or, although present, they had not proved that they had a close tie of love and affection to the immediate victim.

---

[30] Jane Stapleton, "In Restraint of Tort" in P. Birks (ed.), *The Frontiers of Liability* (Clarendon Press, 1994) vol. 2, 94.

[31] See *Frost* v. *Chief Constable of South Yorkshire Police* [1997] 3 WLR 194, CA. The case is being appealed to the House of Lords.

[32] See *Alcock* v. *Chief Constable of South Yorkshire Police* [1992] 1 AC 310.

[33] *Liability for Psychiatric Illness*, Law Com. No. 249 (1998).

[34] [1992] 1 AC 310.

In our view—and this was heavily supported by consultees—the second and third of the above requirements for liability are unjust and unnecessary and should be removed. For the law to distinguish the claim for psychiatric illness of one mother present at the scene of her son's death or at its immediate aftermath from that of another mother who was not present at the scene but came across the aftermath several hours later, or who heard about the accident from a friend or saw it on television, might justly give rise to accusations of arbitrary and insensitive line-drawing.

Our central recommendation, therefore, is that a new statutory duty of care not to cause a recognised psychiatric illness should be owed to a person with a close tie of love and affection to the immediate victim.[35] Certain relationships between the plaintiff and the person injured, killed or imperilled (spouse, parent, child, brother, sister and cohabitant) are deemed to be ones where there is a close tie of love and affection; in other cases that close tie will need to be proved.[36] In addition, although we see the duty of care to avoid psychiatric illness as an "independent" duty, there will be no such duty of care owed to the plaintiff if there was no duty of care owed to the immediate victim, and the (policy) reasons for denying that duty also extend to the claim by the plaintiff for psychiatric illness.[37] For example, a defendant is, in general, not liable for failing to rescue a person even though that failure to act foreseeably causes that person's death. The reasons for denying a duty of care to rescue mean that, correspondingly, the defendant in that situation should not be liable for the foreseeable psychiatric illness suffered by the deceased's loved ones.

Other recommendations we make are, first, to remove the requirement (also laid down in the *Alcock* case) that the psychiatric illness be shock-induced[38]; and, secondly, that it should not be an automatic bar to recovery that the immediate victim is the defendant.[39] The latter would mean that a negligent driver (D1) who injures himself in a car accident could be liable for the psychiatric illness suffered by a loved one consequent on D1's injuries: an important practical consequence of this would be to enable another defendant (D2), who has been partly responsible with D1 for D1's injuries, to recover a contribution from D1 if sued by D1's loved ones for their consequent

[35] Report No. 249, para. 6.16.
[36] Report No. 249, paras. 6.24–6.35.
[37] Report No. 249, paras. 6.36–6.41.
[38] Report No. 249, paras. 5.28–5.33.
[39] Report No. 249, paras. 5.34–5.44.

psychiatric illness. However, deliberate, as opposed to negligent, self-injury raises sensitive questions involving respect for a person's self-determination. That is, it may be thought to restrict unduly a person's choice to injure himself if one imposed a duty of care to avoid the psychiatric illness of a loved one consequent on that deliberate injury. We therefore qualify the removal of the bar to recovery where the immediate victim is the defendant by leaving the courts scope to decide that it would not be just and reasonable to impose a duty of care where the immediate victim has chosen to cause his own death, injury or imperilment.

Our recommendations do not seek to provide a complete legislative code on liability in the tort of negligence for psychiatric illness. So, for example, we do not recommend legislation in relation to rescuers or bystanders who suffer psychiatric illness as a consequence of injuries to strangers, nor in relation to those who suffer psychiatric illness consequent on damage to their property, nor in respect of those who suffer psychiatric illness from stress at work. Liability to those plaintiffs would continue to be governed by the common law. In our view, a codification would result in a freezing of the law at a time before it is ready. Neither medical nor legal understanding of psychiatric illness, its causes and its effects, has developed to a sufficiently mature stage for complete codification to be attempted. Moreover, there are sharply conflicting views on policy in this area between those, on the one hand, who seek to assimilate entirely liability for psychiatric illness and for physical injury and those, on the other hand, who consider that claims for psychiatric illness need to be tightly controlled for fear of opening the floodgates of litigation and allowing exaggerated or fraudulent claims. At this stage in the development of the law, we are anxious not to push the boundaries of liability too far lest we lose wide support for our proposals. Our strategy has therefore been one of recommending minimal legislation: curing by legislation serious defects in the present law, while allowing the law otherwise to be developed by the courts.

(4) Should there be Reform of Joint and Several Liability?

Joint and several liability is the most politically controversial topic with which I have been involved at the Law Commission. It is also the only area in relation to which the task was to carry out a preliminary "team" investigation rather than to undertake a full Law

Commission project.[40] It therefore differs from the other "recently completed" or "ongoing" projects discussed in this essay. It also differs from them because, in my view, joint and several liability does not merit major reform.

Our conclusion, that a replacement of joint and several liability by proportionate liability is not justified, incurred the wrath of many "professionals", especially auditors. Some impression of the hostility which I faced in addressing audiences on the topic can be gleaned from the following extract from the *Financial Times*[41]: "If accountants played the hot air balloon game in which each player has to say who they would first throw overboard in order to stay airborne, there is little doubt Professor Andrew Burrows would be chosen first."

In understanding what all the fuss is about, one first needs to be clear that we are not here concerned with joint and several liability as a principle of partnership law according to which each partner can be held personally liable for the civil wrongs of another partner acting within the scope of the partnership's business. It is in relation to that aspect of joint and several liability that there have been moves for reform so as to allow "limited liability partnerships". I see no objection to such a reform: in principle, the law should facilitate whatever associations people reasonably wish to adopt in order to carry on business.

We are instead concerned with the general legal principle—as relevant to individuals and companies as to partnerships—whereby, if two or more civil wrongdoers (whether tortfeasors, or those committing a breach of contract or breach of trust), while acting independently, cause the same indivisible damage to the same plaintiff, any of those wrongdoers can be sued for the full (legally recoverable) loss caused. For example, if a building has been defectively constructed so that the structure cracks, claims for that indivisible damage may be brought against the builder for breach of contract and against the architect for breach of his or her contractual or tortious duties of care. If liable at all, the builder and the architect will be jointly and severally liable for the economic loss caused to the plaintiff by the defects: each is liable to the plaintiff for 100 per cent of the (legally recoverable) loss.

If the defendants are jointly and severally liable, they have an entitlement to recover contribution from each other (under the Civil

---

[40] *Feasibility Investigation of Joint and Several Liability*, by the Common Law Team of the Law Commission, Consultation Paper issued by the DTI (1996).
[41] Jim Kelly, "Burden of Liability", *Financial Times*, 5 Nov. 1996.

Liability (Contribution) Act 1978), with the amount of that contribution being determined by their respective blameworthiness and the respective causal potency of their wrongs. So at the secondary, contribution, stage there is a regime of "proportionate liability" as between defendants.

Joint and several liability of defendants to the plaintiff, plus contribution as between the defendants, works perfectly well where the defendants are all solvent. The difficulty for professional defendants is that other joint wrongdoers are often insolvent and they, as the deep-pocket defendants, are left with 100 per cent liability to the plaintiff. Hence the call for proportionate liability (to be moved forward from contribution) to replace joint and several liability. If P has suffered a £100,000 loss as a result of the wrongdoing of D1 and D2 who, as between themselves, are equally to blame, then under proportionate liability the liability of D1 and D2 would be limited to £50,000 and there would be no right of contribution between them.

While perhaps at first looking and sounding eminently reasonable, closer investigation reveals that proportionate liability would be contrary to both principle and sound policy. It would, in essence, replace harshness for defendants with glaring unfairness for plaintiffs. There are better, less drastic, ways to help professional defendants and these should be tried first.

The three main objections to proportionate liability may be expressed as follows:

(i) Proportionate liability confuses the just position as between defendants with the just position as between the plaintiff and a defendant. As between each defendant and the plaintiff, joint and several liability is fair because the defendant is 100 per cent responsible for the whole of the plaintiff's loss. The confusion is well illustrated by the oft-cited, but erroneous, statement that joint and several liability means that a defendant may have to pay 100 per cent of damages even if only 1 per cent to blame.

(ii) If one sees the problem as being one of who should bear the risk of D2's insolvency, it is fair that, as between the plaintiff and D1, that risk should be borne by D1. The plaintiff, unless contributorily negligent, is legally blameless for the loss. D1 is, in contrast, a legal wrongdoer.

(iii) Proportionate liability would produce the unacceptable result that a plaintiff is less likely to recover full damages by being the victim of two wrongs (one by a solvent defendant and another by an insolvent defendant) than if he or she had been the victim of just one wrong (by a solvent defendant).

The above three objections are neatly illustrated by comparing two examples. In the first example, P, relying on D1's negligent advice, invests in company X and loses £100,000. Assuming that D1 is legally liable, and that there is no contributory negligence, P is entitled to recover his full loss from D1. The second example involves the same facts, except that P additionally goes to D2, who gives him the same negligent advice as D1. P, relying on both D1 and D2 (but either piece of advice would have been sufficient by itself to induce reliance), invests in company X and loses £100,000. As a matter of language, one can say that D1 and D2 are equally (50 per cent) responsible for P's loss: that is a correct proposition as regards the legal position between D1 and D2. But as against P, D1 and D2 are each 100 per cent responsible and it would surely be unacceptable that, if D2 were insolvent, P could recover only £50,000 from D1, rather than £100,000. If that were the law P would end up worse off in example two than in example one, merely because he has been the victim of two bad pieces of advice rather than one.

There are several further objections to (or fears concerning) proportionate liability:

(i) The determination of a plaintiff's damages would be rendered much more complex under a system of proportionate liability, than under the present law. This would increase the costs of litigation and hamper out-of-court settlements.

(ii) Proportionate liability would not entirely achieve the aim of protecting defendants. In particular, the threat of a single catastrophic claim against a professional defendant would remain because, in contrast to a statutory or contractual cap on liability, proportionate liability depends somewhat arbitrarily on the conduct of other defendants.

(iii) In recent years, English courts have been reluctant to expand duties of care for pure economic loss,[42] and have restricted damages,[43] against professional defendants. If

[42] See, e.g., *Caparo Industries Plc v. Dickman* [1990] 2 AC 605. Cf. *Morgan Crucible Co. v. Hill Samuel & Co.* [1991] Ch. 295; *Bank of Credit & Commerce International (Overseas) Ltd v. Price Waterhouse, The Times,* 4 Mar. 1998. See also 213–6 below.

[43] See, e.g., *Banque Bruxelles Lambert SA v. Eagle Star Insurance Co. Ltd* [1997] AC 191. See 209–11 below.

proportionate liability were to be introduced, the knock-on effect might be to encourage a reversal of that judicial conservatism. The common law's capacity for dynamic growth, and adaptation to new circumstances, means that the gains for professional defendants of a move to proportionate liability may not be as great as at first sight appears.

Rather then replacing joint and several liability by proportionate liability (or modified versions of proportionate liability) the principled and fair way to deal with the liability problems faced by auditors, and other professional defendants, is to allow them to agree contractual limitations on liability with their clients and to recognise clearly that any duties of care owed to third parties can be limited by similar non-contractual disclaimers (of which the plaintiff had notice) limiting liability. This may already be the law,[44] except for auditors who are prevented from excluding or limiting liability by section 310 of the Companies Act 1985. Section 310 should be repealed.[45]

A further reform that might help professional defendants would be to make clearer the extent to which contractual (or non-contractual) terms limiting liability will be struck down as unreasonable under the Unfair Contract Terms Act 1977.[46]

This suggested approach of making clear in statute the extent to which limitation clauses are valid is not a long way from an (excludable) statutory cap, which has been put forward by some professions as a better solution to their problems than proportionate liability. Certainly, an excludable statutory cap is less objectionable in principle and policy than proportionate liability and it has the advantage, as against proportionate liability, of indisputably being a method of preventing the single "wipe-out" claim against a defendant.

It would also seem to be the case that auditors should be making far more than hitherto of the defence of contributory negligence in situations where either the fraud of directors can be attributed to the audited company or, more likely still, the audited company has failed to put in place structures that would have detected and prevented the fraud or incompetence of a director or other official.[47]

[44] This is clearly the position in relation to liability for negligent misstatement: see *Hedley Byrne & Co. Ltd* v. *Heller & Partners Ltd* [1964] AC 465; *Smith* v. *Eric S. Bush* [1990] 1 AC 831; *McCullagh* v. *Lane Fox & Partners Ltd* [1996] 18 EG 104.

[45] *Feasibility Investigation of Joint and Several Liability*, Consultation Paper issued by the DTI (1996), para. 5.26.

[46] *Ibid*. See also 203–4 below.

[47] A lead may be taken here from the Australian case of *AWA Ltd* v. *Daniels* (1992) 7 ACSR 759 (Rogers CJ); (1995) 16 ACSR 607 (Court of Appeal of New South Wales).

No-one would suggest that professional defendants do not face problems with the rising tide of negligence litigation. But legislation to replace joint and several liability by proportionate liability would constitute an unnecessary and unacceptable over-reaction to those problems. This is particularly so when other, less objectionable, possible solutions (for example, contractual and non-contractual limitations of liability) have not been given a fair trial.

3. ON-GOING PROJECTS

I now turn to consider projects on contract or tort where we have not yet produced a report with final recommendations. There are three of these on-going projects: limitation of actions; damages for personal injury and death; and illegal transactions. In relation to the first two, but not yet the last, we have published consultation papers.

(1) *Limitation of Actions*

The law governing the period within which a plaintiff must bring a claim, if he or she is not to lose it, is incoherent, complex and unfair. Confining ourselves here to contract and tort (although our project covers all civil actions, including actions to recover land) we can immediately see the problems of the present law.

Under section 5 of the Limitation Act 1980, a person who sues for breach of contract has a limitation period of six years from the date of the breach if the contract is a simple contract (that is, a contract supported by consideration but not made by deed); whereas, under section 8 of the 1980 Act, he or she has twelve years from the date of breach if the contract is a specialty (that is, made by deed). Moreover, it makes no difference whether the plaintiff knows, or ought reasonably to know, of the breach. Thus the owner of a house, who has a contractual action against the builder for using inadequate materials, is time-barred where the walls of the house start cracking more than six years after completion of the works. This is so even though he or she could not reasonably have known of the breach until the cracks appeared, which was after the expiry of the limitation period.

In tort the position is even more convoluted. Under section 2 of the 1980 Act, the general limitation period is six years from the date of the tort, which for torts actionable on proof of damage (such as negligence and nuisance) means the date when damage or injury was caused. But for negligently caused personal injury, the period laid down in section 11 of the 1980 Act is three years from discoverability (that is, from when the plaintiff knew, or ought to have known, of the facts constituting the claim); and under section 33 the court has a discretion to disapply the three-year period if it is equitable to do so. For claims in the tort of negligence for latent damage, other than personal injury, the period under sections 14A–14B of the 1980 Act is three years from discoverability or six years from accrual of the cause of action, whichever is the later, subject to a long-stop of fifteen years from the date of the defendant's breach of duty; and there is no judicial discretion to disapply those periods. For claims in respect of defective products under Part I of the Consumer Protection Act 1987, the period, laid down by section 11A of the 1980 Act, is three years from discoverability, with a judicial discretion, in personal injury but not property damage cases, to disapply that period, subject to a long-stop of ten years from when the product was supplied. Yet another approach is adopted for defamation and malicious falsehood: under section 4A of the 1980 Act, the limitation period is one year from accrual of the cause of action with a judicial discretion to disapply that period where it is equitable to do so. A further, extremely complex, regime laid down in sections 3–4 of the 1980 Act applies to actions for the tort of conversion, which is designed to balance fairly the claims of the original owner and those of a *bona fide* purchaser for value.

A major purpose of our project is to reduce such complexity and incoherence. We are asking, "Are there good reasons for so many different regimes and periods or, on the contrary, do the differences merely reflect the irrational ad hoc development of the law?"

Another linked purpose is to remove the unfairness that can result not only from time starting to run from a date before the plaintiff could reasonably have known of the action but also from the inevitability that so many different regimes will produce unacceptable inconsistencies. A glaring example of this is sexual abuse. Say, for example, a girl has been sexually abused by her father and, as an adult, suffers from a depressive illness as a consequence. Her action against her father for trespass to the person will be time-barred six years after she was 18.[48] In contrast, if she sues her mother in the tort of negligence for failing to take reasonable steps to stop the abuse, which her

---

[48] *Stubbings* v. *Webb* [1993] AC 498, applying s. 2 of the 1980 Act. Time does not run during minority: s. 28 Limitation Act 1980.

mother knew about, she will have three years from when (after the age of 18) she knew that her illness could be attributed to the abuse; and that period could be disapplied at the discretion of the courts.[49] Surely it cannot be right that the limitation period applicable to actions for personal injury may be less favourable to a victim where the claim is that the injury was inflicted deliberately than where the claim is that the injury was caused negligently.

Our consultation paper, *Limitation of Actions*,[50] was published in January 1998. The main provisional recommendation is that there should be a new core limitation regime of three years from discoverability subject to a long-stop of ten years or, in personal injury cases, of thirty years. This would extend to actions in contract and tort and, subject to some modifications in a few cases, to all actions governed by the Limitation Act 1980. There would be no judicial discretion to disapply the period (so that, for example, the uncertainty inherent in the section 33 discretion, which has led to over 115 appellate decisions, would be removed).

We also make provisional proposals for improving the present law on factors extending the running of time. We suggest: that the plaintiff's mental disability (including supervening disability) or minority should extend the initial limitation period (unless, possibly, there is a representative adult other than the defendant); that mental disability should not extend the long-stop limitation period (and we seek views on whether minority should do so); that deliberate concealment (initial and subsequent) should extend the long-stop; and that acknowledgements and part payments should start time running again but not once the initial or long-stop limitation period has expired.

The law on limitation of actions is of great practical importance and raises many fascinating and difficult questions. Yet it rarely finds a place in law courses and has tended to be overlooked by academics.[51] In general terms, limitation law requires a careful and sensitive balance to be struck between the interests of plaintiffs, defendants and the state. Our work suggests that in many respects the balance struck under the present law is unsatisfactory and that significant improvements can be made.

---

[49] *S* v. *W* [1995] 1 FLR 862, applying s. 11 of the 1980 Act.

[50] Consultation Paper No. 151 (1998).

[51] Significant exceptions include A. McGee, *Limitation Periods* (2nd edn., Sweet and Maxwell, 1994); T. Prime and G.P. Scanlan, *The Modern Law of Limitation* (Butterworths, 1993); M. Jones, *Limitation Periods in Personal Injury Actions* (Blackstone, 1995); D. Oughton, J. Lowry, R. Merkin, *Limitation of Actions* (LLP, 1997).

(2) *Damages for Personal Injury and Death*

An earlier part of this project bore legislative fruit in the shape of the Damages Act 1996, section 150 (and Schedule 2) of the Finance Act 1996, and section 10 of the Civil Evidence Act 1995.[52] This essay concentrates on our on-going work in this area.

As part of the Law Commission's Sixth Programme of Law Reform[53] it was recommended "that an examination be made of the principles governing and the effectiveness of the present remedy of damages for monetary and non-monetary loss, with particular regard to personal injury litigation". Certain matters to which specific consideration was to be given included:

> "(a) deductions and set-offs against monetary loss . . .;
> (b) awards to cover medical, nursing and other expenses incurred by the plaintiff;
> (c) the law relating to fatal accidents, including bereavement damages; . . .
> (e) the award of damages for pain and suffering and other forms of non-pecuniary loss . . ."

In relation to these terms of reference it should be stressed that we were not asked to look at the more fundamental question (examined in 1978 by the Pearson Commission[54]) of whether the tort system for compensating personal injury should be replaced, for example by no-fault state compensation schemes. Rather we were asked to look at the present tort system on the basis that it will continue and to suggest ways in which it might be improved.

Our work has been assisted by empirical research, masterminded for us by Professor Hazel Genn. This focused not on the litigation

---

[52] See *Structured Settlements, Interim and Provisional Damages*, Law Com. No. 224 (1994). We there recommended that the present voluntary system of structured settlements, with its tax advantages, should be rationalised and put on a firm statutory basis; that an award of provisional damages should not bar a Fatal Accidents Act claim; that the "Ogden" actuarial tables for calculating future pecuniary loss in personal injury and death cases should be admissible evidence; and that the rates of return on index-linked government stocks should be used in calculating damages for future pecuniary loss. In respect of the last of these the relevant legislative provision (s. 1 of the Damages Act 1996) differs in merely laying down that the court, in determining the discount rate to be applied in calculating damages for future pecuniary loss, is to take into account a rate which may be prescribed by the Lord Chancellor.

[53] Law Com. No. 234 (1995), Item 2.

[54] Report of the Royal Commission on Civil Liability and Compensation for Personal Injury, chaired by Lord Pearson (1978) Cmnd. 7054-I.

process or on the cost of obtaining compensation, both of which have been well-documented, but on the experiences of victims after receiving damages. This empirical work was published as *Personal Injury Compensation: How Much is Enough?*[55] Although I cannot here do justice to all of that research, there are four findings that indicate the type of help that it gave us. First, it was found that plaintiffs tended to receive inadequate sums to compensate them for future pecuniary loss, especially loss of earnings. In general, predictions of the future were unduly optimistic. Secondly, the pain endured by personal injury victims was surprisingly long-lasting. Four-fifths of victims were still experiencing pain (at the time when interviewed) and two in five were reported as being in more or less constant pain. Thirdly, contrary to what is often thought, plaintiffs tend to be risk-averse with respect to the damages they receive. Finally, a surprisingly high amount of unpaid care is provided to victims by relatives and friends.

We published four consultation papers on damages for personal injury and death during 1996 and 1997. The intention is to draw together the final recommendations in one or two reports within the next year or so.

The first of the four consultation papers, *Damages for Personal Injury: Non-Pecuniary Loss*,[56] examines the principles and methods applied in assessing non-pecuniary loss (that is, pain, suffering and loss of amenity). Plainly one cannot say that any particular level of damages for non-pecuniary loss is right or wrong in the same way as one can for pecuniary loss. Nevertheless one can ascertain what people's views are on whether the present levels are satisfactory; and, perhaps more importantly, one can ask questions about how the levels should be fixed and by whom.

There are three aspects of the present law and practice which should, perhaps, be the focus of our attention in formulating legislative recommendations. The first is that damages for non-pecuniary loss appear to be too low, at least for serious injuries. The present scale runs up to about £130,000. There is a widespread view that this is not high enough. Factors that may be thought of relevance supporting that view are that, first, at least in respect of very serious injuries, damages for non-pecuniary loss have failed to keep pace with inflation when compared with awards of twenty-five to thirty years

[55] Law Com. No. 224 (1994).
[56] Consultation Paper No. 140 (1996). The paper was published on 4 Jan. 1996.

ago.[57] Secondly, practitioners have informed us that it is often embarrassing and difficult explaining to plaintiffs how low damages are for pain, suffering and loss of amenity. Thirdly, research commissioned by the Association of Personal Injury Lawyers to inform their response to us, which involved "focus groups" being presented with case histories, indicated that lay opinion regards the appropriate levels as being significantly higher than those presently applied.[58]

Secondly, if one does believe that an uplift is required, how should that be brought about? A legislative tariff may be thought to have the disadvantage of reducing the degree of flexibility that the judiciary presently has in finely tuning awards to the circumstances of the particular plaintiff. There is also the fear that a legislative tariff might ultimately be used politically to deflate damages. An alternative suggestion is that one should set up a Compensation Board,[59] which would be representative of, or could take representations from, the various interests in personal injury litigation. To "feed in" lay opinion, such a body could be required to take account of, for example, simulated jury trials or the views of "focus groups".

Thirdly, what role should there be for juries? While it is now rare for juries to be involved in fixing damages in personal injury cases, this is still possible. It is most likely to occur where a false imprisonment claim brought against the police also involves a claim for personal injury. In that sort of circumstance we have provisionally recommended that the damages for personal injury should be fixed by the judge not the jury.[60] But in seeking to fix a satisfactory level of damages, a continuing problem has been the discrepancy between damages for non-pecuniary loss in personal injury cases, essentially fixed by judges, and jury awards for non-pecuniary loss in defamation cases. We provisionally recommended that, in fixing damages for defamation, juries should be told of the level of damages for non-pecuniary loss in personal injury cases.[61] While our consultation paper was at the printers, this provisional recommendation was effectively "implemented" by the Court of Appeal in *Elton John* v. *Mirror Group Newspapers*.[62]

---

[57] Consultation Paper No. 140, paras. 4.34–4.51.
[58] See also the National Consumer Council straw poll referred to in Consultation Paper No. 140, para. 4.29.
[59] Consultation Paper No. 140, paras. 4.68–4.72.
[60] Consultation Paper No. 140, paras. 4.82–4.85.
[61] Consultation Paper No. 140, paras. 4.101–4.103.
[62] [1996] 3 WLR 593.

However, one can question whether the *Elton John* case has gone far enough. Jury awards are given without reasons and are unpredictable. Without guidelines, any consistency they achieve is a matter of chance: and guidelines can, in any event, be ignored. Moreover, one can strongly argue that, if the system requires guidelines for juries, any merit in letting lay opinion rule quantum has largely been lost and one may as well assimilate the exceptional areas where jury assessment is still permitted with the vast majority of civil cases where the judge alone assesses damages. In short, there are powerful arguments for supporting the basic view taken by the Faulks Committee[63] in the context of defamation that, while liability may be best left to juries, assessment of damages should always be a matter for a judge not the jury.[64]

But, in a project on damages, there is a limit to what can be achieved in relation to jury trial. Moreover, there may be something to be said for allowing the effects of the *Elton John* case to be felt before removing the assessment of damages from juries. Perhaps the whole question of the role of juries in civil cases should be the subject-matter of a separate Law Commission project.

The second of the four consultation papers, *Damages for Personal Injury: Medical, Nursing and Other Expenses*[65] produced considerable media interest because of our suggestion that there was a case for the National Health Service having the right to recoup its costs of caring for a victim from the tortfeasor (or other wrongdoer). The strongest arguments in favour of this are, first, that if the victim opts for private health care, the tortfeasor must pay damages covering the cost of that health care. And, secondly, if one regards provision of care by the NHS as a state benefit, there is an obvious analogy to the recoupment of social security benefits by the Department of Social Security under, what is now, the Social Security (Recovery of Benefits) Act 1997.

Another major issue looked at in this paper was the assessment of damages where care has been provided free to the victim by relatives or friends. It has long been established that the plaintiff can recover damages for the cost of care even though he or she has not incurred

---

[63] *Report of the Committee on Defamation* (1975), Cmnd. 5909.

[64] Although we were initially persuaded that this split of function was unworkable (because the jury may have come to a finding of fact relevant to both liability and quantum), we now consider that any problems are surmountable (in a similar way to how they are overcome in criminal trials): see Consultation Paper No. 140, paras. 4.96–4.100, *Aggravated, Exemplary and Restitutionary Damages*, Law Com. No. 247 (1997), paras. 5.87–5.90.

[65] Consultation Paper No. 144 (1996).

any expenses because that care has been provided free. According to *Donnelly v. Joyce*[66] the loss was the plaintiff's not the carer's, and the carer had no entitlement to the damages. It therefore made no difference that the carer was the defendant. But the law was changed in *Hunt v. Severs*.[67] In that case, a wife (the plaintiff) was suing her husband (the defendant). The plaintiff had suffered catastrophic injuries as a result of an accident when she had been a passenger on the motor-cycle driven by the defendant. The plaintiff was subsequently cared for by the defendant and they married. The House of Lords considered that the loss in relation to the provision of care is that of the carer not the victim. A victim would therefore hold damages for past cost of care on trust for the carer. As, in the instant case, the carer was the defendant, no damages at all were payable: on the analysis adopted by the House of Lords, to award such damages would be circular as it would involve the defendant paying damages only for them to be held by the plaintiff on trust for the defendant.

In terms of principle, this decision may be correct, but in terms of policy it produces problems. For example, it encourages plaintiffs to enter into contracts with defendant-carers to pay for the care because, in that situation, the plaintiff would be able to recover damages for the expenses incurred (which, of course, he or she would then be free to pass on to the carer). Furthermore, it encourages plaintiffs to have the services performed by someone other than the defendant-carer, whether on a commercial basis, or gratuitously by a friend or relative other than the defendant. Yet that other person may be a less appropriate carer than the defendant and commercial private nursing involves expenses that might otherwise be avoided.

For these reasons, we have provisionally recommended legislation reversing *Hunt v. Severs* so that damages for cost of care can be recovered even if the care has been rendered by the defendant.[68] On the other hand, we are inclined to think that the approach of treating the loss as the carer's, rather than the plaintiff's, is correct.[69]

In the third personal injury consultation paper, *Damages for Personal Injury: Collateral Benefits*,[70] we examined how one should calculate damages where the injured person has already received, or will receive, other payments because of the injury. Say, for example, an

---

[66] [1974] QB 454.
[67] [1994] 2 AC 350.
[68] Consultation Paper No. 144, paras. 3.59–3.68.
[69] Consultation Paper No. 144, paras. 3.43–3.55.
[70] Consultation Paper No. 147 (1997).

employee is injured in a car accident because of another's negligence; and let us assume that the victim receives full sick pay from his employer or a voluntary contribution from his trade union or that he has a personal accident insurance policy or that he is in receipt of a disablement pension. Should the victim be able to recover full damages without account being taken of those payments?

The present law on this issue appears to be in a muddle. Some benefits are deducted while others are not deducted. For example, sick pay[71] and social security benefits (for the first five years[72]) are deducted: whereas charitable payments,[73] insurance payments[74] and disablement pensions[75] are not deducted. This means that if a person is paid long-term sick pay that will be deducted from damages for loss of earnings, but if he or she is paid a disablement pension that will not be deducted.

We found it very difficult to decide what the law ought to be and the consultation paper did not offer a provisionally preferred view. Instead we put forward several options (including leaving the law as it is) on which we sought the views of consultees.[76] The most radical reform would be, in effect, to deduct all collateral benefits from damages which meet the same loss including charitable payments, personal accident insurance and disablement pensions. A second, still radical, option would be to deduct all collateral benefits from damages which meet the same loss except charitable payments. A third, and less radical, reform would be to leave the present law as it is, except that disablement pensions would be deducted.

What we did indicate was that there are strong arguments for favouring greater deduction. First, the basic notion that damages are to compensate the plaintiff, and not to punish the defendant, indicates that *prima facie* collateral benefits should be deducted. That is, compensation equals deduction. Secondly, to deduct collateral benefits would reduce damages and would therefore reduce the cost of the tort system without unduly prejudicing victims, who will be fully compensated in any event. Thirdly, the main policy reasons for non-

---

[71] See, e.g., *Turner* v. *MOD* (1969) 113 SJ 585; *Hussain* v. *New Taplow Paper Mills Ltd* [1988] AC 514.

[72] Social Security (Recovery of Benefits) Act 1997.

[73] *Redpath* v. *Belfast and County Down Railway* [1947] NI 167.

[74] *Bradburn* v. *The Great Western Railway Co.* (1874) LR 10 Exch 1.

[75] *Parry* v. *Cleaver* [1970] AC 1; *Smoker* v. *London Fire and Civil Defence Authority* [1991] 2 AC 502.

[76] Consultation Paper No. 147, paras. 4.79–4.105.

deduction, of, say, insurance payments that have been put by judges—in particular by Lord Reid in *Parry* v. *Cleaver*[77]—may not withstand close scrutiny. For example, to the argument that deduction would act as a disincentive for parties to take out insurance, it can be counter-argued that it is unlikely that the law is known about by those who are about to take out insurance and, even if it were, deduction would not act as a real disincentive because a prudent person would take out insurance anyway. In particular, it would guarantee payment even where the injury is not caused by a legal wrong. Similarly, to the argument that non-deduction ensures that the plaintiff gets what he or she has paid for, one can equally well argue that the plaintiff has not paid for double recovery but has rather paid to ensure that he or she receives full compensation, including in situations where there would be no legal claim for compensation.

What makes this area particularly difficult is that there are three parties involved, so that the position as between the provider of the collateral benefit and the victim or the tortfeasor must be considered, as well as the position as between the victim and the tortfeasor. If there were to be greater deductibility of collateral benefits, one may wish to give the provider of the collateral benefit a restitutionary claim against the tortfeasor for having effectively discharged a liability of the tortfeasor to the victim.[78] Alternatively, if collateral benefits were not to be deducted, so that *prima facie* the victim would be overcompensated, one might wish to give the provider of the collateral benefit a restitutionary remedy against the victim to recover the overcompensation.[79]

Although the issues raised by this paper are of immense difficulty, one must not lose sight of their central strategic importance. If, in other respects, changes in the law will result in higher damages being awarded to plaintiffs, one must carefully consider how those increases are to be paid for (i.e. what the impact on insurance premiums will be). One way in which they could be paid for (i.e. one way of minimising the necessary increases in insurance premiums) would be to deduct collateral benefits so that some victims are not overcompensated.

The final consultation paper, *Claims for Wrongful Death*[80] looks at

---

[77] [1970] AC 1.
[78] Consultation Paper No. 147, paras. 5.3–5.21. This would involve reversing *Metropolitan Police District Receiver* v. *Croydon Corp.* [1957] 2 QB 154.
[79] Consultation Paper No. 147, paras. 5.22–5.26.
[80] Consultation Paper No. 148 (1997).

who can claim damages when another person is wrongfully killed and how much the damages should be. For example, if a person is killed in a car accident or an accident at work as a result of another's negligence, who can claim damages against the negligent person and how much will those damages be? The present law is entirely based on the Fatal Accidents Act 1976.

If we first of all look at damages for pecuniary loss caused by the wrongful death, who can claim? Historically this has been laid down in a fixed list of dependants. In the Fatal Accidents Act 1846 those who could claim were the wife, husband, parent, child, step-parent, stepchild, grandparent or grandchild of the deceased. The Fatal Accidents Act 1959 extended this to include, for example, brother, sister, uncle, aunt and cousin. The list was further extended by the Administration of Justice Act 1982, amending the 1976 Act, to include former husband and wife and a cohabitee, who is defined as a person who lived with the deceased in the same household "as the husband or wife of the deceased" for two years immediately before the death. But the present list still makes unjust omissions. For example, it excludes long-term same sex cohabitees, children of the deceased's cohabitee whom the deceased supported, and a friend of the deceased who was supported by him albeit that they did not have a marriage-like relationship. It is our provisional view that the time has come to abandon an exclusive statutory list which keeps on having to be updated.[81] Instead any person should be entitled to recover who can prove that he or she has lost the financial support of the deceased; or, putting it another way, any person should be entitled to recover who was, or but for the death would have been, dependent, wholly or partly, on the deceased. Proof of a factual dependency has to be made out in any event under the present law by a dependant who is on the fixed list. Our provisional proposal therefore is that one could abandon the first requirement (being on the list) and move straight to the second requirement (proof of factual dependency).

"Damages for bereavement" were introduced in 1982 and are essentially intended to compensate for the dependant's grief and sorrow caused by the death. Two main problems have arisen. The first is that bereavement damages can be claimed by only a very narrow class of people, namely the spouse of the deceased or the parents of the deceased if the child was unmarried and under 18 at the time of his or her death. It is our provisional view that this very narrow list

---

[81] Consultation Paper No. 148, paras. 3.18–3.337.

should be extended to include the deceased's children, brother and sister, and parents even if the deceased was married and over 18; and we seek consultees' views on whether cohabitees in a long-term relationship should also be able to claim bereavement damages.[82] The second problem is the level of bereavement damages, which are fixed at a particular sum, subject to alteration by the Lord Chancellor. The present amount is £7,500, having been uplifted once from the original figure of £3,500. It is our provisional view that there should be a modest increase to £10,000,[83] that that award should be index-linked so that it will not in future fall behind inflation,[84] and that the full sum should be recovered by each of those who can claim, rather than, as at present, being split between parents.[85] The modest increase to £10,000 is based on the need to reflect inflation since 1991 when the £7,500 figure was fixed, and that £10,000 will be consistent with the levels of damages for non-pecuniary loss generally (but taking account of the fact that many consider that those levels are too low). Our provisional view is that a moderate uplift only is appropriate. In particular, it must be borne in mind that grief and sorrow at the death of another are suffered in any event on natural death.

We do not agree with those who argue that bereavement damages should be abolished on the grounds that one cannot properly put a sum of money on grief and sorrow. It is more insulting to relatives to award nothing for grief and sorrow even if one accepts that any award for non-pecuniary loss is imperfect. It must also be remembered that, in other areas, intangible losses are compensated, as for example pain and suffering in personal injury cases and the upset of a ruined holiday caused by a breach of contract.

In contrast to the above concerns, it would seem that some dependants are being overcompensated under the Fatal Accidents Act 1976. This is a result of two provisions. The first is section 3(3) which lays down that, in assessing a widow's damages, her remarriage or the prospects of her remarriage are to be ignored. This means that if a husband is killed, a widow is entitled to full damages even though she has remarried a millionaire. The reasons for this provision, introduced by section 4 of the Law Reform (Miscellaneous Provisions) Act 1971, were essentially to avoid distressing cross-examination of a

---

[82] Consultation Paper No. 148, paras. 3.141–3.157.
[83] Consultation Paper No. 148, paras. 3.162–3.167.
[84] Consultation Paper No. 148, paras. 3.168–3.169
[85] Consultation Paper No. 148, paras. 3.170–3.173.

widow and to avoid the judiciary having to consider a widow's physical attractiveness. Yet no distressing enquiries are required to determine the fact of remarriage. And, even if thought valid today, the argument put forward in 1971 that taking the fact of remarriage into account would encourage "living in sin" cannot stand as a rational objection if, as appears to be the law, the fact of financially supportive cohabitation is taken into account.[86]

The second overcompensating provision is section 4 of the 1976 Act which lays down that all benefits received as a result of the death are to be ignored in assessing damages. This means that a widow who, as a result of her husband's wrongful death, receives full financial support under her widow's pension is still entitled to full damages for loss of support. And, applying a natural interpretation, it would even mean that a child who was supported by the deceased father's investment income and then inherits those investments is still entitled to loss of support from those investments.[87] It is also clear that social security benefits (for example, income support, family credit, widow's pension, widow's payment and widowed mother's allowance) are to be ignored. In general terms, this raises the same issues as we have discussed above in relation to collateral benefits in personal injury cases. There seems no good reason why one should adopt a different approach to collateral benefits as between personal injury claims and fatal accidents claims.[88] Even if one is not willing to adopt a *prima facie* rule of deduction, it would seem preferable to go back to a listing of the benefits that are to be ignored. At the very least, this would ensure that section 4 does not have a wider effect than appears to have been intended by the Legislature.[89]

(3) *Illegal Transactions*

This project is concerned with one of the most complex and technical areas of English law.[90] It focuses primarily on "illegal" contracts

---

[86] See Consultation Paper No. 148, paras. 3.56–3.68, where we set out four main options for reform of s. 3(3).

[87] Cf. *Wood* v. *Bentall Simplex Ltd* [1992] PIQR P332 where that natural interpretation was not taken, it being decided that, as no loss had been suffered, s. 4 had no part to play. For the problems in interpreting s. 4 see, e.g., *Stanley* v. *Saddique* [1992] QB 1 and *Hayden* v. *Hayden* [1992] 1 WLR 686. See, generally, Consultation Paper No. 148, paras. 2.49–2.60.

[88] Consultation Paper No. 148, para. 3.78.

[89] Consultation Paper No. 148, paras. 3.73–3.76.

[90] We hope to publish a consultation paper on this topic by the end of 1998.

but it also covers "illegal" trusts (hence the more wide-ranging title, "illegal transactions"). Practitioners faced with a question on illegal transactions (for example, the effect on the validity of a contract of performance being contrary to a statutory regulation) can be forgiven for being terrified, not least because the writers of text-books differ so much in their exposition of the relevant law.

There are initial problems over definition and classification. The courts have never attempted a precise definition of an "illegal" contract (or trust) and commentators have different views, with some distinguishing between illegal contracts, on the one hand, and contracts that are void as being contrary to public policy, on the other.[91] Closely linked to this is how one should classify "illegal" contracts. There are several approaches. Some writers, for example, distinguish between whether the source of the illegality is statute or common law[92]; some distinguish between contracts to commit crimes or other legal wrongs on the one hand and contracts that are contrary to public policy on the other[93]; and some between whether the contract is illegal as formed or as performed.[94]

These difficulties and differences of opinion should not, however, be exaggerated. While they make the subject needlessly difficult to "access", they are less the concern of the statutory reformer than the text-book writer. If one uses the term "illegality" in a wide sense, illegal contracts are contracts whose formation or performance or purpose is a crime or a tort or is otherwise contrary to public policy. Included within this are contracts that are illegal because tainted by the illegality of a primary contract with which they are linked. And for these purposes a contract should not be regarded as being contrary to public policy, but rather as being void, unenforceable or invalid for another more specific reason, where: (a) it fails to comply with formalities; or (b) there is a factor vitiating consent such as misrepresen-

[91] This distinction is made by, for example, G.C. Cheshire, C.H.S. Fifoot and M.P. Furmston, *Law of Contract* (13th edn., Butterworths, 1996), chs. 11–12; and by P.S. Atiyah, *An Introduction to the Law of Contract* (5th edn., OUP, 1995), chs. 17–18. Cf. E. McKendrick, *Contract Law* (3rd edn., Macmillan, 1997), 291, "this division is a troublesome one" because of the difficulty of deciding which contracts fall into which category.

[92] E.g. Cheshire, Fifoot and Furmston, *Law of Contract* (13th edn., 1996), 362–85; *Anson's Law of Contract* (ed. A.G. Guest) (26th edn., OUP, 1984), 292–339; E. McKendrick, *Contract Law* (3rd edn., 1997), 287, 290–9.

[93] E.g., G.H. Treitel, *The Law of Contract* (9th edn., Sweet & Maxwell, 1995), 389–437; P.S. Atiyah, *An Introduction to the Law of Contract* (5th edn., 1995), 341–5.

[94] E.g., Cheshire, Fifoot and Furmston, *Law of Contract* (13th edn., 1996), 387–406; P.S. Atiyah, *An Introduction to the Law of Contract* (5th edn., 1995), 351–3; E. McKendrick, *Contract Law* (3rd edn., 1997), 287–90.

tation, undue influence, duress, unconscionability or inequality of bargaining power; or (c) one of the parties lacks the capacity to make the contract (including where the contract is *ultra vires* a company). Defined in the above wide sense, illegal contracts include wagering contracts and contracts in restraint of trade.

The project primarily focuses on the consequences/effects of a transaction being illegal. This is the question at the forefront of practitioners' minds. At present, the law on it is complex, uncertain and, in some respects, unfair. In particular, it is governed by technical rules which, on the face of it, may hamper just solutions albeit that, in practice, the courts may very often be willing to manipulate the rules to achieve a desired outcome. Even if the consequence is that correct decisions are reached, they have to be reached indirectly by opaque reasoning, and this process adds to the uncertainty and complexity of the law. Although it may be difficult to devise new rules that give absolute certainty, it would seem that reform should aim to enable the courts to take into account, directly and openly, the factors that should be important in reaching a fair decision as to the consequences of illegality.

Tinsley v. *Milligan*[95] provides an excellent illustration of the problem. Cohabitees put a house in the name of only one of them, despite the fact that both had contributed to its purchase, in order to suggest that the other had no means. The purpose was to defraud the Department of Social Security. When the parties fell out, the "owner" (the plaintiff) argued that the presumed resulting trust, that would normally have given the defendant a share in the house, could not be relied on by the defendant because of the fraud. By a bare majority the House of Lords rejected that argument and held that the presumed resulting trust was valid. Both the majority and minority of their Lordships felt bound to adopt a technical approach, under which they could not weigh up directly the competing policy arguments for upholding, or not upholding, the trust. The majority considered that the relevant technical rule in play was the rule in *Bowmakers Ltd* v. *Barnet Instruments Ltd*,[96] namely that one could not assert title where to do so involved reliance on an illegal transaction. Here the defendant was not relying on the illegal transaction in the sense that she did not need to adduce any evidence of that transaction to establish her equitable title which was rather presumed from her having provided part of the purchase price. The position would

---

[95] [1994] 1 AC 340.
[96] [1945] KB 65.

have been different had she been trying to rebut a presumption of advancement. In contrast, Lords Goff and Keith, dissenting, considered that, in equity, there is an absolute rule that a person who comes to equity "must come with clean hands" and that the *Bowmakers* rule, confining illegality to where one had to rely on it, was a rule of common law only.

None of their Lordships felt free to weigh openly the relevant policy factors in play which included, on the one hand, the need to deter fraud and that the defendant knew that she was engaged in criminal conduct; and, on the other hand, the fact that denial of the equitable title would leave an equally guilty fraudster with a large windfall and would cause the defendant a considerable loss that was disproportionate to the relatively minor crime involved. A weighing of these factors points clearly in favour of recognising the defendant's equitable title. It seems very likely, therefore, that had their Lordships been able to weigh these factors openly, they would have decided (as the majority did) that the defendant's equitable title should be recognised. But in that event the process of reasoning would have been straightforward and transparent rather than opaque and technical.

The problem with applying a technical approach was subsequently avoided in *Tribe* v. *Tribe*[97]—where a presumption of advancement applied in respect of a transfer of shares by a father to his son in order to defeat creditors—only by the fortuity that the father's creditors had not been defrauded. This meant that the father was able to recover the shares on the basis of withdrawal during the *"locus poenitentiae"* (that is, the father could withdraw because, as he had reached an agreement with his creditors, the illegal purpose was not carried into effect).

But in the Australian case of *Nelson* v. *Nelson*[98] there was no such let out. Instead the High Court of Australia launched a scathing attack on the House of Lords' reasoning in *Tinsley* v. *Milligan* and refused to apply such a technical approach. Rather they allowed a mother to adduce evidence of her illegal purpose in order to rebut a presumption of advancement. As McHugh J said, "A doctrine of illegality that depends upon the state of the pleadings or the need to rely on a transaction that has an unlawful purpose is neither satisfactory nor soundly based in legal policy."[99]

[97] [1996] Ch. 107.
[98] (1995) 70 AJLR 47. See N. Enonchong, "Illegality and the Presumption of Advancement" [1996] *RLR* 78.
[99] *Ibid.*, at 87.

Giving the courts the discretion to weigh relevant factors may therefore be the best way forward. However, the temptation simply to give the courts an open discretion to decide what is a just solution in relation to the effects of illegality should, perhaps, be resisted.[100] Some additional certainty would be gained by structuring the courts' discretion. One should perhaps also accept in formulating the discretion—so as to avoid needlessly cutting across common law rules and principles—that generally illegality acts as a defence to what would otherwise be a standard (contractual or restitutionary) remedy or a standard recognition of proprietary rights. That is, one is generally asking whether the remedies or rights, that would apply if the transaction were valid, are to be denied or modified because of the illegality of the transaction. Needless uncertainty might be created if the courts were given a wide discretion to invent new remedies or principles that are inconsistent with those given in relation to non-illegal transactions.

It should be noted, finally, that one clear exception to illegality being a defence to normal remedies and rights is withdrawal during the "*locus poenitentiae*".[101] The law here recognises a special remedy (of withdrawal) that is available only to a party to an illegal transaction. Although there is disagreement on its precise governing rules,[102] the best view would seem to be that the withdrawal remedy is designed to encourage a party to "break" the contract or other transaction where this would have the effect of thwarting, in whole or in part, an illegal purpose.

4. SOME POSSIBLE FUTURE PROJECTS[103]

In this section I offer a personal view, coloured by suggestions made to me, of possible future Law Commission projects in contract and tort. In so doing (some of) the main defects in the English laws of

---

[100] See A. Burrows, *The Law of Restitution* (Butterworths, 1993), 471–2. Cf. New Zealand Illegal Contracts Act 1970, s. 7.

[101] Burrows, *The Law of Restitution*, 333–41.

[102] *Ibid.* In *Tribe* v. *Tribe* [1996] Ch. 107, 135, Millett LJ rejected the view that genuine repentance is required.

[103] These are personal views and must not be taken as suggesting that any of those projects meet all the project-selection criteria applied by the Law Commission: see 165 above. Note also that I do not here mention possible projects in relation to specialised areas of contract. For example, it is arguable that legislative reform is needed in relation to guarantees and indemnities, and in respect of non-disclosure in insurance contracts: see *Sixth Programme of Law Reform*, Law Com. No. 234 (1995), para. 3.2.

contract and tort will be exposed; and, at the same time, we shall see
where (some of) the main future developments in contract and tort
are likely to lie (whether brought about by the Legislature or by the
judges).

The discussion first looks at four areas (consideration, compound
interest, unfair terms and damages for a public authority's *ultra vires*
acts) where legislative reform seems appropriate. It concludes by
examining a number of other possible projects (on defamation,
privacy, damages for negligent valuation, constructive notice and
vitiated transactions, and liability for pure economic loss in the tort
of negligence) where, in my view, legislative reform would be inappropriate at least at the present time.

(1) *Consideration*

The requirement of consideration—that something requested must
be given in return for a promise in order to make it binding—ensures
that only bargain promises, and not gratuitous promises, are enforceable in English law. In civil law systems this is not so and, even in
England, there are a number of exceptions to the need for consideration, which cast doubt on its underlying validity. In particular, a
promise contained in a deed is valid, whether or not there is consideration; proprietary estoppel protects a promisee's expectations of
being given proprietary rights where the promisee has detrimentally
relied on a promise to be given such rights[104]; and promissory estoppel may operate to prevent a promisor breaking a promise to give up
existing rights where the promisee has relied on that promise.[105]
There are also very specific exceptions, for example documentary let-
ters of credit[106] and compositions with creditors.[107]

The decision of the Court of Appeal in *Williams* v. *Roffey Bros. &
Nicholls (Contractors) Ltd*[108] raises further difficulties. In that case it was
held that a head-contractor's promise to pay sub-contracting joiners

[104] E.g. *Dillwyn* v. *Llewellyn* (1862) 4 De G F & J 517; *Inwards* v. *Baker* [1965] 2 QB 29;
Crabb v. *Arun District Council* [1976] Ch. 179; *Pascoe* v. *Turner* [1979] 1 WLR 431; *A–G of
Hong Kong* v. *Humphreys Estate (Queen's Garden)* [1987] AC 114; *Brinnand* v. *Ewens* (1987) 19
HLR 415.
[105] E.g. *Central London Property Ltd* v. *High Trees House Ltd* [1947] KB 130; *Combe* v.
Combe [1951] 2 KB 215.
[106] See Treitel, *The Law of Contract* (9th edn., 1995), 140.
[107] *Ibid.*, 119–20.
[108] [1991] 1 QB 1.

extra money to complete their pre-existing contractual duties on time was a binding promise, supported by consideration, albeit that the promise would have been voidable if made under economic duress. The consideration was deemed to be the "practical benefit" of the work being completed on time even through the head-contractor was already contractually entitled to that and, in one sense therefore, did not receive anything extra or different in return for its promise.

If one accepts that performance of, or a promise to perform, a pre-existing duty is good consideration for a promise to pay extra, it is hard to see why, applying the same logic, part performance, or a promise to perform part, of a pre-existing duty should not be good consideration for a promise to give up an entitlement to full perfor-mance.[109] While one must again be careful not to enforce promises entered into under duress, it would seem that in line with *Williams* v. *Roffey* there is a "practical benefit" to promisors in receiving part per-formance, where the practical alternative may be no performance at all. Yet three Court of Appeal cases[110] since *Williams* v. *Roffey* have adhered to the traditional view, established in *Foakes* v. *Beer*,[111] that such promises are not supported by consideration and are therefore unenforceable. These cases have also either marginalised, or ignored, the potential operation on these facts of promissory estoppel.

The picture is therefore one of incoherence and some uncertainty. It represents English law struggling to decide whether to enforce informal gratuitous promises and deciding that, in some circum-stances but not all, it should do so. The law would be rendered more intelligible and clear if the need for consideration were abolished and gratuitous promises that have been accepted or relied on were held to be binding (subject to the operation of normal contractual rules relating to, for example, the intention to create legal relations, duress, and illegality).[112]

---

[109] For examination of this issue, see Janet O'Sullivan, "In Defence of *Foakes* v. *Beer*" [1996] *CLJ* 219; E. McKendrick, *Contract Law* (3rd edn., 1997,) 91–3; J. Adams and R. Brownsword, *Key Issues in Contract* (Butterworths, 1995), 113–15; Mindy Chen-Wishart, "Consideration: Practical Benefit and the Emperor's New Clothes" in J. Beatson and D. Friedmann (eds.), *Good Faith and Fault in Contract Law* (OUP, 1995), 123–50.

[110] *Re Selectmove Ltd* [1995] 1 WLR 474; *Re C, a Debtor*, unreported, CA, 11 May 1994; *Ferguson* v. *Davies* [1997] 1 All ER 315.

[111] (1884) 9 App. Cas. 605.

[112] Harvey McGregor, *Contract Code drawn up on behalf of the English Law Commission* (Guiffré Editore, Sweet & Maxwell, 1993), 1–3, favours abandoning consideration so that, *prima facie*, every agreement would be binding as a contract unless the persons making the

Wide-ranging reform of consideration was proposed in 1937 by the Law Revision Committee in its Sixth Interim Report.[113] Although not recommending abolition of the doctrine as such, the Committee proposed that a promise should be binding without consideration where, for example, it is in writing, or where it is supported by past consideration, or where it is a firm offer, or where it is a promise to forgo part or all of what was already owed, or where it is a promise to perform a pre-existing duty, or where it has been detrimentally relied on.[114]

Those proposals were combined with recommending abolition of the benefit side of the privity doctrine.[115] Many would argue that these two great traditional features of English contract law—consideration and privity—do indeed go hand-in-glove and that the case for reform of consideration has recently been strengthened by the Law Commission's proposals for reforming privity.[116] Indeed in that report on Privity we accepted that, while formally our proposals did not affect the requirement of consideration, at a deeper policy level they could be regarded as relaxing the importance attached to consideration; and that, taken together with existing exceptions to the need for consideration, the doctrine of consideration might be a suitable topic for a future separate review by the Law Commission.[117] It should also be noted that in *Re Selectmove Ltd*[118] Peter Gibson LJ said, in relation to whether the principle of *Williams* v. *Roffey* should be extended to overturn *Foakes* v. *Beer*, "If that extension is to be made, it must be made by the House of Lords or, perhaps even more appropriately, by Parliament after consideration by the Law Commission."[119]

But while legislative reform of consideration appears justified in order to render English contract law more coherent and certain—and to bring English law more into line with that of civil law systems—it may be argued that the topic has insufficient practical importance to

agreement do not intend to be legally bound by it. See also *Unidroit Statement of Principles for International Commercial Contracts*, Art. 3.1.

[113] *Statute of Frauds and the Doctrine of Consideration* (1937), Cmd. 5449, paras. 26–40, 50.

[114] See, similarly, the proposals of the Ontario Law Reform Committee, *Report on Amendment of the Law of Contract* (1987), ch. 2.

[115] Law Revision Committee, Sixth Interim Report, n. 113 above, paras. 48, 50.

[116] *Privity of Contract: Contracts for the Benefit of Third Parties*, Law Com. No. 242 (1996). See 166–8 above.

[117] Law Com. No. 242, para. 6.17.

[118] [1995] 1 WLR 474.

[119] *Ibid.*, at 481.

merit a Law Commission review. The range of exceptions (including, most recently, the approach in *Williams* v. *Roffey*)—and the fact
that English law recognises that nominal consideration counts—may
mean that, as a practical matter, the need for consideration causes little injustice or difficulty.[120] Nevertheless the doctrine is so deep-
seated that judicial "reform" can only be of a very limited type; and
while reform may not be urgent, the modernisation of English contract law—in line with commercial expectations—surely requires
that, for example, firm offers are binding[121] and that a promise to
accept a lesser sum is binding where not induced by duress (or
another vitiating factor).

(2) *Compound Interest*

There are three non-statutory bases for awarding interest, whether
simple or compound, in English law. First, where a debtor has
agreed, expressly or impliedly, to pay interest on a debt, that interest
is payable as part of the award of the agreed sum.[122] Secondly, while
the general rule is that damages cannot be awarded for the failure to
pay a debt, the plaintiff can recover damages for special loss suffered
(including, e.g., interest payable to a third party) as a consequence of
such a breach of contract.[123] Thirdly, there is an equitable jurisdiction to award interest, including compound interest, in cases of prof-
iting by fraud or breach of fiduciary duty.[124]

In contrast, the statutory discretion under section 35A of the
Supreme Court Act 1981 to award interest on a debt or damages
(which does not apply unless proceedings have been commenced
although, as we have seen, the Government has decided to rectify this

---

[120] Johan Steyn, "Contract Law: Fulfilling the Reasonable Expectations of Honest Men"
(1997) 113 *LQR* 433, 437: "In my view, the case for abandoning the privity rule is made out.
But I have no radical proposals for the wholesale review of the doctrine of consideration. I
am not persuaded that it is necessary."

[121] See Treitel, *The Law of Contract* (9th edn., 1995), 141–2; *Firm Offers*, Law Commission
Working Paper 60 (1975) (firm offer to be binding if made in the course of a business and
expressed to be irrevocable for a definite period, not to exceed six years); Vienna
Convention on Contracts for the International Sale of Goods, Art. 16(2).

[122] *Cook* v. *Fowler* (1874) LR 7 HL 27; *National Bank of Greece* v. *Pinios Shipping Co. No.
1* [1990] 1 AC 637.

[123] *Wadsworth* v. *Lydall* [1981] *1 WLR 598*. See A. Burrows, *Remedies for Torts and Breach
of Contract* (2nd edn., Butterworths, 1994), 97–9; 151 above.

[124] *President of India* v. *La Pintada Compania* [1985] AC 104; *Westdeutsche Landesbank
Girozentrale* v. *Islington BC* [1996] AC 669.

by giving creditors an automatic right to interest after thirty days on unpaid commercial debts[125]) is confined to simple interest only. On the face of it, this seems odd.[126]

Depending on the purpose of the main remedy in question, interest is awarded to ensure full relief. Hence interest on an award of compensatory damages for a civil wrong is designed to ensure full compensation; and in many circumstances the plaintiff's loss will be best reflected in the compound interest rate at which it has had to borrow replacement funds or at which it has had to forgo lending, or otherwise investing, the funds. Similarly interest on a restitutionary award should ensure that the defendant's enrichment at the plaintiff's expense is fully reversed; and this may only be so if the defendant's enrichment through saving the expense of borrowing an equivalent sum at compound interest rates (which matches the plaintiff's loss of the opportunity to lend an equivalent sum at compound interest rates) is reflected in an award of compound interest from the date of the principal unjust enrichment. It follows that for the courts to be confined to awarding simple interest only will often mean that plaintiffs are deprived of full and proper relief.

In *Westdeutsche Landesbank Girozentrale* v. *Islington LBC*[127] the House of Lords had the opportunity to develop the law by awarding compound interest on a common law restitutionary claim for money paid under a void interest rate swap transaction. By a bare majority (Lords Goff and Woolf dissenting) their Lordships refused to do so. To develop the equitable jurisdiction to award compound interest beyond its two recognised categories (fraud or breach of fiduciary duty) was felt to be unacceptable as outflanking the Legislature's decision to allow simple interest only under the Supreme Court Act 1981 (and before that under section 3(1) of the Law Reform (Miscellaneous Provisions) Act 1934). Lord Lloyd also argued that to allow the award of compound interest might cause uncertainty and consequent litigation, for example as to the rate to be awarded. In contrast, Lords Goff and Woolf saw the award of compound interest, in the instant case, as essential in order to achieve full and proper restitution; and there was thought to be no countervailing good reason for refusing to extend the equitable jurisdiction. They cited with approval Hobhouse J's statement at first instance: "Anyone who lends or bor-

<hr>

[125] See 153 above.
[126] For criticism of the present law see, e.g., F.A. Mann, "On Interest, Compound Interest and Damages" (1985) 101 *LQR* 30, 42–6.
[127] [1996] AC 669.

rows money on a commercial basis receives or pays interest periodically and if that interest is not paid it is compounded . . . I see no reason why I should deny the plaintiff a complete remedy or allow the defendant arbitrarily to retain part of the enrichment which it has unjustly enjoyed."[128]

After *Westdeutsche*, therefore, the present law emerges as fragmented and incoherent; and the House of Lords, by a majority, has declared itself powerless to improve the position.

There is an added reason for concern. Section 49 of the Arbitration Act 1996 has given an arbitrator the power to award simple *or compound* interest at such rates and with such rests as it thinks fit. It is hard to see why arbitrators should have that power, while the courts do not. Moreover, a powerful practical reason for the reform in relation to arbitrators, that was relied on by the Departmental Advisory Committee on Arbitration Law, applies equally to the courts. The Committee said, "There is no doubt that the absence of such a power adds to the delays (and thus the expense) of arbitrations and causes injustice, for it is often in a party's interest to delay the proceedings and the honouring of an award, since the interest eventually payable is less than can be made by holding on to funds which should be paid over to the other party, who of course is losing out by a like amount".[129]

But while the case for giving the courts the power to award compound interest is very strong, there are some significant difficulties. In particular, there may be uncertainty as to when compound interest is appropriate. In principle, availability ought to depend on the evidence of the defendant's or plaintiff's actual or likely borrowing or lending. This may require detailed investigation and argument. It may have to yield to a pragmatic (but inaccurate) black-and-white distinction between commercial cases where compound interest is appropriate and non-commercial cases where it is not. A similar objection can be posed in relation to the fixing of the appropriate rate. Absolute accuracy in calculation, geared to the facts of the particular case, may be thought too complex. Again a pragmatic solution might be the best way forward, with use being made of authoritative "multiplier" tables.[130]

---

[128] [1994] 4 All ER 890, 955.

[129] Report on the Arbitration Bill of the Departmental Advisory Committee on Arbitration Law, Feb. 1996, para. 236.

[130] This has been proposed by the Law Reform Commission of Hong Kong, *Report on Interest on Debt and Damages* (1990) and the New Zealand Law Commission, *The Award of Interest on Money Claims* (1994).

(3) *Unfair Terms (Especially Exclusion and Limitation Clauses)*

We have now had twenty years' experience of the Unfair Contract Terms Act 1977, which remains the major legislative contribution to the general principles of English contract law.[131] The Act strikes down, or gives the courts discretion to strike down, unreasonable exclusion and limitation clauses (and indemnity clauses). The statute should be regarded as a success, in that it has transformed thinking about exclusion and limitation clauses without spawning a huge amount of litigation. Indeed there is a dearth of case law on the Act. What there has been has, by and large, shown the judges interpreting the Act without excessive difficulty or controversy. For example, decisions have clarified: the meaning of "written *standard* terms of business"[132] and "*deals* as a consumer"[133]; that section 2 of the Act does not apply to indemnity clauses unless the party bound to provide the indemnity was itself the victim of the other party's negligence[134]; that section 3 does apply to a clause which would restrict the normal right to set off damages for breach of contract[135]; and that a compromise or settlement of one's rights does not fall under the Act (and in particular does not fall within section 10 dealing with secondary contracts).[136]

I therefore do not subscribe to the view that there is a "yawning conceptual void"[137] at the heart of the Act or that a "reconsideration of the whole basis of the Act"[138] is required. These criticisms are principally directed to the fact that the Act essentially treats exclusion and limitation clauses as defences to what would otherwise be a breach of duty: and it does not clarify the extent to which clauses which define obligations or duties are covered by its provisions. But it is doubtful whether one could provide a watertight definition of clauses defining obligations that should be covered by the Act (unless all contract terms are to be covered); and the basic thrust of the Act is comprehensible and clear.

---

[131] The 1977 Act was the product of *Exemption Clauses: Second Report of the Two Commissions*, Law Com. No. 69, Scot. Law Com. No. 39 (1975).

[132] *Chester Grosvenor Hotel* v. *Alfred McAlpine Management Ltd* (1991) 56 Build. LR 115.

[133] *St Albans City & DC* v. *International Computers Ltd* [1996] 4 All ER 481.

[134] *Phillips Products Ltd* v. *Hyland and Hamstead Plant Hire Co. Ltd* [1987] 2 All ER 620 and *Thompson* v. *T. Lohan (Plant Hire) Ltd* [1987] 2 All ER 631.

[135] *Stewart Gill Ltd* v. *Horatio Myer & Co. Ltd* [1992] QB 600.

[136] *Tudor Grange Holdings Ltd* v. *City Bank NA* [1992] Ch. 53.

[137] Cheshire, Fifoot and Furmston's *Law of Contract* (13th edn., 1996), 203.

[138] E. McKendrick, *Contract Law* (3rd edn., 1997), 217.

This is not to deny that improvements can be made in relation to the law on exclusion and limitation clauses. First, there have been a few "rogue" decisions which it may be thought appropriate to over-turn. For example, in *R & B Customs Brokers Ltd* v. *United Dominions Trust Ltd*[139] it was decided that a company deals as a consumer unless it is actually in the business of making the sort of contract in issue. So, on the facts, it was held that a company purchasing a company car for one of its employees was dealing as a consumer because cars were not its business. A preferable approach might be to clarify that a consumer must be a natural person and not a company.

Secondly, because the 1977 Act not only reformed the law but also consolidated some existing legislation concerning exclusion clauses, the Act has some odd features. In particular, the guidelines for the application of the reasonableness test set out in Schedule 2 are, strictly speaking, applicable only in relation to sections 6 and 7 and not in relation to sections 2 and 3.[140] Although the courts have applied those guidelines analogously to sections 2 and 3,[141] it is unnecessarily complex and misleading for that distinction to remain on the face of the statute. Similarly, it is questionable whether the distinction, between those clauses that are rendered void and those that are void only if unreasonable, is justified in terms of policy. For example, should the exclusion of the implied term as to good title in a contract for the sale of goods be void,[142] whereas other exclusion clauses in a contract for the sale of goods can only be struck down, as against a person dealing otherwise than as consumer, if unreasonable?[143]

Thirdly, and perhaps most importantly, the 1977 Act—except for the five general guidelines in Schedule 2—does not purport to lay down factors to be taken into account by the courts in deciding the reasonableness test. It can be argued that, now that the courts have applied the test in numerous cases, it would be appropriate to specify the factors to be taken into account more comprehensively in the statute. In our *Feasibility Investigation of Joint and Several Liability*,[144] we referred to this problem in the specific context of professionals not being sure of the extent to which they can limit or exclude their

[139] [1988] 1 WLR 321.
[140] S. 11(2) of the 1977 Act.
[141] See, e.g., *Phillips Products Ltd* v. *Hyland and Hamstead Plant Hire Co. Ltd* [1987] 2 All ER 620.
[142] S. 6(1) of the 1977 Act.
[143] S. 6(3) of the 1977 Act.
[144] By the Common Law Team of the Law Commission (see 174–9 above), paras. 5.10–5.26.

liability for negligence. It may even be thought appropriate to lay down in the statute examples of terms which will be regarded as fair and reasonable.

This leads on to a further problem with the Unfair Contract Terms Act 1977: its relationship to the Unfair Terms in Consumer Contracts Regulations 1994. The Department of Trade and Industry has been heavily criticised for opting to introduce these regulations by simply copying out the European Directive (Directive 93/13).[145] No attempt to integrate the Unfair Contract Terms Act and the Directive was made. This means that the law is unnecessarily complex. Consumers are protected by two closely similar but not identical notions, namely the test of fairness/good faith under the Unfair Terms Regulations and the test of reasonableness under the 1977 Act. While in practical terms this duality of test may not produce serious problems, it is peculiarly inappropriate for the relationship between two closely-linked consumer-protection statutes to be obscure.[146] An attempt should have been made—and can still be made—to produce a single simplified statute.

(4) Damages for a Public Authority's Ultra Vires Acts

Under the present law, damages cannot be awarded merely because a public authority has caused loss to a person by invalid administrative action. Rather, to recover damages a person has to establish that the public authority is liable for a recognised tort (or other civil wrong), be it, for example, negligence or breach of statutory duty or the special public law tort of misfeasance in public office. Yet those torts cover only a limited range of situations. Moreover, with the exception of the misfeasance tort, the basis of those torts is that a public authority can only be held liable if a private defendant would also have been held liable, an approach which contradicts the whole development of the modern law on judicial review.

As long ago as 1967 the Law Commission drew attention to this area as a suitable one for a project. In the Working Paper on *Administrative Law*, the Commission said, "it has been suggested that

---

[145] See, e.g., F.M.B. Reynolds, "Unfair Contract Terms" (1994) 110 *LQR* 1; S. Weatherill, "Implementing EC Directives on Consumer Protection—Short-Term Choices by the UK" (1998) 3 *Amicus Curiae* 11.

[146] S. Weatherill, n. 145 above, writes, "[T]he law is now intransparent, which is a weakness of especial consequence in the consumer field".

we need a body of law which, *inter alia*, makes the remedy of damages more widely available where administrative acts are found to be unlawful, and which recognises in the field of contract and tort that the administration as a party is different from a private party and, as in a number of other countries, provides special rules of public law accordingly".[147] In the more recent report on judicial review, the Law Commission said the following: "The fact that English law does not provide for [compensation for those injured by invalid administrative action] has long been the subject of criticism, and a number of factors, including developments in European Community Law, suggest that the general unavailability of compensation against public authorities for invalid administrative action requires reconsideration. However, whether compensation should be available and, if so, what its scope should be calls for deeper study than we could conveniently give it in the present exercise. We agree, however, with those consultees to our consultation paper who said that the time is now ripe for such a study."[148]

The judiciary too has occasionally drawn attention to the problem. For example, Schiemann J said in *R. v. Knowsley Borough Council, ex parte Maguire*, "our law in relation to claims for damages for administrative wrongdoing is notoriously unsatisfactory from the claimant's point of view".[149]

Developments in European Community law have given added impetus to the calls for reform. Where there has been a breach of European law by the state, a person who has been caused loss may recover damages under either the doctrine of "direct effects" or "state liability".[150] Moreover, once the European Convention on Human Rights has been incorporated, a court will be able to award damages against a public authority where the *ultra vires* act is incompatible with a person's Convention rights.[151]

A number of examples can be given of the injustice that, on the face of it, individuals suffer under the present law. For example, a

---

[147] Working Paper No. 13 (1967), para. 8. See also *Administrative Law*, Law Com. No. 20 (1969) para. 9; *Remedies for Administrative Law*, Law Com. No. 73 (1976), para. 9.

[148] *Administrative Law: Judicial Review and Statutory Appeals*, Law Com. No. 226 (1994), para. 2.32.

[149] (1992) 142 *NLJ* 1375.

[150] See, in particular, Cases C–6 & 9/90 *Francovich and Bonifaci v. Italy* [1991] ECR I–5357; C–46 & 48/93 *Brasserie du Pêcheur SA v. Germany; R v. Secretary of State for Transport, ex p Factortame Ltd* [1996] QB 404.

[151] See clauses 6 and 8 of the Human Rights Bill now before Parliament. See further notes 160, 169 below.

market-holder whose market licence is revoked by a local authority *ultra vires* can bring an application for judicial review to get the licence back, but is not entitled to damages in respect of loss incurred in the interim period. Where a planning authority imposes a restriction which unlawfully prevents the applicant trading, the applicant can have the decision set aside but has no right to compensation for the loss suffered as a result of the unlawful restriction. And if a local authority acting *ultra vires* refuses to issue a taxi-cab driver with a licence, the taxi driver is able to have the unlawful decision judicially reviewed but he is not entitled to damages for the loss suffered.

This is not meant to suggest that one could simply move to providing compensation for everyone who suffers loss as a result of a public authority's invalid administrative action. This would appear to be too open-ended and would run the risk of opening the floodgates of litigation. A better approach would seem to be to try to carve out areas where compensation seems especially appropriate, while not opening the door to a mass of claims. While it may be that, when incorporated, the courts in applying the European Convention on Human Rights can take a further step towards providing proper redress for the victims of *ultra vires* acts, it would appear that, as under the present law, compensation for the *ultra vires* infringement of Convention rights will not cover all situations where there should be a remedy.[152] Short of the House of Lords laying down that there is a new tort of invalid administrative action, it would seem that legislation is needed to ensure that reform does not leave undesirable gaps in a citizen's protection. On the other hand, the prospects of specific legislation in this area, which would involve the Government extending its own liability to pay compensation, seem particularly slim.

(5) Other Possible Projects?

I here deal briefly with several other areas of contract or tort that have been drawn to my attention as meriting a Law Commission review, but where my personal view is that, while the law may need reform, legislative reform would be inappropriate *at least at the present time*.[153]

[152] For example, it is not clear that the situations referred to in the previous paragraph of the text above involve incompatibility with Convention rights.

[153] This is not intended to cover all suggestions that have been made to me: rather I focus on those that seem the most important.

(a) *Defamation*

It is commonly suggested that the torts of libel and slander require reform.[154] For example, it can be argued that they impose too strict a liability[155]; and that individuals should not be able to sue, as they presently can, for political libels.[156] More generally, the argument for substantive reform is that English libel law excessively restricts free speech.

Yet legislative reform at this point in time would be particularly inappropriate. This is for two main reasons. First, the law has recently been legislatively reformed by the Defamation Act 1996, which implements most of the recommendations of the Neill Committee.[157] It would be premature to legislate further until the impact of that Act has been properly assessed. Indeed the "offer of amends" defence[158] and the summary/fast track procedure[159] have not yet been brought into force. Secondly, the forthcoming incorporation of the European Convention on Human Rights may give the judges new scope to amend defamation law, particularly in relation to political libels, in order to protect the right to free speech.[160] As is suggested in *Gatley on Libel and Slander*, whilst incorporation "probably does not augur a general revolution in defamation law, we would not be surprised to see early [judicial] developments . . . in relation to privilege and statements about persons involved in public affairs".[161]

---

[154] See also 184–5 above for the argument that judges not juries should assess damages for defamation.

[155] See, e.g., E. Barendt *et al.*, *Libel and the Media, The Chilling Effect* (OUP, 1997), 194–6; G. Bindman, "A Tale of Two Russians" (1998) 148 *NLJ* 307.

[156] See e.g. F. Trindade, "'Political Discussion' and the Law of Defamation" (1995) 111 *LQR* 199; K. Williams, " 'Only Flattery is Safe': Political Speech and the Defamation Act 1996" (1997) 60 *MLR* 387; I. Loveland, "Political Libels and Qualified Privilege: A British Solution to a British Problem" [1997] *PL* 428. F. Trindale, "Defamation in the Course of Political Discussion—The New Common Law Defence" (1998) 114 LQR 1. Organs of government (*Derbyshire CC* v. *Times Newspapers Ltd* [1993] AC 534) and political parties (*Goldsmith* v. *Bhoyrul* [1998] 2 WLR 435) cannot sue for defamation.

[157] Supreme Court Procedure Committee, *Report on Practice & Procedure in Defamation* (1991), chaired by Neill LJ.

[158] Defamation Act 1996, ss. 2–4.

[159] Defamation Act 1996, ss. 8–10.

[160] Freedom of expression is guaranteed by Art. 10 of the ECHR. The Human Rights Bill, now before Parliament, gives individuals direct rights against public authorities. By cl. 6 of the Bill, it is unlawful for a public authority (which is defined to include a court and "any person certain of whose functions are functions of a public nature") to act in a way which is incompatible with rights conferred by the Convention.

[161] *Gatley on Libel and Slander* (9th edn., Sweet & Maxwell, 1998), vii.

(b) *Privacy*

English law has no tort of privacy; this means that there is no tort protecting individuals from the disclosure or publication of personal matters which, although true,[162] are not in the public interest.[163] The best known authority for this is *Kaye* v. *Robertson*,[164] in which it was held that the plaintiff, a well-known television actor, was not entitled to an injunction preventing publication of a photograph of, and "interview" with, him while he was lying critically ill in hospital recovering from brain surgery. Reporters had entered his room without permission. On the other hand, the equitable wrong of breach of confidence will protect individuals from disclosure or publication of *confidential* information (that is, information impressed with an obligation of confidence) unless the disclosure is in the public interest.[165] English law—through breach of confidence—comes very close to a tort of privacy, with the distinction turning on whether the information or matter is merely private, as opposed to being confidential.[166]

The burning question is whether the law should go one step further to a full-blown tort of privacy.[167] But whatever the pros and cons of this, legislation at this stage would be inappropriate.[168] First, there is no obstacle preventing the courts themselves developing a tort of privacy (for example, by giving a very wide interpretation of

[162] It is this that distinguishes privacy from defamation. A true statement is not defamatory.

[163] The right to privacy may also underpin related issues, such as whether evidence obtained by bugging or phone-tapping is admissible evidence: see *R.* v. *Khan* [1997] AC 558. Note also the new statutory tort of harassment created by the Protection from Harassment Act 1996.

[164] [1991] FSR 62, CA.

[165] The Law Commission's Report on *Breach of Confidence*, Law Com. No. 110 (1981), which essentially recommended codifying the law on breach of confidence and putting it on a tortious, rather than equitable wrong, basis, has not been implemented.

[166] A further possible difference is that confidentiality is lost when widely disclosed: but the same may not be true of personal information, so that a plaintiff may well be able to restrain a further infringement of privacy when he would not be able to restrain a further breach of confidence. For the close link between breach of confidence and privacy see *Stephens* v. *Avery* [1988] Ch. 449, where information about the plaintiff's lesbian relationship was told to a friend in confidence. There are obiter dicta which in effect eliminate a distinction between confidence and privacy: *A-G* v. *Guardian Newspapers Ltd* [1990] 1 AC 109, 255 (*per* Lord Keith); *Hellewell* v. *Chief Constable of Derbyshire* [1995] 1 WLR 804, 807 (Laws J).

[167] A statutory tort of privacy was provisionally recommended by the Lord Chancellor's Department and the Scottish Office in a consultation paper *Infringement of Privacy*, July 1993.

[168] The present Government has made clear that it does not intend to legislate.

what constitutes confidential information). Secondly, the courts may be given scope for addressing this issue afresh with the incorporation of the European Convention on Human Rights.[169]

(c) Damages for Negligent Valuation

How one assesses contractual or tortious damages for a negligent valuation has been thrown into confusion and doubt by the decision of the House of Lords in *Banque Bruxelles Lambert SA* v. *Eagle Star Insurance Co. Ltd.*[170] The central question at issue was the extent to which, if at all, valuers who had negligently overvalued property provided as security for loans were liable in damages for the losses suffered by lenders consequent on the collapse of the property market in the early 1990s. For example, let us assume that plaintiffs had advanced £11 million on the security of a property valued by defendants at £15 million. The property's actual value at the time of valuation was £5 million and the plaintiffs ultimately realised £2.5 million on resale. At first instance Phillips J held that the plaintiffs were entitled to be put into as good a position as if they had not entered into the loan transaction but that, on grounds of causation, they were not entitled to damages for the fall in the property market.[171] They were therefore entitled to the money lent (£11 million in the above example) minus the actual value of the property at the date of valuation (£5 million in the above example) plus interest from the date the money was lent. This was reversed by the Court of Appeal which held that, applying a "no transaction" approach, the plaintiffs were entitled to damages for the fall in the market.[172] They

---

[169] The right to respect for private and family life is protected by Art. 8 of the ECHR. For the Human Rights Bill, see n. 160 above. The Press Complaints Commission is, on the face of it, a public authority. Moreover, by cl. 6 of the Bill, a court is a public authority and, although damages cannot be awarded against a court (cl. 9(3)) this would not shield a court from having to exercise a discretion (e.g. whether to grant an injunction) in line with Art. 8. It appears that a court (because a public authority) has a duty to ensure compliance with the ECHR in actions between private parties (i.e. that the Bill is intended to have "horizontal" as well as "vertical" effect) albeit that this, to some extent, negates the Bill's emphasis on public authorities. See *Hansard*, House of Lords Official Report, 24 Nov. 1997, cols. 781–7. See generally, P. Milmo, "Human Rights, Privacy and the Press" (1997) 147 *NLJ* 1631; and the excellent paper by Murray Hunt, "The Impact of a Bill of Rights in English Law" presented to the Third Clifford Chance Conference organised by the Oxford Centre for the Advanced Study of European and Comparative Law on 28 November 1997.

[170] [1997] AC 191. Also known as *South Australia Asset Management Corp* v. *York Montague Ltd*.

[171] [1995] 2 All ER 769.

[172] [1995] QB 375. Five other decisions, some contrary to Phillips J's, were also on appeal.

were therefore entitled to the money lent (£11 million in the above example) minus the value ultimately realised (£2.5 million in the above example) plus interest from the date the money was lent.

The House of Lords took a mid-position. Unfortunately Lord Hoffmann's speech, with which the other Law Lords agreed, is difficult to interpret. It appears to lay down an approach to the assessment of damages in this area which is hard to assimilate with long-established principles. At one level, the reasoning can be expressed quite simply. A lender will be entitled to be put into as good a position as if it had not entered into the loan transaction but can never recover a greater measure than the difference between the represented value of the property and its actual value at the date of the valuation (plus interest). So in the above example the plaintiffs would be entitled to the £8.5 million (£11 million minus £2.5 million) plus interest because that falls within the outer limit of £10 million (£15 million minus £5 million) plus interest. But had the property been valued at £13 million rather than £15 million a maximum of £8 million (plus interest) would have been recoverable.

The central puzzle lies in determining whether and, if so, why that is the correct measure.[173] Lord Hoffmann thought that the answer lay not in remoteness or causation or a cap on liability but rather in analysing at the outset the scope of the valuer's duty of care: the scope of that duty did not extend to protecting the lender against a loss that would have been a consequence of the transaction even if the representation had been true. Or in Lord Hoffmann's words, in an attempt at clarification in the subsequent decision in *Nykredit plc* v. *Edward Erdman Group Ltd*,[174] "he must show that his loss is attributable to the

---

[173] In the words of Jane Stapleton, "Negligent Valuers and Falls in the Property Market" (1997) 113 *LQR* 1, 5, "[W]hy should two lenders who lend the same amount and suffer the same loss due to the fall in the market recover different amounts simply because the extent of the inaccuracy of the relevant careless valuations is different in the two cases?" Much of Stapleton's note is concerned with Lord Hoffmann's admittedly misleading comment about there being a paradox if damages for breach of a warranty as to value were lower than damages for breach of a duty to use reasonable care in giving a valuation. But, with respect to Stapleton, this point was not central to Lord Hoffmann's reasoning. In any event, the recoverability of loss due to a fall in the property market is just as problematic in respect of damages for breach of warranty as it is to damages for breach of a duty to use reasonable care in giving a valuation.

[174] [1997] 1 WLR 1627. This decision focused on the date on which the cause of action accrued for the purpose of interest. Interest was allowed from when the lender had sustained its full allowable loss. Peculiarly their Lordships focused entirely on tort. In contract the accrual date would indisputably have been the date of the negligent valuation, although the appropriate date for interest purposes would presumably still have been the date when the full allowable loss was sustained.

overvaluation, that is, that he is worse off than he would have been if it had been correct."[175]

A number of additional difficult questions arise. Is *Banque Bruxelles* applicable to all instances of negligent misrepresentation or is it confined to property valuations or statements relevant to a property's value?[176] Does it extend beyond damages for negligent misrepresentation to the assessment of damages in other areas?[177] Is the scope of the duty restriction best seen as a new separate restriction on damages or as merely an aspect of remoteness[178] or causation? Was Lord Hoffmann justified in abandoning the distinction developed by the courts[179] between a "no transaction" case (where but for the wrong the lender would not have lent at all) and a "successful transaction" case (where but for the wrong the lender would have lent less)?

Such is the confusion, particularly among practitioners, that it has been suggested to me that legislation is urgently required. But while the decision in *Banque Bruxelles* is a difficult one, and its ambit is far from clear, subsequent cases can be expected to iron out the problems. Moreover, it is not obvious that the decision is incorrect.[180] In my view, therefore, legislation would not be the appropriate way forward.

[175] *Ibid.*, at 1638.

[176] It would appear, for example, that *Naughton* v. *O'Callaghan* [1990] 3 All ER 191 cannot now stand. There the plaintiffs had bought a horse for 26,000 guineas on the basis of an incorrect statement as to the pedigree of the horse. The actual value of the horse at the date of purchase was 23,500 guineas but two years later, after it had failed to be placed in various races, its actual value was £1,500. Waller J awarded as damages (for negligent misrepresentation or breach of warranty) the difference between the price paid, and the horse's actual value at date of trial. If *Banque Bruxelles* applies, it appears that the damages should be restricted to the difference between 26,000 guineas and 23,500 guineas.

[177] Lord Hoffman left open whether a different rule applies to the tort of deceit (or to s. 2(1) of the Misrepresentation Act 1967): [1997] AC 191, 215–16. Subsequently in *Smith New Court Securities Ltd* v. *Scrimgeour Vickers (Asset Management) Ltd* [1997] AC 254 the House of Lords made clear that for deceit the wider "direct consequence", rather than "reasonable foreseeability", rule of remoteness (and the traditional reliance/status quo measure), laid down in *Doyle* v. *Olby (Ironmongers) Ltd* [1969] 2 QB 158, applies. It was left open whether the rule for deceit should apply also to damages under s. 2(1) of the Misrepresentation Act 1967 (as was held to be the law in *Royscot Trust Ltd* v. *Rogerson* [1991] 2 QB 297).

[178] It can be interpreted as nothing more than a revival of the narrow remoteness test of "accepting liability for a risk as a term of the contract" put forward in, for example, *British Columbia Sawmill Co. Ltd* v. *Nettleship* (1868) LR 3 CP 499: see Burrows, *Remedies for Torts and Breach of Contract* (2nd edn., 1994), 55–6.

[179] This terminology was first used by Staughton LJ in *Hayes* v. *James & Charles Dodd* [1990] 2 All ER 815.

[180] While, at first sight, Phillips J's more conventional approach at first instance is attractive, it fails to take account of the different "cushions" against falls in property values that lenders give themselves. It would seem unjust that, applying Phillips J's approach, the greater the cushion a lender gives itself the lower its damages. See Tony Dugdale, "*South Australia Asset Management*: Answers and Questions" (1996) 12 *PN* 71, 72.

(d) *Constructive Notice and Vitiated Transactions*

In *Barclays Bank plc* v. *O'Brien*,[181] the House of Lords dealt definitively with an issue that has been perplexing the courts a great deal in recent years. Cast in general terms, the issue is this. Where D has entered into a contract with P, as a result of undue influence or misrepresentation or duress against P by a third party, X, can P rescind the contract? Probably the commonest example is where, induced by her husband (X), a wife (P) guarantees to a bank (D), secured by a charge over the matrimonial home, the debts to the bank of her husband (or the debts of her husband's company).

In *O'Brien*, their Lordships held that P can rescind where either X was acting as D's agent in procuring the contract[182] or where D has actual or constructive notice of X's conduct inducing the contract. Lord Browne-Wilkinson, with whom the other Lords agreed, spelt out what constitutes constructive notice in this situation. There are three main elements: (i) D must be aware that P is in a relationship of trust and confidence with X; (ii) the transaction on its face must not be to the financial advantage of P; (iii) D must have failed to take reasonable steps to be satisfied that the transaction was entered into by P freely and with knowledge of the full facts (as, for example, where D has failed to advise P to take independent legal advice).

Unfortunately, Lord Browne-Wilkinson's statement of principles—while admirably clear—has spawned a mass of case law. Decisions have dealt, for example, with what types of relationship are covered,[183] with what transactions are disadvantageous on their face,[184] and with what constitutes the reasonable steps that a bank must take (for example, how far is a bank entitled to trust solicitors to comply with their duties[185] including where the plaintiff's solicitor is also the bank's solicitor[186]).

---

[181] [1994] 1 AC 180.

[182] Cases prior to *O'Brien* had artificially enlarged the scope of agency in this context. Subsequent to *O'Brien*, there is no need for that artificiality. It should be, and now is, rare for agency to be made out.

[183] *Massey* v. *Midland Bank* (1995) 27 HLR 229 (CA); *Barclays Bank* v. *Rivett* (1997) 29 HLR 893 (CA); *Crédit Lyonnais Bank Nederland NV* v. *Burch* (1997) 29 HLR 513 (CA).

[184] *CIBC Mortgages Plc* v. *Pitt* [1994] 1 AC 200 (HL); *Goode Durrant Administration* v. *Biddulph* [1994] 2 FLR 551; *Scotlife Home Loans (No. 2) Ltd* v. *Hedworth* (1996) 28 HLR 771 (CA).

[185] *Massey* v. *Midland Bank* (1995) 27 HLR 227; *Banco Exterior International* v. *Mann* (1995) 27 HLR 227 (CA); *Bank Baroda* v. *Rayarel* (1995) 27 HLR 387 (CA), *Barclays Bank* v. *Thomson* [1997] 1 FLR 156 (CA).

[186] *Halifax Mortgage Services Ltd* v. *Stepsky* (1996) 28 HLR 522 (CA); *Barclays Bank* v. *Thomson* [1997] 1 FLR 156 (CA); *Royal Bank of Scotland* v. *Etridge* [1997] 3 All ER 618 (CA).

Commentators have also raised theoretical doubts about aspects of *O'Brien*. It has been said, for example, that constructive notice is an inappropriate concept to use when one is simply talking about setting aside a transaction (albeit induced by a third party)[187]; and it has been queried whether, although *O'Brien* itself was a misrepresentation case, Lord Browne-Wilkinson's principles are appropriate for a case of misrepresentation (where awareness of vulnerability would seem irrelevant), as opposed to undue influence.[188]

A further series of cases has dealt with the precise meaning of rescission in this context. Rescission on the terms of being bound to a different contract has been rejected,[189] albeit that severance of the unobjectionable part of the instrument from the objectionable is possible.[190]

It can be argued that, to stop continuing litigation on *O'Brien*, there should be legislation codifying and clarifying the law on constructive notice and vitiated transactions. But many of the difficult questions seem now to have been resolved, and indeed many of the cases relate to banking practice before *O'Brien* was decided. Banks have subsequently amended their practice in the light of *O'Brien* so that there is now less likelihood of their being held to have had constructive notice. In any event, it is far from clear that legislation now would be any less likely to throw up litigation than the rulings of the courts.

(e) *Liability for Pure Economic Loss in the Tort of Negligence*
Over the last twenty-five years, no area of civil liability has proved more troublesome than pure economic loss in the tort of negligence. It is in respect of this area of negligence, above all, that the courts dramatically pushed forward the boundaries of negligence and then, equally dramatically, backtracked with the overruling of *Anns* v. *Merton London Borough Council*[191] in *Murphy* v. *Brentwood District Council*.[192] The apparent underlying explanation for the backtrack

---

[187] E.g. Mindy Chen-Wishart, "The *O'Brien* Principle and Substantive Unfairness" [1997] *CLJ* 60; Janet O'Sullivan, "Undue Influence and Misrepresentation After *O'Brien*: Making Security Secure" (Warwick SPTL conference 1997). This derives support from the integration into Scots law of *O'Brien* by relying not on constructive notice but on good faith dealing: *Smith* v. *Governor and Company of Bank of Scotland* [1997] 2 FLR 862, HL.

[188] O'Sullivan, n. 187 above. See also Lord Jauncey's speech in *Smith* v. *Governor and Company of Bank of Scotland* [1997] 2 FLR 862, 866.

[189] *TSB* v. *Camfield* (1995) 27 HLR 205.

[190] *Barclays Bank* v. *Caplan*, *The Times* 12 Dec. 1997.

[191] [1978] AC 728.

[192] [1991] 1 AC 398.

was a judicial fear that negligence liability was out of hand and that, by following Lord Wilberforce's "principled" approach of there being a duty of care where loss to the plaintiff was reasonably fore-seeable, subject to good policy reasons to the contrary, the judiciary had unacceptably abandoned conventional control mechanisms. The modern approach to the duty of care, as laid down in *Caparo Industries Plc* v. *Dickman*,[193] in which it was held that no duty of care was owed by auditors of a company to investors in that company who had relied on the auditors' accounts in making their investments, requires a plaintiff to establish not only that the loss was foreseeable but also that there is "proximity" between the parties and that it is just and rea-sonable to impose the duty of care. Although the last two concepts merge into one another, the underlying importance of this three-fold test is that it has enabled the courts to return to traditional incremen-tal development of pure economic loss recovery in the tort of negligence.[194]

The present position is, therefore, one in which pure economic loss recovery has been reined in. There are two main liability situa-tions. First, where the defendant has made a negligent misstatement on which the plaintiff has detrimentally relied suffering pure eco-nomic loss. This is the narrow principle laid down in *Hedley Byrne & Co. Ltd* v. *Heller and Partners Ltd*[195] and elaborated on, in terms of the representation having to be plaintiff-specific and purpose-specific, in *Caparo*.[196] The second situation is where the plaintiff has contracted for beneficial services from the defendant which the defendant has negligently performed causing pure economic loss. This tortious duty of care was recognised, and formed the basis for the acceptance of concurrent liability, in *Henderson* v. *Merrett Syndicates Ltd*[197] (as regards the direct Lloyds Names). In Lord Goff's view, giving the leading speech, the tortious duty of care rests on the wide "assump-tion of responsibility" principle espoused in *Hedley Byrne*.

---

[193] [1990] 2 AC 605.

[194] For an interesting analysis of the link between the threefold test, "assumption of responsibility" (discussed in the next three paragraphs of the text below) and the incremen-tal approach, see *Bank of Credit & Commerce International (overseas) Ltd* v. *Price Waterhouse, The Times* 4 Mar. 1998 (*per* Sir Brian Neill).

[195] [1964] AC 465.

[196] See also *Reeman* v. *Department of Transport* [1997] 2 Lloyd's Rep. 648. Cf. *Smith* v. *Eric S Bush* [1990] 1 AC 831; *Welton* v. *North Cornwall DC* [1997] 1 WLR 570.

[197] [1995] 2 AC 145. See Essay 2 above. There are many examples of this duty of care sit-uation including, e.g., valuers' negligence: see *Banque Bruxelles Lambert SA* v. *Eagle Star Insurance Co. Ltd* [1997] AC 191, 209–11 above.

In addition, claims will exceptionally be allowed for the defendant's negligent performance of services under a contract with X causing pure economic loss to the plaintiff. The best example is *White v. Jones*.[198] Here delay by a solicitor in carrying out his client's instructions to draw up a new will meant that the client died without that new will having been executed. It was held (Lords Keith and Mustill dissenting) that a duty of care was owed by the solicitor to the beneficiaries who would have benefited under the new will. Lord Goff again based his reasoning on the "assumption of responsibility" principle, albeit that on the facts he regarded that assumption as deemed by law to exist; and his primary justification for the decision was that there was no other satisfactory way of filling the gap whereby the person who had suffered the loss could not otherwise sue and the person who could sue had suffered no loss.[199] Lord Browne-Wilkinson agreed that a duty of care arose from an extension of the principle of "assumption of responsibility" (which he saw as having its historical roots in fiduciary relationships).

At this moment in time, therefore, the law in this area is probably more certain than it has been for over twenty years. Admittedly the "assumption of responsibility" principle is vague and open to manipulation.[200] Practitioners and their clients may still have good grounds for fearing that the concepts are insufficiently tight to prevent future expansion and uncertainty. It may further be true to say that the courts are not directly and openly addressing the policy concerns that, in her seminal article[201] in this sphere, Jane Stapleton has persuasively argued would be the best way of rendering the tort of negligence coherent.

It may be thought that legislation could eliminate uncertainty in this area. But it would seem that it could only do this by introducing a blunt recovery/no-recovery distinction. While this may ultimately prove necessary, it would seem particularly inappropriate to give up the quest for finely-tuned justice, and to opt for such an across-the-board legislative solution, at a time when the law on pure economic

---

[198] [1995] 2 AC 207. See also the claims of the indirect names in *Henderson* v. *Merrett Syndicates Ltd* [1995] 2 AC 145.

[199] Hence *White* v. *Jones* does not apply (i.e. there is no duty of care owed to disappointed beneficiaries) in relation to inter vivos transactions because the error can be rectified (*Hemmens* v. *Wilson Brown* [1995] Ch. 223) or where the estate has an action to recover the loss (*Carr-Glynn* v. *Frearsons* [1997] 2 All ER 614).

[200] See 28–33 above.

[201] Jane Stapleton, "Duty of Care and Economic Loss: A Wider Agenda" (1991) 107 *LQR* 249. See also B. Hepple, "Negligence: The Search for Coherence" (1997) 50 *CLP* 69, esp. 94.

loss is more certain and controlled than it has been for many years. And while the specific area of pure economic loss from defective building is one where legislation might be attractive (for example by amending the Defective Premises Act 1972[202]) it would seem premature to reform that area unless and until the Law Commission's recommendations on privity of contract have been implemented.[203]

5. CONCLUSION

Since its creation in 1965 the Law Commission has made a rich contribution to improving the laws of contract and tort in this country. One thinks, for example, of the Animals Act 1971,[204] the Congenital Disabilities (Civil Liability) Act 1976,[205] Part I of the Administration of Justice Act 1982,[206] the Supply of Goods and Services Act 1982,[207] the Occupiers' Liability Act 1984,[208] the Civil Liability (Contribution) Act 1978,[209] the Minors' Contracts Act 1987,[210] the Carriage of Goods by Sea Act 1992,[211] the Sale and Supply of Goods Act 1994,[212] the Sale of Goods (Amendment) Act 1995[213] and, most important of all, the Unfair Contract Terms Act 1977.[214]

It is in relation to contract and tort—precisely because they are at the heart of the common law—that the role of statutory law reform raises particularly interesting and difficult questions. At root one must ask when, if at all, should legislation be recommended, given the common law's capacity for incremental, modernising development?:

---

[202] See, e.g., Duncan Wallace, "Anns Beyond Repair" (1991) 107 *LQR* 228, 242–7.

[203] See *Privity of Contract: Contracts for the Benefit of Third Parties*, Law Com. No. 242 (1996), para. 7.55. See 166–8 above.

[204] *Civil Liability of Animals*, Law Com. No. 13 (1967).

[205] *Report on Injuries to Unborn Children*, Law Com. No. 60 (1974).

[206] *Report on Personal Injury Litigation—Assessment of Damages*, Law Com. No. 56 (1973).

[207] *Law of Contract: Implied Terms in Contracts for the Supply of Goods*, Law Com. No. 95 (1979).

[208] *Report on Liability for Damage or Injury to Trespassers and Related Questions of Occupiers' Liability*, Law Com. No. 75 (1976).

[209] *Law of Contract: Report on Contribution*, Law Com. No. 79 (1977).

[210] *Law of Contract: Minors' Contracts*, Law Com. No. 134 (1984).

[211] *Rights of Suit in Respect of Carriage of Goods by Sea*, Law Com. No. 196, Scot. Law Com. No. 130 (1991).

[212] *Sale and Supply of Goods*, Law Com. No. 160, Scot. Law Com. No. 104 (1987).

[213] *Sale of Goods Forming Part of a Bulk*, Law Com. No. 215, Scot. Law Com. No. 145 (1993).

[214] *Exemption Clauses: Second Report of the Two Commissions*, Law Com. No. 69, Scot. Law Com. No. 39 (1975).

and if recommendations for legislation are to be made, how do they relate to the common law? My time working at the Law Commission, and grappling with generalised once-and-for-all legislative solutions, has done nothing to diminish my admiration for the flexible and finely-tuned common law approach to "reform".

In this essay I have sought to explore, through the Law Commission's recently-completed, on-going and possible future projects, some of the worthwhile reforms that should, or might, be made to contract and tort.[215] But, given the distinction between worthwhile law reform and law reform that merits legislation, we must to a large extent continue to rely on the judges, through principled, progressive and sensitive decision-making, to keep the central strands of the common law in line with modern conditions and ideas.

---

[215] In relation to a public authority's *ultra vires* acts, privacy and defamation, I have also touched on the topic that may dominate much of the legal scene in the next few years, namely the effect of the incorporation of the European Convention on Human Rights.

Index

two